The Meaning of Work

Bulletin of Comparative Labour Relations

VOLUME 119

Founding Editor

The series started in 1970 under the dynamic editorship of Professor Roger Blanpain (Belgium), former President of the International Industrial Relations Association. Professor Blanpain, Professor Emeritus of Labour Law, Universities of Leuven and Tilburg, was also General Editor of the International Encyclopedia of Laws (with more than 1,600 collaborators worldwide) and President of the Association of Educative and Scientific Authors Authors. He passed away in October 2016.

General Editor

In 2015 Frank Hendrickx, Professor of labour law at the Faculty of Law of the University of Leuven (Belgium) joined as a co-Editor. Frank Hendrickx has published numerous articles and books and regularly advises governments, international institutions and private organisations in the area of labour law as well as in sports law. He is the Editor-in-Chief of the European Labour Law Journal and General Editor of the International Encyclopaedia of Laws.

Introduction

The Bulletins constitute a unique source of information and thought-provoking discussion, laying the groundwork for studies of employment relations in the 21st century, involving among much else the effects of globalization, new technologies, migration, and the greying of the population.

Contents/Subjects

Amongst other subjects the Bulletins frequently include the proceedings of international or regional conferences; reports from comparative projects devoted to salient issues in industrial relations, human resources management, and/or labour law; and specific issues underlying the multicultural aspects of our industrial societies.

Objective

The Bulletins offer a platform of expression and discussion on labour relations to scholars and practitioners worldwide, often featuring special guest editors.

The titles published in this series are listed at the end of this volume.

The Meaning of Work

A Labour Law Perspective

Editors

Frank Hendrickx
Christina Hiessl

Contributors

Tania Bazzani
John Bolte
Filip Dorssemont
Elena Gramano
Frank Hendrickx
Christina Hiessl
Rüdiger Krause
Julia López López
David Mangan
Stefania Marassi
Adalberto Perulli
Sophie Robin-Olivier
Simon Taes
Manfred Weiss

General Editor

Frank Hendrickx

Founding Editor

Roger Blanpain

Wolters Kluwer

Published by:
Kluwer Law International B.V.
PO Box 316
2400 AH Alphen aan den Rijn
The Netherlands
E-mail: lrs-sales@wolterskluwer.com
Website: www.wolterskluwer.com/en/solutions/kluwerlawinternational

Sold and distributed by:
Wolters Kluwer Legal & Regulatory U.S.
920 Links Avenue
Landisville, PA 17538
United States of America
E-mail: customer.service@wolterskluwer.com

ISBN 978-94-035-0579-4

e-Book: ISBN 978-94-035-0589-3
web-PDF: ISBN 978-94-035-0599-2

Notes on Contributors

Tania Bazzani, holding a doctorate in Labour Law and a qualification of a lawyer, works as a researcher at the Europa University Viadrina, Germany. Previous Marie Curie Fellow, she actively contributes to interdisciplinary projects and is specialized in European employment policy, comparative labour law and social policy, with a focus on the impacts of digitalization and labour market transformations. Additionally, she has led collaborations with trade unions, industry, policy sectors, and EU institutions, including the last report on Telework for the DG Employment (2024), for which she works as the leading expert for the legal part.

John Bolte, Professor of Smart Sensor Systems at The Hague University of Applied Sciences (THUAS) and senior scientific advisor innovative monitoring at the National Institute for Public Health and the Environment of the Netherlands (RIVM). He is a registered occupational epidemiologist and has a PhD in Physics. He worked on various practical measures, guidelines, and transposition of the EU directive on protection against potential health effects from exposure to electromagnetic fields in the workplace. He works on several projects in engineering, policy, and epidemiology. His research group performs studies on exposure to physical and chemical agents with wearable exposimeters.

Filip Dorssemont (1970) is full professor of Labour Law at the Faculty of Law of the *Université catholique de Louvain* (in Louvain-La-Neuve). He is President of the School of Labour Sciences (Uclouvain) (2019-2025). He is a member of the Transnational Trade Union Rights Expert Network (ETUI). He has read law, studied philosophy and history of Art.

Elena Gramano is an Assistant Professor of Labour law in the Department of Legal Studies at Bocconi University. Previously, she served as a research Fellow at Goethe University of Frankfurt, the Institute for Labour and Civil Law, and the University of Roma Tre. She is the author of several scientific articles in the field of labour law.

Frank Hendrickx is a Professor of Labour Law and director of the Institute for Labour Law – KU Leuven, Belgium. He is president of the Belgian Association of Labour Relations, editor of the Bulletin of Comparative Labour Relations and editor-in-chief of the European Labour Law Journal. He is also the general editor of the International Encyclopaedia of Laws.

Christina Hiessl (Hießl) is a Professor of Labour Law at KU Leuven (Belgium), an Invited Professor of Social Welfare at Yonsei University (Seoul), and a Consulting Expert at the European Commission's Centre of Expertise in the Field of Labour Law (ECE). She has worked and/or studied in eight countries, focusing on comparative social law and policy research. She is a board member of the European Labour Law Journal, scientific advisory board member of the Frankfurt Law Review, European correspondent of the 국제사회보장리뷰 (Int'l Social Security Review) and managing board member of the honours programme 'KU Leuven Engage'.

Rüdiger Krause is a full professor of civil law and labour law and director of the Institute for Labour Law at the Georg-August-University Göttingen. He has written numerous articles on German and European labour law and he is the author of the report for the 71st German Lawyers Conference on the digitalization of work (2016) as well as two further reports for the German Federal Ministry of Labour and Social Affairs on employee data protection (2017 and 2023). He is the co-editor of the German journal *Soziales Recht* ('Social Law') and the speaker of the German Association for Labour Law Research.

Julia Lo´pez Lo´pez is a Professor of Labour Law and Social Security Law and senior researcher of the group for Labour and Social Security Law GREDTISS (Consolidated Research Group, Agaur, 2022/2025, UPF). Her work has been published by Oxford University Press, Cambridge University Press, Russell Sage Foundation, Wolters Kluwer, Lavori i Diritto, Comparative Labor Law and Policy Journal, Bomarzo. Her main research topics are collective labour rights, gender equality and social protection, inclusive solidarity, remote work and employment regulation.

David Mangan is based at Maynooth University's School of Law & Criminology. He also has adjunct positions at Osgoode Hall Law School (Professional Development) and the Catholic University of Lyon. At the time of writing, he is a Visiting Professor at the University of Warsaw and at the University of Modena and Reggio Emilia.

Stefania Marassi, Senior Lecturer in European Labor Law and researcher with the Smart Sensor Systems research group at The Hague University of Applied Sciences (THUAS). She is also an external PhD student at Leiden University, writing a dissertation on the use of wearable technology in the workplace. Stefania Marassi is a member of the editorial board of the International Labor Rights Case Law Journal and worked as an independent expert for European projects on the impact of technological developments on the work floor and transnational collective labour relations.

Adalberto Perulli is a Professor of Labour Law at Ca' Foscari University in Venice, where he directs the Master in Labour Law and Social Security. He is a visiting professor at the Universities Paris Nanterre and Paris 1 Sorbonne and is the E.MA Director of the European Master in Human Rights and Democratization at the Global Village. He has twice been a speaker at the World Congress of Labour Law (ISLSSL Paris 2006, Turin 2018) and has published more than 200 papers in national and international scientific journals. He is on the board of the Labour Law Community.

Sophie Robin-Olivier is a professor at the Sorbonne School of Law (University Paris 1 Panthéon Sorbonne). She is the Director of IREDIES (*Sorbonne Research Institute for International and European Law*). Her research focuses on EU law, International and European labour law, anti-discrimination law, and, more recently, the impact of climate change on social justice.

Simon Taes graduated as a Master of Psychology and a Master of Laws at KU Leuven. He obtained his Doctor of Law degree at KU Leuven in 2023. He works as a postdoctoral researcher at the Institute for Labour Law – KU Leuven and cooperates in iCERIS, the Interdisciplinary Centre for Ethics and Regulation in Integrity of Sport (KU Leuven). He also works as a lawyer at the Brussels bar at ELL. Law. He has been coordinating the EU's Erasmus + funded COSMOS-study (2022-2024) on the Cooperation of Stakeholders on the Manipulation of Sport Competitions.

Manfred Weiss is a Professor Emeritus at the Law School of the J.W. Goethe University in Frankfurt, Germany.

Summary of Contents

Table of Contents

In Commemoration of Roger Blanpain

Manfred Weiss

Even if already seven years ago Roger Blanpain died, his inspirations are still with us and will remain with us. A lecture in his honour is held at regular intervals at the Law Faculty of the Catholic University in Leuven. And this year for the third time, Roger's pupil and successor Frank Hendrickx has organized a symposium in commemoration of him. The program as well as the prominent participants demonstrate the high esteem Roger still enjoys in the international community of labour law, social security and industrial relations.

This estimation is well-founded. Let us remember just a few highlights to get a feeling for this exceptional. A special sign for the recognition Roger enjoyed in the scholarly community was certainly the Presidencies of both international associations in our field of scholarship: the International Society of Labour Law and Social Security and the International Industrial Relations Association, now renamed International Labour and Employment Relations Association. Roger, of course, was not only President of both associations but also among the founding fathers. And he always has been very active therein.

The success in both associations is an indication of something else: Roger's approach has been an interdisciplinary one, integrating the realities and dynamics of industrial relations and of the labour market into labour law. He was not primarily interested in the law in the books but much more in the law in practice. He always understood his academic work as a contribution to improve the reality of working life.

This multidisciplinary and practice-oriented approach had important implications for his comparative work where he was not merely comparing rules, instruments and institutions but functions, thereby showing that similar normative patterns in different countries may have totally different effects in actual practice.

Roger served as an expert for international organizations, in particular the OECD and the International Labour Organization (ILO). His contribution to the development of European law barely can be overestimated. He was involved in the elaboration of many Directives. Most important were his efforts to pave the way for the Fundamental

Social Rights which now are contained in the Charter of Fundamental Rights of the European Union (EU).

Roger has helped us to keep track of the rapidly growing internationalization of all aspects of working life up to globalization. Much earlier than others he understood the need to respond in his scholarly work to these factual developments. One of the latest books he co-edited is called *The Global Workplace*, thereby indicating the denominator of his international perspective. Nobody more than him was better aware of the implications of globalization for labour law and industrial relations.

The number of his books and articles exceeds by far the output of other colleagues in our field. When in 1998, we dedicated to him a liber amicorum, the by far longest chapter was his list of publications. This list afterwards until his death still grew impressively.

Roger was not only a well-known author but also a splendid organizer of scholarly publications. He created the giant project *Encyclopedia of Laws* where scholars from all over the world describe their legal system in English and, thereby, provide for all of us a chance to broaden our horizons. The *Encyclopedia*, now continued by Frank Hendrickx, still maintains its dominant worldwide role. The same is true for the Bulletin of Comparative Labour Relations, also continued by Frank Hendrickx, where Roger initiated discussions between scholars from different countries on many topics. Quite often these Bulletins were the result of conferences organized by himself. It is a very important sign of commemorating Roger that the contributions of this year's symposium are published in the Bulletin.

Organizing conferences was one of the core activities of Roger. For many years he succeeded in bringing scholars from different countries together to exchange ideas in seminar style with each other and make a joint contribution to the resolution of burning problems. In addition to these smaller-scale seminars, Roger proved to be a splendid organizer of big international conferences, for example, the 8th World Congress of the International Industrial Relations Association in 1989, the 4th Regional European Congress of the International Society for Labour Law and Social Security in 1993 and the World Law Conference 'Law in Motion' in 1996. Of course, Roger participated in many more international conferences all over the world. His contributions in these conferences always were outstanding, not only when he was listed as a speaker but also in the discussions. His mere presence always has made a big difference. Without him, such conferences were only half as interesting and much less fun. One year before his death in 2015 he still participated actively in the World Congress of the International Society of Labour Law and Social Security in Cape Town. Many wonderful memories come to my mind. It has been difficult for Roger to cope with the many invitations as a lecturer in all kinds of meetings. If you had him as a speaker the success of the event was guaranteed. A lecture by him was not only an intellectual joy but also always full of entertainment. Another important dimension of Roger's contribution to our field of scholarship refers to his teaching. He was a gifted and also very entertaining teacher. In this capacity, he not only was a visiting Professor at many universities abroad but he also succeeded in establishing something more important. In the years when he was a Professor and Dean at the Catholic University, Leuven he made his chair a sort of Mekka for young students and scholars. In a sort of pilgrimage, they came in huge numbers to profit from his knowledge of international, comparative and European Labour Law. He always did everything to support young students and scholars. In this capacity, he also taught in the international summer schools in Szeged, Hungary and in Bologna, Italy. Many international scholars of today owe their careers to Roger. So when in the title of his memoirs he asked 'What can I do for you?' this was by no means a merely rhetorical question. It was the motto of his life. He always tried to share his knowledge with others, thereby supporting them. And this in particular applies to the younger generation, the students and young scholars. In this context, it might be mentioned that Roger every year went with students to Geneva to the ILO to offer these students a chance to get acquainted with the work of this prestigious international organization.

Not only young scholars came to Leuven profiting from Roger but he also gave peers a chance to teach and do research in Leuven. I also had the privilege to come here as a visiting Professor in the early eighties. On this occasion, I could learn what outstanding hospitality for visiting scholars means. I not only got splendid accommodation in the Beguinhof in Leuven but was also treated like a king by Roger and his wife Lina. Thereby, I understood that for Roger international and comparative labour law was not only an intellectual exercise but that he always was also passionate about closely collaborating with other scholars and developing friendly relations with them. This was the basis for uncomplicated and close cooperation among the members of this international scholarly community to which nobody has contributed so much as Roger did. Without him, the international scholarly community would not be what it is today.

His contribution cannot be overestimated. Of course, it was and is not always easy to be integrated with the many projects Roger was pushing forward. If it came to deadlines he could be a real slave driver. However, one has to admit that this determination guaranteed the success of all these projects.

There was one characteristic feature of Roger I admire most: his independence and intellectual integrity. In times when academic independence more and more became and still becomes replaced by opportunistic thinking, pleasing the powerful and those who are funding research, Roger stayed like a rock in the waves. Throughout his life, he kept his ability to strongly criticize wrong developments, no matter what the impact on him might have been. Such a critical approach exclusively based on scholarly insight is more needed than ever. In this respect, Roger should be a role model for all of us.

Roger definitely would have been an important voice in the deliberations on the transformation of the world of work caused by digitalization and decarbonization. His creative and innovative mind might have helped us to find the answers to the many questions that are now arising. This year's programme on 'the meaning of work' in this new environment would have been an ideal topic for his ideas. For me, Roger was not only a great scholar but also an admirable human being and a wonderful friend. I should not hide how much I personally profited from his friendship.

Many years ago I was in a very serious health condition. It was uncertain whether I would survive. In this situation, Roger contacted all our common friends and colleagues worldwide and asked them to contact me and support me. This happened and had an enormous impact on my recovery. Can you think of a better friend? I am more than grateful for his friendship.

We can be proud to have worked with Roger. His outstanding scholarship has been honoured many times, be it by honorary doctorates or by other high-level decorations. Now we are commemorating and honouring him by the lectures and symposia, organized so splendidly by our friend Frank Hendrickx.

Introduction

Frank Hendrickx & Christina Hiessl

This book is the result of the 3rd Conference in Commemoration of Professor Roger Blanpain, organized by the Institute for Labour Law of KU Leuven (Belgium), on 5 and 6 September 2023. The concept of the conference is to bring together labour law and industrial relations scholars around the world and to examine evolutions, ideas and new challenges with a major impact on the way how we understand and approach labour law.

In this book, presented as a collection of papers resulting from the conference, the contributors are looking into 'the meaning of work'. The world of work is undergoing rapid change, due to main challenges, including globalization, demographic evolution, technology, the climate, Industry 4.0 (and even 5.0), and periods of crisis, in such a way that it is time to ask ourselves a number of basic questions: how do we approach work, what exactly is work, the object of study in labour law? And how are work, the workplace or the 'worker' developing and to be seen in (and beyond) legal terms? The aim was to consider contemporary discussions related to the new world of work, such as dependent work, precarious work, invisible or fragmented work, autonomous work, telework, working with smart technology and artificial intelligence, the concept of working time versus rest time, work-life-balance, the place of work, the relationship between work and private life, or generally our idea or understandings about work. In short, now that traditional approaches to the workplace, and the traditional view of working time, or subordinated work, are challenged, the questioning becomes directed to work itself: what is work, and what is the meaning of work? The book aims to reach for a better insight into the problems, questions and challenges and, where possible, explore new pathways and answers.

The contributions can briefly be outlined as follows.

Adalberto Perulli's chapter, 'The Meaning of Work between Labour Law and Philosophy,' offers a profound exploration of how the rapid transformations in work, driven by social, economic, and technological innovations, particularly within Industry 4.0, reshape our understanding of work's purpose. Perulli delves into a philosophical-legal discourse, presenting work as a factor of freedom and self-realization. He challenges the traditional frameworks that often reduce work to mere subordination and control, advocating instead for an evolution of labour law that enhances freedom and dignity. By examining the smart factory's technological, social, and organizational aspects, Perulli situates work within the broader paradigm of Sustainable Development. His analysis progresses towards viewing the worker not just as a functional entity but as a person, whose dignity and freedom – both within and from work – must be central to any legal discussion. Perulli's contribution thus redefines the relationship between labour law and the individual, proposing a transformative vision where labour law becomes the law of social freedom, intrinsically linked to personal development and social recognition.

In her chapter 'The Future of Work,' Sophie Robin-Olivier reflects on the intricate and evolving relationship between working conditions and labour law in the context of profound social, economic, technological, and ecological transformations. She argues that labour law must adapt to the 'new climate regime,' a concept reflecting the societal shifts induced by climate change, and extend its protections beyond the human worker to include the environment. Robin-Olivier critiques the anthropocentric nature of current labour laws, advocating for a framework that acknowledges the interdependence of human and ecological systems. By proposing concepts like 'just transition' and 'decent work,' she envisions a labour law that not only upholds human dignity but also fosters sustainable and meaningful interactions with our planet. Her chapter prompts us to reconsider the foundational principles of labour law, urging a broader understanding of work that integrates ecological sustainability as an essential element of meaningful work.

Filip Dorssemont's chapter, 'Making Sense (of the Artistic Representation) of Labour,' takes an innovative approach by exploring the depiction of labour in art as a means to reconstruct the meaning of work across historical and social contexts. Dorssemont argues that artworks serve as critical reflections on the socio-political dimensions of labour, offering insights into the evolving nature of work through different eras. By using Erwin Panofsky's iconological approach, Dorssemont links these artistic representations to broader philosophical and ideological contexts, highlighting the deep connection between labour, corporality, and social justice. His analysis underscores that the meaning of work is not only a legal or economic concept but also a cultural and ideological one, reflected and shaped by art. This chapter invites us to consider how cultural representations of labour influence our legal and social understandings of work, contributing to a richer, more nuanced narrative of labour law.

Elena Gramano's chapter, 'Smart and Autonomous Work: When Autonomy Reaches Subordination,' examines the blurring boundaries between employee and autonomous worker classifications in light of technological advancements. Gramano highlights the inadequacies of traditional legal categories to address the hybrid nature of smart work, where autonomy and subordination coexist. Her chapter reflects on the need to rethink labour law frameworks to accommodate these new forms of work, ensuring that both employees and self-employed workers receive adequate protection.

By questioning the binary distinctions of labour law, Gramano's contribution challenges us to redefine the legal concepts of autonomy and subordination in a way that reflects the complexities of the modern workplace. Her analysis points to a future where labour law must evolve to protect the nuanced realities of work, maintaining the balance between autonomy and control that is essential to meaningful work.

Tania Bazzani's chapter on 'Telework and the Right to Disconnect' critically examines the challenges posed by the widespread adoption of telework during the COVID-19 pandemic, particularly the erosion of boundaries between work and personal life. Bazzani explores how telework, while offering flexibility, also exacerbates the 'always-on' culture, raising significant concerns about workers' well-being and the preservation of a work-life balance. She discusses the potential for a unified European Union (EU) directive on the right to disconnect as a means to restore balance and protect workers from the encroachment of work into personal time. Her chapter reflects on the broader implications of technological advancements for work-life balance, suggesting that the right to disconnect is not just a legal necessity but a fundamental aspect of maintaining the dignity and autonomy of workers. Bazzani's insights encourage us to view labour law as a tool for protecting the human aspects of work, ensuring that flexibility does not come at the cost of personal well-being.

In 'Work-Life Balance: Well-balanced with Equal Opportunity Goals?' Christina Hiessl addresses the persistent challenges of achieving a balanced work-life dynamic in the face of increasing professional demands and evolving family care responsibilities. Hiessl's chapter explores the gendered nature of work-life balance issues and critiques the existing EU and national policies that fail to address these disparities effectively. She argues for a reformed approach that better aligns with the realities of informal care, particularly as the ageing population grows. Hiessl's analysis underscores the need for labour law to evolve in ways that promote gender equality and support a fairer distribution of care responsibilities. Her chapter reflects on the broader social implications of work-life balance, suggesting that true balance is integral to the meaning of work, as it enables individuals to fulfil their professional and personal roles without compromising either. This holistic approach to work-life balance is essential for achieving a more equitable and meaningful work environment.

David Mangan's chapter, 'Privacy and Labour Law Traditions,' explores the evolving intersection of privacy and labour law in the digital age, focusing on the challenges posed by technological advancements. Mangan argues that traditional labour law frameworks, which often neglect modern privacy concerns, must be re-evaluated to protect worker privacy in an era of heightened surveillance. His chapter reflects on privacy as a fundamental aspect of personal freedom and autonomy, emphasizing the need for legal systems to adapt to contemporary challenges. Mangan critiques the tendency to compromise privacy for economic efficiency, advocating instead for a labour law that balances technological progress with robust privacy protections. His analysis highlights the critical role of privacy in preserving the dignity and autonomy of workers, suggesting that it is a cornerstone of meaningful work in the digital age.

Rüdiger Krause's chapter, 'Protection of Workers' Personal Data between General Data Protection Law and Labour Law,' examines the complex relationship between data protection and labour law in the context of increasing digitalization and workplace surveillance. Krause contrasts sector-specific and cross-sectoral regulatory approaches, highlighting the challenges of reconciling the General Data Protection Regulation (GDPR) with labour law requirements. His chapter reflects on the necessity for clearer and more concrete national regulations to protect workers' personal data effectively. Krause's analysis underscores the importance of data protection in safeguarding workers' privacy, autonomy, and dignity, emphasizing that a robust legal framework is essential for maintaining the integrity of work in an increasingly digitalized world.

In their chapter, 'Wearable Technology to Monitor Workers' Health and Safety: Benefits, Risks, and Legal Considerations,' Stefania Marassi and John Bolte explore the implications of integrating wearable technology into occupational health and safety monitoring. While recognizing the potential benefits of wearables for enhancing worker health and safety, they also highlight significant legal and ethical concerns related to privacy and data protection. Marassi and Bolte's chapter reflects on the dual regulatory frameworks governing wearables, arguing that while these technologies can improve workplace safety, their deployment must be carefully regulated to protect workers' fundamental rights. Their analysis points to a broader reflection on the role of technology in the workplace, suggesting that the integration of new tools must be balanced with the need to preserve the dignity and autonomy of workers. Marassi and Bolte's insights contribute to the ongoing discussion about the humanization of work, emphasizing the importance of a legal framework that both leverages technological advancements and safeguards workers' rights.

In 'Subsidiarity and Technology: The Case of Remote and Platform Workers,' Julia López López examines how the principle of subsidiarity influences the regulation of remote and platform labour within the context of labour law. Subsidiarity, a key distributive and cooperative principle, plays a crucial role in balancing the distribution of competences between international, European, and national labour frameworks. The chapter explores how technological advancements, particularly in remote and platform work, redefine employment relations by shaping working conditions, rights, and legal frameworks. López López highlights the Spanish case as a model of platform labour regulation, emphasising its innovative presumption of employment for platform workers and algorithmic transparency requirements. The chapter also delves into how the hybridisation of employment – combining locational and technological elements – has complicated traditional distinctions between remote and in-person work. This hybridisation, driven by technological innovation, necessitates new regulatory approaches. The chapter argues that subsidiarity and proportionality continue to play an essential role in shaping regulatory approaches, for instance to collective bargaining for remote workers or the presumption of employment for platform workers. The author concludes by calling for the adaptation of regulatory frameworks to accommodate the increasing complexity and hybridisation of modern labour relations.

Simon Taes discusses the increasing use of 'smart' or autonomous robots across various industries and its implications for the nature of work, particularly from a legal perspective. Taes reflects on the challenges posed by robotization, noting that while robots can enhance efficiency, they also raise significant questions about the quality of work and the adequacy of current labour laws. His chapter explores the complex interaction between humans and robots, highlighting the need for labour law to evolve to protect the human aspects of work. Taes argues that the humanization of work, which protects workers from being reduced to mere components of a production process, is essential in a robotized workplace. He suggests that combining occupational safety and health principles with data protection laws could provide a robust framework for safeguarding workers' autonomy and dignity in the face of increasing automation. Taes' contribution encourages a broader reflection on the meaning of work in an era where human and machine interactions are becoming increasingly intertwined, underscoring the need for labour law to adapt to these new realities.

Finally, Frank Hendrickx discusses, in his contribution on 'How privacy shapes the meaning of work', the right to privacy in light of its growing importance in the context of freedom and autonomy in the employment relationship. Hendrickx reflects on the evolving dynamics of work, shaped by technological advancements and the shift towards more flexible and digitalized environments, which bring privacy, freedom, and autonomy into sharper focus within labour law. His chapter emphasizes that, as the lines between personal and professional life blur, privacy must be understood not only as a legal right but also as a fundamental aspect of the human experience that underpins the meaning of work. Hendrickx's contribution suggests that labour law must evolve to develop freedom and autonomy and integrate it in the future for labour law. This should in his view entail the protection of values such as freedom, autonomy, identity, self-development and self-determination, ensuring that privacy remains central to the narrative of meaningful work in an era of unprecedented technological change. His insights highlight privacy as a cornerstone of the modern work experience, essential for navigating the complexities of contemporary work life.

In conclusion, this book provides a comprehensive exploration of the evolving meaning of work in the face of unprecedented global, technological, and social transformations. The diverse contributions illuminate how traditional understandings of work, shaped by subordination and control, are being challenged by contemporary developments such as Industry 4.0, the climate crisis, new forms of work and flexibility, work-life demands, and the rise of autonomous technologies.

As for the language in labour law in relation to the meaning of work, it is clear that different notions and perspectives come to the fore, such as freedom, autonomy, dignity, human and environmental well-being, the cultural dimensions of work, work-life balance gender-sensitivity, privacy, humanization and sustainability.

Together, these contributions advance our understanding of work by highlighting its multifaceted nature and the necessity for legal frameworks to evolve in response to major shifts and developments in the world of work. We hope with these insights to grasp the new complexities of labour law and offer a crucial foundation for reimagining labour law in ways that uphold the true essence of work in the twenty-first century.

CHAPTER 1

The Meaning of Work Between Labour Law and Philosophy

Adalberto Perulli

§1.01 INTRODUCTION

I am going to try to make a critical reasoning on the transformations of work in the light of the social, economic and technological current innovations in the so-called Industry 4.0 or smart factory, highlighting the most relevant issues for a new philosophical-legal perspective of labour law: that is to make work a factor of freedom and self-realization. Moreover, labour law often suffers from a distance between theoretical models concerning its basic components (the enterprise, the employment relationship, the state, etc.) and the reality of social processes, with their routines and resistance to change. I am well aware that the reality of work is complex and cannot be entirely boiled down to a unique positive model. Therefore in my reasoning, there is a problematic challenge, that is to ensure that work should evolve towards the goal of freedom and self-realization of persons and not towards subordination, control, digital and algorithmic evaluation: all the negative elements that are often cited in support of the thesis regarding the difficulties, if not impossibility, of a positive evolution of work towards the goal of freedom and human dignity.

The first segment of my reasoning concerns the phenomenological reality of work within the smart factory, as a technological, social, and organizational reality in which Work 4.0 takes place within the paradigm of Sustainable Development.

The second segment concerns the worker as a person with her values of dignity and two particular forms of freedom: a freedom *within work*, which I link to the concepts of self-realization of the person and of Recognition, and a freedom *from work*, which I link – among others – to a new idea of free time as active idleness.

The third segment is represented by political/moral philosophies that promote the values of personal freedom and which can be a source of inspiration and justification for labour law as the law of social freedom. These philosophies express three forms of freedom: non-domination (as a typical idea of neo-republicanism), social freedom (as a neo-Hegelian idea of Recognition) and capability (as an idea of the capabilities approach).

The objective of my reasoning is to intersect these three segments to create: (a) a project for the transformation of the meaning of work in its material and organizational reality, that is the smart factory; (b) a project for the valorization of the persons and their freedoms (*within* and *from* work) which is realized through (c) labour law as the law of social freedom.

§1.02 THE FIRST SEGMENT: THE SMART FACTORY

In the last century, Taylor-Fordism transformed work into jobs devoid of any knowledge, which only require skills and a job dominated by technique and by conventional work ethics based on values such as duty, commitment, obedience, destiny, necessity, sacrifice: all values which legitimized the conditions of domination and subordination of work in the Fordist factory.

Nowadays, the smart factory and the 4.0 work environment need independent, creative, responsible work; in a word, they need 'free' work (of course as far as it is possible within the sphere of work, which is aimed at production and is still subordinate work).

Does this view reflect the reality of the changing enterprise, or is it a groundless narrative, a kind of rhetoric that conceals a reality in which the enterprise continues to employ labour as a factor of production without any valorization of the worker's freedom? Here two basic visions are confronted, one more optimistic and the other pessimistic, that is to say, a future without value for work. If we choose the pessimistic path, we will soon come to a stop, at least in terms of the philosophical-juridical conception of work: work persists in being subordinated, alienated, biblical damnation in a modern key.

If we choose the more optimistic path, we may critically think the smart factory is actually capable of marking a historical change in the conception of work, with profound ethical, anthropological and legal implications.

What are the vectors of this possible positive transformation?

First of all, an environment characterized by a new collaborative relationship that takes place between the person and the machine made flexible by digitization in an unprecedented way. Second, a non-hierarchical but participatory organization and a managerial culture that recognizes the active and central role of workers, and their personal involvement, recovering the subjectivity that Taylorism and Fordism had radically denied. Third, the production processes that are expressed by Cyber-Physical Systems (CPS), that is a set of interconnecting technologies within an organization that produces goods through communication. Fourth, technological and organizational innovations valorize language: work thus becomes a performative linguistic act. Austin defines as performative utterance the 'saying' that accomplishes 'things', that is acts, actions: things are done through words. Work 4.0 does not only produce acts but also physical realities, objects and services: the Aristotelian separation between *praxis* and *poiesis* is overcome. Thanks to enabling technologies, saying (which is *praxis*) is also doing (which is *poiesis*).

§1.03 NEXT: SUSTAINABLE BUSINESS MODELS AND LABOUR LAW

These four vectors of the evolution of organizational models and business structure are accompanied by other evolutionary factors, which revolve around the paradigm of sustainable development. Sustainability - environmental, social, cultural - is the fundamental strategic framework: it is not a question of aiming at the multiplication of goods, but at quality production, in a context of economic value generation attentive to human values.

Innovative companies tend less and less to acquire working time - the *'faciendi necessitas'* in which the traditional concept of worker subordination is resolved - and more and more to seek the ability to realize projects. A company that involves its employees in the project of improving productivity and creating extraordinary products through socially and culturally meaningful working relationships can be an important element in changing the idea of production and prosperity, according to an increasingly attentive interpretation of the economics of sustainability.

The topic of Enterprise 4.0 thus constitutes a discontinuity factor with respect to the traditional conception of the subordinate employment relationship. The digital revolution, which makes it possible to promote and concretely practice a different organization of work and production, lays the conditions for an effective re-appropriation of work time and content not only in terms of greater freedom and self-determination in its execution but also - and above all - in the perspective of a different arrangement of interests between the parties according to the individual capabilities of the provider, useful for redesigning the boundaries between life time and projects and work time. This is a prospect still largely to be explored, especially if looked at in the light of the economic theories of the enterprise, firmly tied to an individualistic-proprietary vision and refractory to any reinterpretation in terms of workers' social capacity. In reality, it is precisely the reversal of a different conception of the enterprise that could pave the way for the construction of new bonds of solidarity in the places of production, such as to revive the aspiration, to which labour law has undoubtedly contributed, to realize social freedom in the economic sphere: a conception in which freedom is rethought in a solidaristic and less individualistic sense, where the realization of one's own freedom goals is not hinged on the individual but on the community of solidarity.

Business scholars who take sustainability seriously point to the emergence of a new type of business model called the 'well-being business model'. It refers to companies that intend to put the well-being of workers at the centre, prioritizing health, safety and well-being. As such, this model translates into actions with a high impact on the well-being of workers and their families, as well as on the territories to which they belong, emphasizing the following aspects: health and safety at work, corporate climate, clarity of corporate roles and functions; transparency, participatory or horizontal systems; professional and personal growth programmes for workers; work-life balance; corporate welfare or benefits systems; human-centred spaces and technologies.

This model is based on the awareness that a positive corporate climate, made up of people who are valued and enabled to 'feel good' not only in the workplace but also in their personal lives, increases employee motivation, representing a great asset for the company itself. Well-being becomes a determining capital in the company's internal processes and external relations and also helps to attract and retain talented personnel. Focusing on the potential needs of workers also means building new opportunities, providing conditions for growth – professional and personal – and opening up space for unexpressed potential and creativity. This model is flanked by the 'green and circular business model', which emphasizes respect for ecosystem regulation mechanisms within production processes, and the 'fair-trade business model', represented by companies that manage the supply chain with the paradigms of ethics, sustainability and innovative partnerships.

In the latter model, control over the supply chain makes it possible to mitigate the risks of unethical behaviour (towards workers and the environment) by reducing forms of exploitation in commercial relations, human rights violations and environmental damage, promoting fairness in the market. Finally, the 'social need business model' finds its highest expression in the proposal of Muhammed Yunus. In this model, instead of profit maximization, business focuses on the achievement of social objectives such as poverty reduction, health care for the poor, social justice, and global sustainability, while seeking psychological, emotional and spiritual satisfaction.

The common denominator of these sustainable business models is the new focus on people that can be directly translated into operational practices for companies in all sectors and of all sizes, with relevant effects on social and environmental aspects.

What are the possible effects of such changes in the different spheres – ethical, anthropological, legal – that can be detected in the logic of a change in the meaning of work?

On the ethical level, the hierarchy of values of conventional ethics changes: traditional values, based on discipline and subordination, are discredited and considered ethically illegitimate, to the advantage of other values, based on autonomy, creativity, and responsibility of the worker.

On the anthropological level, work – intertwined with knowledge, collaboration and unprecedented elements of freedom – aspires to represent the self-realization of the person who works, a tool for the transformation of persons and their environment. Work, unlike in the past, provides life with meaning.

On the juridical level, a new regulatory model centred on the development of the person, capable of overcoming the many old dichotomies of the culture of work: worker/citizen, subordination/autonomy, manual/intellectual work, productive/unproductive work, *homo faber/animal laborans*, etc.

§1.04 FREEDOM *WITHIN* AND *FROM* WORK

The second segment is that of freedoms, which have characterized philosophical reflection on work: the first is freedom in work (which can be linked to Hegel), and the second is freedom from work (which relates to Marx's thought).

For Hegel, freedom *within* work coincides with autonomy and self-realization (*Selbstbewußtsein*): the subordination of the servant turns into freedom when consciousness finds itself in the 'form' (Form) assumed by the matter transformed by work. Hegel writes that 'with labour, consciousness comes out of itself to pass into the element of permanence'; the negative relationship with the object now becomes the 'form' of the object itself and becomes something permanent, precisely because the object has autonomy in the eyes of the one who processes it. Thus, consciousness reaches its own self-realization within work, in the intuition of the object it produces as an independent being.

Here, however, the Marxian critique of alienation comes into play: work cannot produce self-realization because it is alienated, the servant cannot recognize the product of his/her work as 'one's own'; the worker is denied both the 'joy of production' and the 'enjoyment of the product'. As the craftsman of the Platonic Republic is excluded from any directivity and is placed outside any immediate relationship with rational values and is, therefore, an employed – χειροτεχνης, a mere agent incapable of true knowledge and virtue, the *homo faber* within the process of capitalist valorization has lost his/her theoretical approach, his/her extraneousness to the productivity scheme, his/her freedom (since freedom is guaranteed only by knowledge, which belongs to the intellectual elite governing the issues related to the polis). Work is now part of what Marx associates with capital and land within the 'Trinity formula' described in the third Book of Capital, in the context of the 'mysteries of the process of social production': work is a 'ghost', an abstraction that in general does not exist per se, but one through which man makes possible 'the interchange with nature', 'as an expression and confirmation of life which the still non-social man in general has in common with the one who is in any way social'. According to Marx, just as the savage must struggle with nature to satisfy his/her needs, to preserve and reproduce life, the 'civilized' is also forced into this struggle, 'in all forms of society and under all possible ways of production'. The term 'production' absorbs here that of work, in the philosophical-anthropological meaning of 'industry' (often employed by Marx in his writings, as well), and it indicates instrumental production, or work in its most developed stage: a productive activity equipped with the most advanced technology. 'up to now, any human activity has resulted as work, and therefore industry, that is, an activity made alien to itself', Marx wrote. Only outside the sphere of necessity does the sphere of freedom begin, where human capabilities develop; a sphere which, however, can only thrive on the basis of the sphere of necessity.

It is also true, however, that in the *Grundrisse* (1857-1858), Marx approaches the issue from a different point of view, discussing the nature of the activity of the medieval craftsman, and says that 'Here work itself is still half artistic, half an end in itself (*Selbstzweck*). Mastery.' In this Aristotelian excerpt, Marx defines artistic activity as having its own end in itself, that is, as a non-instrumental activity. If the non-instrumental production, that is 'free', should be in all respects of an artistic nature, it is evident that this does not take place at all in the forms (even juridical-formal) of employment and self-employment. Then he introduces the theme of freedom *within work* as a historical-utopian perspective: the subjective and objective conditions have not yet been created for work to be the 'self-realization of the individual'.

However, the conditions for this work can be *concretely conceived* and become actual. We can therefore argue that – under certain conditions – both for Marx and Hegel, work can be understood as the activity through which the human beings exteriorize their being and realize themselves.

Also in Alexandre Kojève's Hegelian reading the Servant, with his/her transforming action of Nature, accomplishes history: 'The human ideal, born within the Master, can be realized and revealed – can become truth – only in and by Slavery.' Within this fulfilment of history, the Master being its simple catalyst, the Servant fully participates in the social and historical nature of human work, in its specifically human activity, and by transforming Nature he also transforms his/her own Nature. Moreover, this happens as a function of an unnatural idea, that is, the possession of a technique, of a science, which the Greeks attributed both to the craftsman and to the artist (τεχνιτης).

Now, this is the question: can the smart factory and Work 4.0 create the conditions that make freedom *within* work possible? Of course, these are not the activities 'with an end in themselves' carried out with the 'joy' (Genuss) of the craftsman that Marx saw as lost in alienated labour. But it is nonetheless a fundamental change with respect to Fordist work. In Work 4.0, the collaborative human-machine relationship, the role of knowledge, the productive power acquired by language, the reduction of the distinction between employed and self-employed work and between manual and intellectual work, *are all elements that push towards a paradigm of work which makes persons free, which tends towards the self-realization of the persons*. Work that creates freedom *within* work is quality work, advocating autonomy, creativity and responsibility. Of course, we know that in the world of work, there are also neo-Fordist models, digitally hetero-directed, poor in quality, carried out by workers whose rights are denied on a daily basis. However, we cannot deny that the *smart factory* paradigm has elements that tend towards self-realization.

Let us now consider freedom *from* work. In his main work, the Capital, Marx does not place the emphasis on self-realization and freedom *within* work but on freedom *from* work, to be understood in quantitative terms, such as a reduction in working hours and redistribution of work.

However, the transformation of Work 4.0 changes the perspective of freedom *from* work, that is: it turns this freedom into something other than simple non-work. In the Fordist era, the time freed from work was as opposed to the time dedicated to work. Moreover, it is time dedicated to rest and consumption, therefore it is not functional time for the development of the person but actually for the *market*. In short: within Fordism, the free time that creates *leisure* is only a compensation, a balancing of the fatigue of work, of the alienation of the assembly line and at the same time an opportunity for the consumption of the goods produced by work.

But if Fordism is overcome by the smart factory - which changes the nature of work and creates work allowing people to free themselves *within* work - the leisure that is produced by freedom *from* work also changes. In this way, an unprecedented and powerful connection is created between freedom *within* work and freedom *from* work, a connection that becomes circular. Freedom *within* work and freedom *from* work are no longer antagonistic but complementary and tend to overlap. The free work of the smart factory is a different free time compared to that of Fordism. It is an active free time, to be devoted to recreational practices in the ancient sense of the Latin *otium* and the Greek *scholé*, that is to say, it consists of the generalization of the techniques of the self and of the others, it is not mere non-work, but it is *Bildung*, which refers to the German tradition of self-cultivation, an occasion for personal development, freedom to develop a wide variety of talents and abilities and this requires personal agency. Free time is the de-automation of everything that makes life worth living, it is knowledge, understanding, affection, human relationships, culture, sports, and religion.

Now, the issue I would like to address is that in this new model of freedom, work and idleness, work (*poeisis*) and contemplative activity tend to interpenetrate. Freedom is neither in work nor in idleness but in the ability to find the personal form of being within both. If we want to identify a model of this union between work and leisure in human history, we can think of Hesiod, the independent farmer from Boethia who wrote Works and Days, in which he narrates his passion for his work. Hesiod is the first worker who writes a poem about his work during his idleness, so he employs his idleness not as a simple time of non-work or rest, but as creative idleness, and lives in a balance between work and idleness as a not antagonistic activity.

Another example is that of Benvenuto Cellini, who on the one hand carries out manual work at levels of full autonomy and self-realization of the person, while on the other, in his spare time, writes his 'Life'. This is an autobiographical work which contains perhaps the most complete narration of this type of self-fulfilment in manual work, in which we find three key elements of extraordinary power and relevance: the personal relationship with work, freedom (understood both as a choice of what work to undertake and as a method and choice of places and conditions in which to work), training and continuous updating.

The smart factory should valorize all possible elements to realize spaces of freedom and autonomy in work that generate spaces of freedom from work. Starting from the idea of personal autonomy proposed by Joseph Raz as 'the vision of people controlling, to some degree, their own destiny, fashioning it through successive decisions throughout their lives', it was proposed to relate the worker's autonomy to work itself through job satisfaction and job security that derives from the personal experiences at the workplace or arises from the worker's ability to control his or her working life. In this perspective, the worker's autonomy presupposes a plurality of conditions, such as the mental ability to identify and know how to resolve issues that affect his/her working life, the access to information to generate a range of options for workers, the independence from coercive power and the modes of participation that empower the worker to effect changes in his/her working life.

Another key element in this perspective is the concept of trust and new forms of organization that grant employees more trust and autonomy, reducing the level of control. An example in this sense could be offered by remote work, which introduces a regulatory model based on trust rather than control and personal responsibility rather than hierarchy, granting the worker greater autonomy in terms of place and time. Changing 'how' and 'where' to work should not be the result of heteronomous rules imposed by company management. Collective bargaining can play a decisive role in the preparation of a framework of shared rules for the planning of remote work itself. According to the International Labour Organization (ILO), collective bargaining can be a good tool for designing teleworking practices and inclusive hybrid work, reconciling the preferences of employers and those of workers in terms of flexibility and autonomy, on the one hand, and guaranteeing decent conditions for remote work on the other hand.

Now, it is clear that this new project that I would define as 'neo-humanistic' of valorizing freedom *within* and *from* work certainly cannot be entrusted to the spontaneous forces of the market or to the rationality of capital. The promotion of Work 4.0 expressing freedom *within* work, as well as the techniques creating freedom *from* work, is not only the result of technological determinism but must also be guided by normative rationality and extra-economic values.

§1.05 PHILOSOPHICAL APPROACHES TO LABOUR LAW FROM THE PERSPECTIVE OF SOCIAL FREEDOM

This is where the third segment comes into play: labour law interacting with contemporary philosophies can help carry out this function of promoting the freedom of the working person. There are three main currents of thought that can come into play in this perspective of freedom in and from work: (1) the neo-republican political philosophy of non-domination; (2) the neo-Hegelian moral philosophy of recognition and social freedom (and, for me, participation); (3) the capabilities approach.

The first political philosophy orientation is the well-known *neo-republican* approach, which theorizes freedom as non-domination. This concept is fundamental if you want to develop a regulatory project based on the freedom of the worker as freedom *within* work: only if the worker is not dominated can they express their person within work, can they be as creative and autonomous as the smart factory demands them to be. But what is non-domination? It is an articulated political ideal that closely concerns labour law in its function of reducing social uncertainty and regulating the subjection of workers to employer power, with the aim of expanding the spaces of positive freedom of the subject. Although domination (in the republican sense) and subordination (in the legal sense) are not superimposable concepts, there is a connection, a bi-univocal correspondence between the two concepts: in fact, an increase in freedom as non-domination affects the morphology of subordination, just as normative changes to subordination (which is still a form of 'normative domination') in the direction of greater worker autonomy redefine the sphere of domination.

While the freedom of liberalism produces social insecurity and contrasts the law as being a factor of interference, neo-republican freedom is based on the protective function of law and on the distributive function of the State, both in domestic relations and in the workplace, where domination can be very intense and widespread.

Negative freedom maximizes non-interference, regardless of the worker's condition of social vulnerability – in fact, vulnerability is fully compatible with the worker's condition of negative freedom.

On the contrary neo-republican freedom requires compliance with constitutional directives and norms which insure workers against arbitrary acts of interference on the part of the employer. For this reason, freedom – in neo-republican terms – coincides with the protection offered by the law, which should never be labelled as 'paternalistic', but as the means to provide the subject with a power to counter the domination of others and to enable the subject to exercise basic freedoms without depending on the permission of others.

The fact that freedom (as non-domination) is a function of the subject's power has crucial implications on the possibility of acquiring a higher degree of non-domination through policies which are aimed at guaranteeing justice *in* the distribution of power. Freedom as non-domination is therefore combined with another key value of labour law: equality. While freedom as non-interference is anti-egalitarian, the link between maximizing the condition of non-domination and equality constitutes one of the main features of neo-republicanism. Neo-republicanism combines freedom not only with equality – *egalité* – but also with *fraternité*, the modern social solidarity. Freedom as non-domination – differently from freedom as non-interference – is for this reason a 'community good', shared by every single class of vulnerability. The cause of freedom is a social cause, not concerning isolated subjects in selfish competition, but the *united community* recognizing itself in the State, the only institution capable of guaranteeing the highest degree of non-domination.

Therefore, labour law as a security system based on heteronomous sources (law and collective bargaining) finds full theoretical justification in the neo-republican perspective, with non-domination as a demanding goal for social and political institutions. Far from expressing an oppressive paternalism, labour law is a guarantee of freedom for workers. In neo-republican terms, not only does labour law give workers control over interference but also a more advanced form of positive freedom, which is implemented with workplace republicanism. In this perspective, a legal system that is consistent with positive freedom ought to not only embed procedural protections for its citizens vertically vis-à-vis the State but also in respect of private social relationships, and in particular in the relationship between worker and entrepreneur.

Neo-republicanism requires the State to provide citizens *with both* the 'resilient right' to question decisions, and the right to share the influence and control of decision-making mechanisms in order to prevent 'uncontrolled interference' and legitimize 'collective order'. And now we get to the point: if these prerogatives are to characterize the *status* of free citizens in terms of non-domination in their relations with the State, they should be granted similar powers in the context of their 'economic citizenship', and in general in all the main spheres of life, because the domination citizens can suffer in private spheres is no less substantial than that within public power relations.

The second current of moral thought that must be considered, and possibly linked with neo-republicanism, is the theory of social freedom. Social freedom is based on the Hegelian idea of Recognition. Recognition plays an equally essential role as non-domination in the development of the person and of freedom understood as social freedom, that is, intersubjective. This social freedom is manifested in the world of work in two ways: in collaborative relationships and in the participation of workers in corporate decisions.

Unlike the liberal tradition, in 'freedom-as-recognition' the relations with other subjects have a positive value: this freedom must be found *in the other*. This is the freedom Hegel refers to when speaking of '*being-with-oneself in the other*' (*Bei-sich-Selbst-Sein-im-Anderen, Philosophy of Right §7*).

The Hegelian philosophy of recognition outlines the founding characteristics of historical development in the differentiated spheres of modern society, by delivering to our human consciousness a normative project of future transformation.

The legal systems implementing co-determination achieve social freedom in the sphere of labour through discursive mechanisms helping workers to deploy their cooperative activity. Social freedom requires that all actors in the labour market are able to carry out a cooperative activity in view of a common good transcending the strategic and selfish behaviour of the actors. Moreover, for this reason, they must be placed in a position to influence both strategic and organizational business decisions: because strategy concerns the development of the firm as a social institution, and because the organization contributes to the 'humanization of work'. The latter constitutes, together with the discursive mechanisms of cooperation, the second regulatory prerequisite for achieving social freedom.

If social freedom is identified with the 'relationships of recognition' that characterize our life in common, co-determination definitely represents the tool to achieve social freedom in the economic sphere, and for this reason, it must be promoted within social institutions, and in particular within the firm. This contravenes both the classical liberal vision that attributes an absolute value to individual contractual autonomy, and to the standard economic vision that considers that private ordering is more economically efficient than state-sanctioned rules. In fact, as Honneth believes, there is an intrinsic social normativity of the economic sphere (compared to the previous era) capable of reuniting the idea of freedom with that of justice. However, freedom and social justice are conceptualized as conditions that demand 'non-domination' in a private bilateral relationship. Consequentially a space is opened to revisit the theory of the employment relationship as a relation of subordination, which obviously is linked to the different conceptions of the firm and its governance in democratic terms. In essence, a new perspective opens up to consider the employment relationship in a different light from that described by the great twentieth-century sociology at the dawn of the Fordist era, that is, in terms of the full subjection of the worker to the domain of the entrepreneur, and one space opens to rethink both the scope of the economic domination and the structure of the labour market, and, finally, the strategic role of the labour in the organizational dimension of productive activity. According to Honneth, social freedom is closely related to the institutional dimension and to the idea of mutual recognition that lives in the ethical-moral dimension of the market through a *normative functionalism* that, according to a line of thought that leads from Hegel to Durkheim and Polanyi, is capable to legitimize the market by forcing all actors to follow principles of fairness and justice.

The conditions for achieving social freedom in the context of the market economy are the following: first, 'the purely individual self-interest constitutive of market behaviour must be able to fulfil the normative condition that all participants can understand it as a suitable means for the complementary realization of their own respective purposes'. Second, market institutions must 'institutionally reflect these underlying claims to social freedom, thus ensuring that the participants remain aware of these claims'. Third, '(e)xpressed in terms of recognition, this means that economic actors must have recognized each other as members of a cooperative community before they can grant each other the right to maximise individual utility'. This last step is very important for the legitimization of the board-level employee representation both from the point of view of the theory of the firm and from the point of view of the employment relationship. From this last perspective, it is clear that the participation of workers represents a device capable of rebalancing the status of subordination to the extent that the coordination of individuals can be successful only if they 'recognize each other not only legally as parties to contract but also morally or ethically as members of a cooperative community'.

Finally, the capabilities approach. A careful reading of Sen's work clarifies that capabilities are 'positive' freedoms conceived as real opportunities: in this sense means that one has all the required means necessary to achieve that doing and being if one wishes to. That is, it is not merely the formal freedom to do or be something, but the substantial opportunity to achieve it.

This approach looks at freedom as a concrete possibility for the person to act through choices of alternative functioning. More than 'primary goods', functions are therefore the concrete expression of the freedom of the persons, who can be said to be free because they can choose. Among these capabilities, there is one fundamental for our analysis, and that is training. Training is the capability to learn and through this knowledge to develop one's functions.

The smart factory needs people who have developed such capabilities. Beware: it is not about acquiring and updating skills in the interests of the company, as a function of productivity, like in the Fordist factory; it is actually about training that enables the working person to participate and to be actively involved in the processes. As a matter of fact, without constant training, the working person cannot be involved in such innovative processes. But participation and involvement are the person's experiences, not their skills. The theory of capabilities places the cultural conflict under the spotlight rather than the economic conflict and puts the issue of freedom on the top of the list as the choice of one's own functioning. We need this to develop regulatory strategies for training as a driving force for further and larger capabilities, to stimulate the growth of the person. The challenge is to create capabilities through training to be used by companies and thus to create companies that put forward knowledge and a labour law that guarantees new rights of freedom and self-fulfilment through knowledge.

But there is more, because the capabilities approach, in my opinion, also constitutes a justification for the participation of workers in company decisions. In fact, this tension towards the creation of individual capabilities requires institutional vectors capable of transforming abstract principles into effective rules: in the theory of capabilities the problem consists in the translation of subjective preferences into substantial freedoms – that is to say in individual capabilities – through a series of 'conversion factors' operating at different levels. Among these conversion factors, the organizational and life context of people, together with social and legal norms, play an essential role, so that the participation of workers should act as a factor of concretization and conversion to support the creation of capabilities for the worker in the specific business context and, therefore, to implement concrete forms of democratization of the employment relationship. Board-level workers' participation should, in short, be part of a systemic project consisting of promoting substantial freedom in the workplace and ensuring that each person can best fulfil himself in the performance of tasks useful to himself and others. In the current phase of changing labour law, its levels of protection and its own objectives and values, the participation of workers can therefore be a useful tool to make sense of the employment relationship in a direction that can bring together the efforts to redefine a social citizenship increasingly threatened by the deconstruction of the social rights and solidarity typical of the industrial era.

I conclude by saying that if we put together the three segments I have discussed, and if these three segments really do go together, then we would have both a new concept of work, very different from that of Fordism, and a new idea of freedom of the person (*within* work and *from* work) and, finally, a new function for labour law, that of truly becoming the law of freedom.

CHAPTER 2
The Future of Work

Sophie Robin-Olivier

For labour law scholars, reflecting on the future of work is not an easy task. What we are used to considering is not work but labour law, its structure, its notions and its rules. Although the nature and modalities of work cannot be ignored by a discipline that intends to regulate work relations and protect workers, work often remains an abstract concept in labour law. However, the concrete conditions under which it is achieved are essential to the determination of a legal regime of protection. When these conditions change, the conceptual framework that labour law constitutes, as well as the categories of workers it covers, should evolve in tandem. This is imperative unless the fabric of labour law is sufficiently flexible to adapt. That is why, without pretending to be any kind of a visionary, it is vital, in a time of substantial social, economic, technological, and, above all, 'ecological' transformation,[1] to identify how these factors impact work and its modalities, and the ways labour law can adjust to a new system of production. *Vice versa*, as institutionalists would contend, work is also determined by the law that regulates its operation. The future of work depends on the future of labour law. This chapter will therefore examine the future of work from the perspective of factors of transformation lying both outside and within labour law.

Among the factors transforming the world of work, one stands out today as particularly influential. Latour calls it the 'new climate regime'.[2] It is anticipated that the reforms necessitated by climate change, often euphemized by the term 'green transition', will profoundly alter the fundamental structure of society.[3] According to Latour, the 'new climate regime', which 'shakes the cosmic order', will inevitably

---

1. The ILO Declaration on the Future of work (2019) referred to 'technological innovations, demographic shifts, environmental and climate change, and globalization' as factors of transformation of the world of work.
2. B. Latour, 'After the Lockdown: A Metamorphosis', Duke Polity Press, 2021.
3. The European Commission Green Deal (2019) acknowledges the need for a global transformation of the EU economy.

transform the political order as well.[4] This mutation, which has only recently attracted the attention of labour law scholars,[5] is not an isolated phenomenon. Rather, it is inextricably linked with the other social, economic, and technological transformations that have affected work and labour law since the beginning of the twenty-first century: the deregulation of the labour markets, fragmentation of the category of workers, increased inequalities and precariousness, and the exploitation of the most vulnerable workers around the world.

A central, although relatively new question, for labour law, in the 'new climate regime', is the role it can, and should, play in the definition of new ways to inhabit the Earth.[6] Meant to protect workers in a system based on exploitation of natural resources, the field of labour law was not originally designed to accommodate the existence of entities other than humans, whether living or non-living. How can it endorse a new role in an ecological perspective that no longer ignores relationships with non-humans? How can it serve to recognize and ensure, in the world of work, 'attachment to the other beings that are necessary for existence'[7]? This would entail, as Baptiste Morizot suggests, taking into account relations with non-humans and with other livings' territories, and diplomatically dealing with entanglements and attachments.[8] This approach is markedly distinct from the prevailing paradigm of labour law, which is primarily concerned with the interpersonal dynamics between workers and between workers and firms within a system designed to serve the interests of humanity. It requires a re-examination of the concept of work that forms the basis of labour law.

One initial step in this direction consists in reconstructing the relationships within the category of workers that have been impaired as a consequence of processes of deregulation, globalization and, more recently, digitalization. Fragmentation of forms of work, and the invisibilization of vulnerable workers in global supply chains, and in the informal economy, have led to the exclusion of larger categories of workers from the protection granted by labour law. Instead of making relationships and dependencies visible, and including them in its perspective, labour law has contributed to the separation of groups of workers. The future of work thus depends on the capacity of labour law to include workers currently left outside its field of application. This is one way to reconnect the pieces of the divided world of work, but it is not sufficient to account for the ecological transformation, which also requires connections with non-human entities. In this chapter, we will start with a description of the state of work, a state of fragmentation,[9] and the difficulties in the way towards a more inclusive

4. B. Latour, 'Critical Zones: The Science and Politics of Landing on Earth', MIT Press, 2020.
5. Among early research on the role of labour law in the context of the 'green transition', *see*, in particular: David J. Doorey, 2017. Just Transitions Law: Putting Labour Law to Work on Climate Change. *Journal of Environmental Law and Practice* 30(2): 201.
6. On the notion of 'ways to inhabit the Earth': Latour, 'Critical Zones …', *supra* n. 4.
7. B. Latour, 'An Inquiry into Modes of Existence', Harvard University Press, 2013.
8. B. Morizot, 'Les Diplomates, Cohabiter avec les loups sur une autre carte du vivant', Wildproject, 2016.
9. On the state of fragmentation and the challenges it represents for international labour law, *see* Etienne Pataut & Sophie Robin-Olivier (eds), 'White Paper on the Future of Labour Law', International Law Association, 2023, https://www.ilaparis2023.org/en/white-paper/labour/.

labour law. In the second part of this analysis, we will consider the more comprehensive reconceptualization of work, and labour law, that is necessary to account for the climate mutation.

§2.01 FRAGMENTED WORK AND THE STRUGGLE TOWARDS A MORE INCLUSIVE LABOUR LAW

This section distinguishes between two different aspects of fragmentation. The first results from the diversification of forms of work, which goes hand in hand with more precarious work arrangements. The second aspect of fragmentation is the effect of 'deterritorialisation' of work. This is a territorial modality of fragmentation that results from the localization of work in different jurisdictions. The ability of labour law to reduce these fragmentations remains uncertain, despite recent evolutions in this direction.

1) Diversification of Forms of Work

Forms of work relations have diversified, with more and more flexible working arrangements being used as modalities of work, leading to a fragmentation of forms of work.[10] In 2024, this is nothing really new.[11] The emergence and spreading of so-called atypical contracts have been a core issue for labour law in the past decades.[12] Nevertheless, the distinction between standard and non-standard (or atypical) work arrangements, with a multitude of nuances within the category of the 'non-standard' forms (from part-time, fixed-term, and temporary work contracts to self-employment or a combination of the former), and the growing proportion of the workforce engaged in alternative employment arrangements, continues to challenge the efficacy of labour law in ensuring the protection of all workers. These multiple categories introduce a rather rigid division between the most privileged workers, who benefit from the full range of social rights, and the more precarious groups. This division has led to competition between workers and a race to the bottom that threatens the most advanced protections.[13]

In recent years, the rise of digital platforms has facilitated this shift towards fragmentation, creating more opportunities for those engaged in the gig economy,

10. According to the ILO, non-standard work (in particular, reliance on temporary or casual workers) has recently increased, including in segments previously associated with standard jobs (ILO, 'Non-standard Employment Around the World: Understanding Challenges, Shaping Prospects', Geneva, 2016, p. 2).
11. On this topic, *see* namely: K. Stone & H. Arthurs (eds), 'Rethinking Workplace Regulation: Beyond the Standard Contract of Employment', Russel Sage Foundation, 2013; D. Weil, 'The Fissured Workplace: Why Work Became So Bad for So Many and What Can Be Done to Improve It', Harvard University Press, 2014; S. Robin-Olivier, 'Les contrats de travail flexibles', Presses de SciencesPo, 2016.
12. For an analysis in European Labour Law, *see*: Antonio Lo Faro & Sophie Robin-Olivier, 'Atypical Forms of Employment', in T. Jaspers, F. Pennings & S. Peters (eds), European Labour Law, Intersentia, 2024, p. 327.
13. Such as, for instance, the protection against unfair dismissal, which has been called in question in many European jurisdiction, in the last decades.

among whom platform workers. When they are considered self-employed, these workers fall outside the scope of traditional employment protections (minimum wage, regulation of working time, protection against unfair dismissal, and the right to collective action, in particular), which are structured around the concept of an employment relationship where the employer has significant control over the employee's working conditions. Many studies have described in detail the very precarious situation of most platform workers.[14]

As a result of, namely, fragmentation, poverty at work has increased,[15] and become a more central concern, namely at the European Union (EU) level.[16] However, for now, law developments concerning poverty at work have been limited. The most recent action, at the EU level, focused on wages, and it has resulted in the adoption of the Directive on minimum adequate wages.[17] To be sure, this directive can be considered an important step forward, especially if it manages to reactivate sectoral collective bargaining in a sector where poverty at work is more rampant. However, this piece of legislation aiming at decent wages does not provide solutions for workers who are the most precarious, including platform workers under very flexible work arrangements, who only work for limited hours, often as self-employed. Poverty at work cannot be efficiently combatted by a conception of minimum wage, which does not take into account new forms of low-paid or unpaid 'work' resulting from digitalization. As explained by Zoe Adams and Nicola Contouris,[18] digitalization has resulted in a new category of work that has been defined as 'heteromated work'. This is a form of low-cost work or free labour in computer-mediated networks from which economic value is extracted.[19] Heteromated forms of work include work in the gig economy, the user-generated data extracted by digital platforms, or customer work in the context of self-service machines, for instance.[20] The integration of technology and machines

---

14. For a recent study, *see* C. Marzo (ed.), 'Réinventer la protection sociale des travailleurs de plateformes numériques: Étude pluridisciplinaire des fondements de la protection sociale à la lumière du travail de plateformes', Mare&Martin, 2023. Among numerous publications on the topic, *see*, for a comparative approach: Isabelle Daugareilh, Christophe Degryse & Philippe Pochet, 'The Platform Economy and Social Law: Key Issues in Comparative Perspective', ETUI, working paper 2019-10, https://www.etui.org/sites/default/files/WP-2019.10-EN-v3-WEB.pdf.
15. On the impact of fragmentation on in-work poverty, *see* Oliver de Schutter, 'The Working Poor: A Human Rights Approach to Wages', Report of the Special Rapporteur on extreme poverty and human rights, A/78/175.
16. *See* namely the European Parliament Resolution of 10 February 2021 on Reducing Inequalities with a Special Focus on In-Work Poverty (2019/2188 (INI)). Luca Ratti & Antonio Garcia-Muñoz, 2022. In-Work Poverty, and Vulnerable Workers. *European Law Open* 1: 734. *See also* S. Robin-Olivier, La pauvreté au travail: nouveau sujet et nouvelle méthode de la politique sociale de l'Union, 2021. *Revue trimestrielle de droit européen* 2: 497.
17. Directive (EU) 2022/2041 of the European Parliament and of the Council of 19 October 2022 on adequate minimum wages in the EU, OJ L 275, 25 October 2022, p. 33.
18. Zoe Adams & Nicola Contouris, 'Heteromated Labour in 21st Century Computing Capitalism: A Critical Conceptualisation of "Work"', ILO RDW 2019 Conference, 9 July 2019.
19. H. Ekbia & B. Nardi, 'Heteromation, and Other Stories of Computing and Capitalism', MIT Press, 2017, p. 1.
20. Adams & Contouris, *supra* n. 18.

makes the nature of the work, and its beneficiary, much harder to identify in order to ensure wealth redistribution.[21]

More recently, telework has become a more and more frequent modality of work, and another possible source of fragmentation. To be sure, telework does not require the same type of reconceptualization of work as 'heteromation'. But it represents a novel form of work that has emerged with particular prominence in the context of the COVID-19 pandemic, which challenges the traditional organization of work. Not only is the existence of subordination less obvious since physical presence, direct supervision, and fixed working hours are indeed less apparent but also the definition of working conditions, and the issues related to digitalization, which telework depends on (the right to privacy,[22] to disconnect, the extraction of data produced by workers ...) raise a number of questions still unanswered. In States, which have started to regulate telework, the law recognizes the existence of this particular category of workers, with specific needs and rights.[23] Telework is not only a source of concern for labour law and social rights' protection but it is also, as opposed to other forms of precarious work previously envisaged, considered a social advantage by many workers. In the future, telework, under different modalities, might well become a standard modality of work, for many workers, all the more so as climate change policies are a justification for limiting mobility. The fragmentation that will result, as far as it is concerned, will be one between workers who can benefit from this modality of work and others.

All in all, it is beyond dispute that a significant proportion of workers are no longer able to achieve work within the parameters of the 'general form' of employment relationship as defined by the Court of Justice (employment contracts of indefinite duration).[24] Forms of work have diversified, which would require that labour law extends its scope of application in order to ensure that all workers, or a larger group of workers, receive adequate protection, regardless of their employment status. In recent years, labour law has begun to evolve in this direction, albeit at a gradual pace and in a limited manner. At the EU level, for instance, the directive on transparent and predictable working conditions[25] aims at improving the situation of very precarious workers. In EU Member States, courts have sometimes reclassified platform workers as employees to ensure their protection,[26] and legislations, including at the EU level, have

---

21. *Ibid.*
22. On privacy and telework, *see* in particular: Frank Hendrickx, 'Privacy@Work: A Systemic Introduction', in Frank Hendrickx et al. (eds), Privacy@Work, A European and Comparative Perspective, Kluwer, 2023, p. 50.
23. *See* in France, for instance: Ordonnance No. 2017-1387 of 22 September 2017 (the law defines teleworking arrangements and establish rights and obligations for both employers and teleworkers, but it mostly relies on contractual provisions and collective agreements for determining working conditions).
24. *See* namely: ECJ, C-109/09, *Kumpan*, ECLI: EU: C:2011:129, para. 30.
25. Directive (EU) 2019/1152 of the European Parliament and of the Council of 20 June 2019.
26. *See*, for instance: the *Uber* case decided by the French Cour de cassation (20 March 2020, n° 19-13.316); the decision of the UK Supreme Court in *Uber v. Aslam* (2021) UKSC 5, and, more recently, the *Deliveroo* Judgment of the Dutch Supreme Court (ECLI:NL:HR:2023:44, 24 March 2023).

also evolved in order to guarantee a certain degree of protection to platform workers.[27] More importantly, a redeployment of labour law is currently going on at the EU level to cover various forms of 'personal work' that are not performed under employment contracts.[28] These recent evolutions are still only light touches, but they contribute to bringing within the sphere of labour law more complex and diversified work relationships.

2) Deterritorialization of Work

Social law traditionally applies within States: States' territories have been the scope and the limit of labour law, and social security law. Work that labour law covers takes place on one national territory, where rights are protected and social security benefits are granted.[29] This territoriality of social law has led to a 'deterritorialisation' of work driven by global supply chains, and more recently, platform work, which allow firms to resort to workers living and working in locations remote from the place where the goods are consumed or services delivered.[30]

This deterritorialization of work is the outcome of existing gaps between labour law regimes that businesses can exploit.[31] Free trade and technological advancements have thus made it possible for companies to resort to workers across the world who do not have to leave their home country, but, as a result, cannot claim the benefit or a more protective labour law than the one applicable in that country. Or, when they leave for short-time migration, for instance, in the framework of free provision of services within the EU, they remain legally covered by the law of their home state.[32] Fragmentation and competition take place between workers in (or from) the 'Global South', who contribute to the production of goods or services for firms incorporated in the 'Global North', and workers in the 'Global North'. The critics against this form of

27. The Directive on improving working conditions in platform work has been adopted by the European Parliament on 24 March 2024 but still needs to be formally adopted by the Council. The Directive is not only aiming at facilitating reclassification of platform workers as employees: but it will also extend the rights of workers submitted to algorithmic management to self-employed workers and, in general, all those who operate via a digital platform.
28. For a synthesis of recent EU law evolutions converging toward 'personal work' as the condition of protection, *see* Adalberto Perulli, 2024. A New Category Within European Union Law: Personal Work. *European Labour Law Journal* 15(1): 184-210 https://doi.org/10.1177/20319525231221225. For a more general analysis of personal work, as an analytical framework to further worker rights in today's world of work, *see* Nicola Contouris, Valerio De Stefano & Marc Freedland (eds), 2019. Testing the 'Personal Work' Relation: New Trade Union Strategies for New Forms of Employment. *ELLJ special issues* 10(3).
29. On this construction of labour law, *see* namely: Guy Mundlack, 2009. De-Territorializing Labour Law. *Law & Ethics of Human Rights* 3(2): 189 https://doi.org/10.2202/1938-2545.1037.
30. *See* namely: C. Gammage & T. Novitz (eds), 'Sustainable Trade, Investment and Finance', Edward Elgar Publishing, 2019, Chapter 1, https://china.elgaronline.com/edcollchap/edcoll/9781788971034/9781788971034.00006.xml.
31. On this topic, *see* namely: Myriam Cherry, 'Regulatory Options for Conflicts of Law and Jurisdictional Issues in the On-demand Economy', ILO Conditions of work and employment series No. 106, 2019.
32. For a critic of this form of exploitation, *see* namely: Sophie Robin-Olivier, September 2022. Posting of Workers in the European Union: An Exploitative Labour System. *European Law Open* 1(3) https://doi.org/10.1017/elo.2022.38.

labour exploitation, which has neo-colonialist overtones,[33] are all the more justified as the most vulnerable workers in the global supply chains are subjected to violations of their fundamental social rights, including forced labour and child labour.[34]

Deterritorialization of work requires a reevaluation of the scope of labour law and social security rules to ensure protection of all workers in the chain of production, including those working on territories where they risk exploitation or are subjected to forms of mobility which make them vulnerable and leaves them unprotected. Different ways to extend labour law protection outside national territories have been explored: international labour standards, which is the primary endeavour of the International Labour Organization (ILO); integrating labour law into international trade law[35] and developing non-territorial regulation for the protection of workers through non-binding corporations' code of conduct.[36] Transnational collective agreements have also been experimented with as a possible instrument of protection of a globalized workforce.[37]

In addition to these still relatively constrained approaches, a more ambitious development of the law is emerging, which constitutes a more efficient method to blur the divide between the different categories of workers involved in production at a transnational level. In the EU, social regulation of global supply chains is currently taking place in the framework of 'sustainable' reporting[38] and sustainable due diligence[39] imposed on big corporations. The introduction of these new requirements places an obligation on businesses that depend on a deterritorialized workforce to consider and strive to enforce social standards benefiting all workers involved in the production process, including self-employed and employees of subcontractors. Indeed, this process creates new distinctions among workers: 'own workforce', 'workers in the value chain' and 'affected communities' are not granted the same consideration.[40] There is a gradation in terms of responsibility of big companies, depending on their particular relation with the different categories of workers in the chain. However, all

33. For a critic of global supply chains as instruments of imperialism, *see* namely: Intan Suwandi, R. Jamil Jonna & John Bellamy Foster, 'Global Commodity Chains and the New Imperialism', 2019, https://www.jussemper.org/Resources/Economic%20Data/Resources/GlobalCommodityChains.pdf.
34. On forced labour in global supply chains, *see* namely: F. Bodendorf, F. Wonn, K. Simon & J. Franke, 'Indicators and Countermeasures of Modern Slavery in Global Supply Chains: Pathway to a Social Supply Chain Management Framework', Business Strategy and the Environment, 2022, pp. 1-29 and the Commission Proposal for a regulation of the European Parliament and of the Council on prohibiting products made with forced labour on the Union market COM(2022) 0453.
35. For recent evolutions of the EU trade agreements, to better protect social rights through 'sustainability chapters', *see* namely: Marc Jütten, 'Trade and Sustainable Development in the EU Free Trade Agreements', EPRS, European Parliament, 2023.
36. On these different paths: Mundlack, *supra* n. 29.
37. On this topic, *see* Etienne Pataut, 'Les accords collectifs internationaux', in K. Chatzilaou & N. Mihman (eds), La figure du travailleur à l'épreuve de l'internationalisation du droit du travail, CY Cergy Paris Université, 2022.
38. Directive 2022/2464 of 14 December 2022 on Corporate Sustainability Reporting and Commission delegated regulation 2023/2772 of 31 July 2023 on sustainability reporting standards.
39. Directive 2024/1760 of 13 June 2024 on corporate Sustainability due Diligence.
40. This typology is derived from the Commission delegated regulation 2023/2772 of 31/0//2023 on sustainability reporting standards.

workers in the chain must be taken into account, which contrasts with the strict separation of workers on the basis of their territorial situation. The fragmentation resulting from a deterritorialization of some workers is no longer ignored, but this is not so simple for labour law to embrace this evolution.

3) Labour Law Challenges in Overcoming Fragmentation

Among the challenges that labour law faces, in order to adapt to fragmentation, one central one is its ability, and legitimacy, to bridge the gaps resulting from the definition of its own categories and borders. The decline of the standard employment model upon which labour law was constructed, coupled with the weakness of the 'labour' class and movement, poses a risk of erosion of labour law as a legal field.[41]

In recent times, it has become clear that the regulation of work relations was more and more taken over by other branches of law. If we consider the diversification of work arrangements and globalization effects on the segmentation of workers, the most recent developments confirm that important evolutions take place outside the realm of labour law. This is particularly obvious in so far as global supply chains are at stake. Regulation through sustainable reporting and due diligence mentioned above is not achieved under the auspices of labour law. Labour law instruments, such as international labour convention or transnational collective agreements, although not negligible, are not the driving forces. International trade law and corporate law are the domains in which major changes take place. Similarly, collective bargaining of platform workers depends, for a part, on changes in the domain of anti-trust law.[42]

This is not necessarily problematic if the objectives of labour law can be achieved in these different legal fields. When looking at the conception of workers according to the EFRAG standards,[43] labour law scholars could rejoice that they reflect a progressive conception of workers, whose working conditions have to be taken into account in the process of production. However, there is a potential for loss or dilution when labour concepts are transferred from their original context to another field. The interpretation of notions such as equality and non-discrimination, freedom of association, or the right to privacy, to take just a few examples, have a long history, through which their interpretation, in the context of work relations, has been developed and refined. What happens when social rights are conceived and interpreted in a legal framework which is disconnected (partly or fully) from labour law? With regard to novel concepts such as the notion of 'own workforce', 'workers in the value chain' and 'affected communities', they are not categories of labour law. Consequently, unless labour law manages to incorporate them, they continue to exist beyond the scope of its legal framework.

Similarly, labour law cannot ensure an appropriate regulation of 'heteromated labour': social security law, family law, tax law, and even competition and company

41. On this evolution, *see* G. Davidov & B. Langille (eds), 'Boundaries and Frontiers of Labour Law', Oxford, Hart Publishing, 2006.
42. Cf. the Communication from the Commission 'Guidelines on the application of Union competition law to collective agreements regarding the working conditions of solo self-employed persons', 2022/C 374/02, 29 September 2022.
43. Which have become binding through the Commission delegated regulation 2023/2772 of 31/0//2023 on sustainability reporting standards.

law, must be involved in order to ensure that all workers receive a socially necessary wage in practice.[44] If platforms do not remunerate their users directly, one way to ensure that the profit resulting from the use of the data collected is to tax them in order to fund public services and social assistance, and/or to require that they make that data available for public use.[45] When, in particular, work is provided, for free, by consumers using self-service machines, consumer law, contract law and tax law are more appropriate regulatory frameworks than labour law. These legal fields seem better placed than labour law to ensure that cost-saving obtained by firms be passed on to the consumer in the form of lower prices, and/or to charge a license fee for the use of such machines, and to use the sums obtained for public purposes.[46]

Fragmentation also weakens trade unions and the labour movement itself. The ability of trade unions to represent the various categories of workers, and possibly consumers too, is uncertain. Other forms of representation emerge besides trade unions to defend the rights and interests of non-standard workers, especially platform workers.[47] Although this is not always straightforward, given the differing histories and objectives of these organizations, trade unions and NGOs can form alliances. Such alliances between organizations representing different types of interests seem particularly necessary from an ecological perspective, which requires consideration for more extended categories of interests.

§2.02 RETHINKING WORK IN AN ECOLOGICAL PERSPECTIVE: ATTACHMENTS, DEPENDENCIES AND DECENT WORK

Work fragmentation imposes a new type of regulation capable of encompassing the variety of forms and diversity of places of work, and creating relationships, possibly complex ones, instead of divisions. In the same line, the ecological perspective on work is about links and dependencies, but it goes beyond relationships between the different categories of workers.[48] The ecological take on work requires further reconceptualization of work and working conditions to include the impact ***on*** work, and the impact ***of*** work on non-human entities, living and non-living. In light of the various proposals put forth in this direction, we propose the addition of an extended notion of decent work that could encapsulate the ecological concerns for attachments and dependencies.

1) Two Bifurcations

The ecological perspective on work involves two major shifts in the ideological foundations of labour law. First, as already mentioned, it imposes setting aside the

44. Adams & Countouris, *supra* n. 18.
45. *Ibid.*
46. *Ibid.*
47. On this topic *see*: Isabelle Daugareilh, 'Formes de mobilisation collective et économie des plateformes: Approche pluridisciplinaire et comparative', Rapport de recherche CNRS; Université de Bordeaux., 2022, p. 558.
48. On rethinking work in an environmentalist perspective, *see* the different approaches suggested in N. Räthzel, D. Stevis & D. Uzzell (eds), 'The Palgrave Handbook of Environmental Labour Studies', Palgrave Macmillan, 2021.

human-centred approach. Work, as labour law initially conceived it, aims at fulfilling human needs. Labour law's main focus has been the protection of people not 'nature'.[49] In its Declaration on the Future of Work, and factors that determine this future, including climate change and sustainable development, the ILO insisted on the notion of 'human' dignity. This is an illustration of the human-centred approach that continues to prevail in the ILO approach to work. In an ecological transformation, labour law should take into account humans and non-human entities ('nature'),[50] and address the relationship between work, workers, and the socio-ecological system. A redefinition of work is necessary to take into account the impact of this human activity on the existence of other living and non-living, within an ecological system encompassing these various modes of existence. This represents a radical transformation of the programme of labour law, which must include reflections on the ways in which workers can relate to non-human entities with which they are coengaging, coworking and cotransforming, and on the quality of that relation.[51]

The second bifurcation concerns the use of resources in the process of work. Reducing the impact of human activity on the planet requires sobriety. In contrast, work, when viewed through the lens of productivism, entails an extensive exploitation of (natural and human) resources. From an ecological perspective, work and working conditions are no longer guided by the objective of increasing productivity but rather revolve around the central objective of saving resources.

2) Just Transition and Green Jobs

Just transition aims at ensuring that 'no one is left behind in the transition'. It is concerned with the impact of climate change and climate change reforms on the most vulnerable groups and individuals.[52] It seeks greening the economy 'in a way that is fair and inclusive to all concerned by maximizing the social and economic opportunities of environmental actions, including climate action and protecting biodiversity, while minimizing and carefully managing the negative impact on workers and enterprises'.[53] It aims 'to support workers, enterprises and communities affected by economic shifts away from certain sectors and regions'.[54] According to the ILO, a just transition framework for all should namely promote the creation of more decent jobs through anticipating impacts on employment, adequate and sustainable social protection for job losses and displacement, skills development and social dialogue, including the effective exercise of the right to organize and bargain collectively.[55]

49. On this disconnect of labour law from the sphere of 'nature', or the socio-ecological system, *see* Ania Zbyszewska, 2018. Regulating Work with People and 'Nature' in Mind: Feminist Reflections. *Comp. Lab. L. & Pol'y J.* 40: 20.
50. On the problem with separation of 'nature' and society, *see* namely Zbyszewska, *supra* n. 49 and Supriya Routh, 2018. Embedding Work in Nature: The Anthropocene and Legal Imagination of Work as Human Activity. *Comp. Lab. L. & Pol'y J.* 40: 29.
51. *Ibid.*
52. EU Green Deal (2019), *supra* n. 3.
53. *See* namely: ILO, UNEP & IUCN, 'Decent Work in Nature-based Solutions', Geneva; 2022, p. 18.
54. *Ibid.*
55. ILO Guidelines for a just transition towards environmentally sustainable economies and societies for all, 2015.

This, however, constitutes a minimal version of the transformation of work and work regulation in the context of the 'new climate regime'. It focuses on the development of green jobs and green skills to cope with future job loss in sectors that may disappear or suffer substantial shrinks due to regulatory requirements in greenhouse gas reduction targets. The objective of 'just transition' is to better match labour supply and demand and avert the labour market, social, and economic consequences of the green transformation.[56] This could indeed justify the emergence of a 'Just Transition Law' conceived as a new legal field bringing together environmental law, environmental justice, and labour law in order to elaborate legal responses to climate change.[57]

However, this concept of just transition does not focus on relationships and dependencies. It has also prompted criticism, primarily due to its failure to challenge the underlying model of production and the role of work.[58] To be sure, 'just transition' does not challenge the logic of growth and productivity: it relies on green growth, which entails the decoupling of economic growth from resource use[59] but does not question growth itself. As such, the creation of green or sustainable jobs is an ineffective strategy for contributing to the development of a new ecological model of work that takes into account the interconnections and interdependencies between humans and other living and non-living entities.

3) Decent Work in the Ecological Perspective

Forms of work not governed by the objective to increase production and productivity already exist. These work practices that already deviate from productivism have been proposed as a starting point to design ecological transition trajectories.[60] Social economy, and in particular not-for-profit cooperatives, belongs to this different paradigm.[61] Reconceptualization of work beyond productivism has inspired a series of other innovative proposals.[62]

A promising path in the direction of rethinking labour/work in a degrowth society consists of considering not only paid labour but also work in general, including unpaid work.[63] The implications of such an extension of the concept of work are far-reaching, extending beyond the aforementioned fragmentation of forms and places of work. Another way to rethink work in consideration of social and ecological local contexts is the notion of 'job guarantee', currently experimented with in different

56. *See* Zbyszewska, *supra* n. 49, p. 25.
57. On this proposal: Doorey, *supra* n. 5.
58. *See* Zbyszewska, *supra* n. 49, p. 26.
59. Cf. the ILO Guidelines and the European Green Deal.
60. Elise Dermine & Daniel Dumont, 2022. A Renewed Critical Perspective on Social Law: Disentangling Its Ambivalent Relationship with Productivism. *International Journal of Comparative Labour Law and Industrial Relations* 38(4): 237 https://doi.org/10.54648/ijcl2022012.
61. Support at the EU level has increased in recent time. *See* namely: European Commission Action Plan for the social economy, Luxembourg, Publications Office of the European Union, 2021.
62. On this idea, *see* the contributions in N. Bueno, B. ter Haar & N. Zekic (eds), 'Labour Law Utopias: Post-Growth & Post-Productive Work Approaches', OUP, 2024. On the world of work beyond capitalism, *see also*: T. Jackson, 'Post Growth: Life after Capitalism', Polity Press, 2021, namely Chapter 8, 'The Return to Work', p. 108.
63. Anna Saave & Barbara Muraca, 'Rethinking Labour/Work in a Degrowth Society', in Räthzel, Stevis & Uzzell (eds), *supra* n. 48, p. 743.

regions of the EU.[64] In recent years, the 'job guarantee', consisting of government provision of basic, relatively low-paid, and public-good-oriented jobs to all those willing to work, has been proposed as an environmental project. It aims at providing employment in conjunction with addressing significant societal needs that are not currently met by the State or the market, which includes jobs aiming at environmental sustainability.[65] Building renewable energy infrastructure, rehabilitating polluted land, and rebuilding cities to expand public transit and improve energy efficiency are seen as possible objectives.[66] The 'job guarantee' is also described as an inherently green policy because of its organic connection with the climate conservation movement and because it is supposed to remedy the neglect and squandering that come with economic distress, unemployment and precarious work.[67] The notion of 'job guarantee' also connects with the idea of a work as a 'meaningful work', which does not only imply a contribution to the lives of other humans but also, more generally, connections with a larger environment within which work takes place.[68]

In labour law terminology, this notion of 'meaningful work' that depends on the connection of work with the wider ecological system it belongs to and is participating in, could be encompassed in the notion of decent work and decent working conditions. Decent work is defined by the ILO as 'a multidimensional aspirational concept that is central to achieving social justice'.[69] According to the ILO, the concept of decent work implies a fair income; security in the workplace and social protection for families; better prospects for personal development and social integration; freedom for people to express their concerns, organize and participate in the decisions that affect their lives; and equality of opportunity and treatment for all.[70] To be sure, decent work does not, so far, take into account the impact of work on other entities from an ecological perspective. But the concept of decent work is flexible enough to accommodate this new dimension.

In parallel, the fundamental right to work could also evolve to become a right to decent work, including the ecological perspective. Similarly, the notion of decent working conditions could include, in addition to health and safety of workers, the health and safety of the world around them, composed of living and non-living entities. So far, labour law has limited itself to the immediate environmental hazards that productive activity poses to people in the course of work, without taking into account

64. Cf. Territoires Zéro Chômeur de Longue Durée (TZCLD) project in France; the Job Guarantee pilot and Aktion programmes in Austria; Actiris in Brussels, and Kinofelis in Greece.
65. On this potential of the job guarantee, *see* namely: O. de Schutter, 'The Employment Guarantee as a Tool in the Fight Against Poverty', Report of the Special Rapporteur on Extreme Poverty and Human Rights, A/HRC/53/33, 2023. *See also*: Pavlina Tcherneva & Aurore Lalucq, 'A Job Guarantee for Europe', Foundation for European Progressive Studies Policy Brief, 2022.
66. Mathew Forstater, 2006. Green Jobs: Public Service Employment and Environmental Sustainability. *Challenge* 49(4): 58 https://doi.org/10.2753/cha0577-5132490405.
67. Tcherneva & Lalucq, *supra* n. 65.
68. On this idea, *see* Caleb Althorpe, 'What Is Meaningful Work? A Philosopher's View', Social Europe, 30 April 2024, https://www.socialeurope.eu/what-is-meaningful-work-a-philosophers-view.
69. *See* namely: ILO, UNEP & IUCN, 'Decent Work in Nature-Based Solutions', Geneva, 2022, p. 17.
70. *Ibid.*

the impact of particular models of work and working practices for the broader environment, beyond the workplace, that also affects people and non-human others.[71] A new, much more extensive conception of decent working conditions could be promoted from an ecological perspective. In this context, basic or universal income has a role to play in emancipating workers from the necessity to accept work or working conditions that are inconsistent with the ecological perspective. This path is not, however, without problems for labour institutions. In particular, the existence of a basic income creates a risk of disempowerment of workers, and trade unions, which would no longer have the capacity to fight for better terms and conditions.[72] The role of the labour movement in defending the right to ecological work could be compromised, and so would the necessary alliances between the labour movement and environmental justice movements.[73]

§2.03 CONCLUSION

Fragmented forms and places of work have shattered the frontiers of labour law. The construction of a more inclusive labour law is underway, but the current state of work presents a challenge for labour law, which is overshadowed by other regulatory frameworks. Against this backdrop, climate transformation can be regarded as an opportunity for labour law to undergo a paradigm shift from the human-centred productivist model, in order to accommodate the necessity to limit the exploitation of resources and incorporate the complex relationships with other forms of life and modes of existence. Different paths are currently explored for a reconceptualization of work beyond productivism (the development of social economy, job guarantee, or basic income, for instance), which opens the way to forms of work consistent with the ecological transformation. As this chapter suggests, a reinterpretation of the notion of decent work, the fundamental right to work and decent working conditions is another way to design an ecological future for work.

71. Zbyszewska, *supra* n. 49, p. 21.
72. Adams & Countouris, *supra* n. 18, p. 30.
73. On the necessity, and possibility, of such alliances, *see* namely: Stefania Barca, 2019. The Labour(s) of Degrowth. *Capitalism Nature Socialism* 30(2): 207-216 https://doi.org/10.1080/10455752.2017.1373300. *See also* Nora Räthzel, Society-Labour-Nature: How to Think the Relationship., in Nora Räthzel, Dimitris Stevis and David Uzzell (eds), *The Palgrave Handbook of Environmental Labour Studies*, Palgrave Macmillan, 2021, 1, p. 793.

CHAPTER 3

Making Sense (of the Artistic Representation) of Labour

Filip Dorssemont

§3.01 INTRODUCTION

This contribution seeks to examine whether one can use works of art representing labour as tools to reconstruct 'the meaning' of work. It is better to refer to *a* meaning at a given time and in a given space. In the first section, I will deal with the question of *how* to look for such images and what it means to look for their meaning. The second section will deal with the question of *where* to find and contemplate such images. Special attention is given to the decoration of the first seat of the International Labour Organization. In a subsequent section, I want to discard the idea that Labour was solely depicted in the nineteenth century. Special attention is given to representations of labour in what can be called history painting, including religious painting, as opposed to so-called genre painting. This section takes us from the Middle Ages to the verge of the nineteenth century. The nineteenth century constitutes to some extent a turning point. For the very first time, labour constitutes a subject 'in its own right'. It is not enshrined in history painting nor can it be seen as genre painting as we knew it. The number of subjects which is represented is much more elaborated. They are in touch with a number of key issues of the employment relation of the industrial and even post-industrial era. Some conclusions will be drawn, which do not pretend to be exhaustive or final. This contribution seeks to stimulate further research.

§3.02 FROM THE *CORPUS* TO THE MEANING

Artists have represented labour since times immemorial. Thus, Bruno Debaenst in his PhD thesis on the history of the legal regulation of work accidents, has pointed out the existence of a mural painting in the tomb of the Egyptian architect Ipy, dating back to

1200 BC (Figure 3.1). It shows a number of accidents taking place in the construction sector, affecting the limbs and even an eye of construction workers.[1]

This contribution examines whether these works of art are helpful in reconstructing the 'meaning of work'. The meaning of work is not a transhistorical or anthropological concept which can be dissociated from time and space. Neither can an iconological analysis of works of art be dissociated from time and space. Hence, the question can solely be whether works of art can be helpful to reconstruct 'the meaning of work' in *a specific society in a specific period.*

Such an exercise requires a two-tier approach. First, one has to identify a *corpus* of works in time and space representing labour. Second, one has to identify their meaning which might not per se be related to the meaning of the work which is represented. For the sake of this study, I will be looking primarily at paintings and sculptures. The period under examination will run from the late Middle Ages to the start of the First World War, at a moment when art was still primarily figurative. *Ratione loci*, I will look for works of art created on the European continent.

Brevitate temporis, it is impossible to build the *corpus* of works representing labour in a systematic or complete way. Research on the representation of work is rare. It constitutes a niche in iconographical studies. The most comprehensive encyclopaedia has been composed by Klaus Türk. In his *Bilder der Arbeit, Eine ikonografische Anthologie*, the author has collected about 1,400 images representing labour.[2] Whereas the first eight chapters are thematic, the last six chapters follow a more chronological sequence, albeit intertwined with thematic subsections. It would be wrong to state that the Iconology of Labour has evolved into an academic subdiscipline. However, at a national or a local level, especially in the aftermath of the Second World War, numerous exhibitions have been organized focusing on the representation of labour.[3] The exhibition catalogues are a precious source to find representations of labour. In 1957, the International Labour Organization (ILO) organized an international exhibition in commemoration of their first Director-General Albert Thomas. It was staged in

1. D. Avenel-Treguier, *Les accidents du travail et les maladies professionnelles dans l'Egypte pharaonique*, Histoire des accidents du travail, 1984, 149-150, quoted by B. De Baenst in the Introduction of his PhD thesis (B. De Baenst, *Een proces van bloed, zweet en tranen!: Juridisering van arbeidsongevallen in de negentiende eeuw in België*, Brussels, Koninklijke Vlaamse academie van België voor Wetenschappen en kunsten, 2011, 503 p.).
2. K. Türk, *Bilder der Arbeit. Eine ikonografiche Anthologie*, Wiesbaden, Westdeutscher Verlag, 2000, 400 p.
3. For Belgium, *see, inter alia*: 1997; L. Schoonbaert, *Nood zoekt brood*, Antwerpen, KMSKA, 1987, 44 p., X., *Het volk ten voeten uit. Naturalisme in België en Europa 1875-1915*, Gent, Ludion, 1996, X., *Travail et Vie. Un siècle d'art belge 1848-1948*, s.l., Pandora, 192 p., (*See also*: M. Renard, *Le Travail dans l'Art*, Bruxelles, Editions Serge Baguette, 1948, 159 p.). *See also, inter alia*, the following exhibitions outside Belgium: E. Delapierre & B. Tillier, *Les Villes ardentes 1870-1914. Art, Travail, révolte*, Gent, Snoeck, 2020, 199 p., S. Douce de la Salle & P. Le Nouëne, *Exigences de réalisme dans la peinture française entre 1830 et 1870*, Chartres, Musée des Beaux-Arts de Chartres, 1983, 175 p.; M. Margozzi, L. Martini & A. Negri, *I costruttori; Il corpo del lavoro in cento anni di arte italiana*, Milano, Skira, 2006, 293 p.; A. Von Specht, *Streik. Realität und Mythos*, Berlin, Deutsches Historisches Museum, 1992, 174 p. and G.P. Weisberg, *Illusie en werkelijkheid. Naturalistische schilderijen, foto's theater en film, 1875-1918*, Brussel, Mercatorfonds, 2010, 223 p. For an exhibition in the field of contemporary art: C. Jankowsky, *What People Do for Money. Manifesta 11*, Zürich, Lars Müller Publishers, 2016, no numbered pages.

the *Musée d'art et d' histoire* of Geneva. Not less than 783 pieces are enumerated in the catalogue, from thirty countries in Asia, America and Europe. In the introduction, Pierre Bouffard had to admit that the catalogue was not up to the standards of a scientific publication.[4] In sum, the catalogue does not contain any essay and no information about the numerous pieces indicated. They are just enumerated by a technical description (title, materials, measures and the collection from which they originated).

All these catalogues of exhibitions are precious tools to compose the *corpus*. At the level of States, databases have been elaborated on the works of art present within the national boundaries, usually in public collections.[5] These databases can be screened on the basis of key concepts stemming from the world of labour.

On the basis of these sources, it is possible to analyse a sample of paintings and sculptures which are representative or emblematic. This analysis will be undertaken to understand the intrinsic meaning of these works of art. Such research is called iconological in the meaning intended by the seminal publication of Erwin Panofsky (1892-1968). Panofsky made a distinction between a more descriptive, *id est* iconographical analysis and an iconological one, able to reveal what he called the intrinsic meaning. This approach is not essentially different from the approach lawyers might adopt. Whereas lawyers interpret language in search of the meaning, art historians interpret another type of sign, *id est* images.

According to Panofsky, an iconographic analysis is primarily concerned with 'images, stories and allegories', over and above the representation of 'motifs', which is the subject of pre-iconographic analysis.[6] The iconographic interpretation tools recommended by Panofsky concern literary resources.[7] Panofsky then invites us to delve into the 'intrinsic meaning' that brings these representations into a more symbolic order, inviting the researcher to articulate the work of art with 'documents bearing witness to the political, poetical, religious, philosophical and social tendencies of the personality, period or country under investigation'.[8] Paradoxically, the sources for discerning the intrinsic meaning lie outside the work itself.

§3.03 LOCATIONS: A CATHEDRAL FOR LABOUR

The most obvious places to look for works of art representing labour are Musea. In the end, a lot of works representing labour ended in these 'cemeteries'. They became the object of musealization. The best catch might be musea specialized in 'modern art', focusing on the nineteenth century, the golden age for these kinds of works. Other museums might cover both ancient and modern masters. The growing digitalization of

4. X., *Art et Travail*, Genève, Musée d'art et d'histoire, 1957, 23.
5. *See*, for example, the database Balat for Belgium, https://balat.kikirpa.be; Joconde for France, https://www.pop.culture.gouv.fr/search/list?base=%5B%22Collections%20des%20mus%C3%A9es%20de%20France%20%28Joconde%29%22%5D and the database of RKD for the Netherlands, https://www.rkd.nl/collectie/beeldmateriaal.
6. E. Panofsky, *Studies in Iconology*, New York, Harper & Row, Publishers, 1939 (reprint 1972), 11.
7. E. Panofsky, *Studies in Iconology*, New York, Harper & Row, Publishers, 1939 (reprint 1972), 11.
8. E. Panofsky, *Studies in Iconology*, New York, Harper & Row, Publishers, 1939 (reprint 1972), 14.

these collections facilitates the exploration of these collections. Publications on these collections through the lens of labour are rare. A remarkable exception is the volume produced by a collective of Professors of Spanish labour law and law and social security law as well as Spanish Judges, who have screened the collections of ancient and modern painters of the Prado.[9] Industrialization pushed an interest in these kind of paintings and sculptures, filled with working heroes. Musea specialized on the issue of (the representation of) Labour or monographic musea specialized in artists known for the representation of labour are *rari nantes*. For Belgium, one might refer in this respect to the *IndustrieMuseum*[10] and to the Museum dedicated to the unsurpassed master of the representation of labour in painting and in sculpture, Constantin Meunier.[11] In France, the Musée *La Piscine* (*Musée de l'Industrie et de l'Art*) in Roubaix could be mentioned.[12] In Germany, there is the *Bergbaumuseum* in Bochum.[13] In the Netherlands, the Museum Helmond has collected more than 1,500 works related to 'Man and Labour'.[14] In Italy, *Palazzo Romagnoli* at Forli is home to the Galleria Verzocchi. From 1949 to 1950 Giuseppe Verzocchi commissioned the production of seventy-two paintings from 'great and small' Italian artists representing the various arts and crafts, preindustrial and industrial. He also ordered to submit a self-portrait and a short description. The only 'artistic' limitations which were being imposed, were the imposed size (70 cm × 100 cm) and the necessity to integrate a representation of a brick of his company, recognizable by the stamp 'V & D'. Some artists adopted a horizontal, others a vertical format. Hence, the collection offers a time capsule of what contemporary Italian artists produced in a very short time frame. Some of the artists are very well known (Carlo Carrà, Giorgio de Chirico and Gino Severini, some of which had already abandoned the style (e.g., futurist) which made them famous). Hence, it pays witness to the variety of styles which were 'fashionable' at that time, some more avant-garde than others. The album curated by Giuseppe Verzocchi to this collection was dedicated 'To all who work'.[15]

Although some of these musea have not selected paintings and sculptures or artefacts primarily on the basis of artistic criteria, their collections can contain precious works of art and images which are relevant for visual culture studies.

The question arises where to find these representations in their *natural* environment, outside musea, still kept 'in situ', The answer is: on the place for which they have been commissioned. This can be inside non-museal institutions or in the case of Monuments to Labour, in the public space. A lot of these works, especially starting

9. V. Sempere Navarro, *Una mirada laboralista a la pintura del Prado*, Madrid, 2020, 660 p. (It can be consulted online: Una mirada laboralista a la pintura del Prado (boe.es)).
10. https://www.industriemuseum.be/nl and https://fine-arts-museum.be/nl/de-musea/musee-meunier-museum.
11. https://fine-arts-museum.be/nl/de-musea/musee-meunier-museum. *See also*: D. Depelchin & F. Vandepitte, *Musée Constantin Meunier*, Gent, Snoeck, 2021, 123 p.
12. https://www.roubaix-lapiscine.com.
13. https://www.bergbaumuseum.de/montandok/museale-sammlungen.
14. https://museumhelmond.nl.
15. G. Verzocchi, *Il lavoro*, Milano, 1950, 463.

from the nineteenth century and beyond, were created for the market. There was no pre-established location for these 'emancipated' works of art.

Just as it seems obvious to look for religious art, in religious institutions, like Churches, one of the most obvious places to look for works representing labour, are institutions which are intertwined with the very idea of labour. The most obvious and most prestigious institution to look for such representation might be the International Labour Organization. The first Palazzo constructed as the seat of the ILO (inaugurated in 1926), is primarily a source for the iconography and iconology of the idea of *Social* Justice. Representations of Social Justice are at the heart of its decoration. This is hardly surprising. Thus, the Preamble of the ILO's Constitution, enshrined in the Treaty of Versailles starts with the following recital: *Whereas universal and lasting peace can be established only if it is based upon social justice.*

This is probably the first reference to the philosophical concept of social justice in a legal text. The Preamble does not define the notion of social justice, but the objectives and the tripartite governance of the ILO make it clear that it is about justice in employment relations and to some extent in social security.

The idea that justice and peace go hand in hand has already been expressed in Psalm 85, verse 11: *Misericordia et veritas occurrerunt iustitia et pax osculatae sunt.*

In former centuries, the union between peace and justice gave rise to a rich iconography. An allegorical painting of *Palma the Younger* from Venice (1548-1628), now exposed in the Modena *Gallerie estense,* pays witness to this idea (Figure 3.2). It was painted in the 1620s. Another example of this power couple is a painting which has decorated the rooms of the Academy of Fine Arts of Antwerp (founded in 1663), but which dates back to the late sixteenth century. It is a work of Jacob De Backer (ca. 1555-1585) (Figure 3.3).[16] In neither of these paintings, the allegorical ladies are actually working. They are not represented as working heroines. The focus is on Justice, not on Social Justice. The text of the ILO Constitution innovates by adding the word 'social' to justice.

The first building (1923-1926) which was created as a seat for the ILO is now occupied by the WTO.[17] A number of the works of art of the original building can still be seen *in situ*. They are in fact impossible to move. Another object which did not move was a parchment which was integrated underneath the first three stones of the new building and which contained the Latin words *Si vis pacem, praepara iustititiam* (If you want to secure peace, promote justice).

Prior to entering the old building, one is confronted with two seated sculpted figures. (Figure 3.4) A woman with a child at the left offering his mother a leaf of an olive tree represents Peace, whereas another non-blindfolded woman, holding both a serpent to be combatted in her right and a dove in her left hand, represents Justice. Both statues enter in a dialogue with one another. They are the work of the Swiss artist Luc Jaggi (1887-1976).

16. https://kmska.be/nl/meesterwerk/gerechtigheid-en-vrede.
17. For a description of the interior and the exterior of the original building of the ILO: X., *Le Centre William Rappard*, OMC, Genève, 2011 and R.H. Graf, *Le Bureau international du travail. Les œuvres d'art et les dons reçus par cette institution*, Genève, 1951, 183.

Another work of art could be construed as conceptual art *avant la lettre*. It is a panel of about 2,000 tiles, covering the wall behind a reception desk in the central hall (Figure 3.5). The tiles were created in the still functioning Workshop of the *Porceleyne Fles* in the city of Delft. Around a central medallion showing a 'blue collar' worker dressed in a red tunica, four panels describe the text of the preamble of the Constitution in the three official languages of the ILO as well as in German. The tiles have been hand painted on the basis of a design by the talented Dutch artist Albert Hahn Jr (1894-1953). They were a gift made in 1926 of the International Federation of Trade Unions, which was based upon socialist or social democratic convictions. When the building was occupied by the administration of the GATT, their director ordered the immediate covering up of this monumental panel. Did they have a problem with the idea of Social Justice or did they dislike the idea expressed in the Declaration of Philadelphia (1944) stating that '*all national and international policies and measures, in particular those of an economic and financial character, should be judged in this light (read: social justice) and accepted only in so far as they may be held to promote and not to hinder the achievement of this fundamental objective*'?

Paradoxically, the first works of art representing Social Justice are thus not working men, but allegorical representations of virtues. The latter are represented by women. In an allegory, the *genus* of a noun determines the choice of the gender of the allegorical person. In sum, a tradition is being followed.

However, representations of working men are not absent. In 1931, the competing International Confederation of Christian Trade Unions donated an impressive painting which decorates the central staircase of the old ILO building. In line with the ideological convictions of the confederation, it represents Jesus Christ in the workshop of his father, a carpenter. Although the painting serves as a wall painting it is not executed in the *affresco* technique. It is an oil painting on canvas. Jesus is the central *dramatis personae* of the painting. Although he sits on a (sufficiently high) balustrade while teaching, his head reaches the same level as the people listening to him. The verticalizing pine trees behind him accentuate a vertical line, which distinguishes the image of Jesus Christ from the rest. The people attending are contrary to Jesus Christ not painted *à l'antique* but in contemporary clothing. The board members of the Confederation are represented within the public listening as white- or blue-collar workers. They are an example of a *portrait historié*, since they are a part of the scene. The painting was realized by the famous French artist, Maurice Denis (1870-1943), one of the founders of the Nabis groupe. The title of the painting *The Dignity of Labour* is consistent with the *ethos* of the Preamble (Figure 3.6).

Some objects of the old building did move. Thus, the Belgian Government donated two bronzes to be integrated into the great staircase. They now serve outside at the entrance of the new ILO building in a way similar to the statues of Justice and Peace of the former seat. The exact date of this donation could not be found. Both statues have been modelled by Constantin Meunier (1831-1905) in view of the Monument to Labour, which was only realized twenty-five years after he died.[18] The

18. *See* references in *infra* n. 70.

statue of the seated puddler (Figure 3.7) was first exposed as a plaster at the Salon of Paris in 1885 and was moulded in bronze a couple of years later. The so-called kneeling miner dates back to the end of Meunier's life. It was moulded in bronze in 1903 (Figure 3.8). He adopts a dignified and introspective attitude, whereas the puddler clearly shows signs of fatigue. The latter lacks some decorum by opening of his mouth. The kneeling miner represents a blue-collar worker in all his dignity in a pose which is reminiscent of Rodin's *penseur*. In both cases, Constantin Meunier wanted to do justice to the dignity of the worker. For two reasons, he opted for workers having a break, suspending their work. First, Meunier does not try to show these workers as *purely* manual workers. His miner is presented as a philosopher. In a way, he thus challenges the distinction between manual and intellectual workers, at a time it was not yet fully institutionalized in law. The bodies of the blue-collar workers do not show signs of exploitation. In fact, they are shown in partial heroic nudity. Second, there is a practical reason, why these free-standing statues cannot represent people *at work*. Both the miner as well as the puddler are dependent on an industrial environment and infrastructure, contrary to, e.g., agricultural workers. Hence, only the sculptural technique of the relief would have allowed the sculptor to represent miners in action. In his Monument to Labour, Meunier had recourse to four reliefs. In one of the reliefs, he was thus able to represent miners at work.[19]

§3.04 THE REPRESENTATION OF LABOUR AND THE ISSUE OF THE GENRES OF PAINTINGS

Ever since the eighteenth century, it has been customary to distinguish 'genres' (categories) in the art of painting. One of these genres is called paradoxically genre painting, which is usually defined as a genre rendering scenes of daily life.[20] Other genres are History Painting (based upon a narrative, whether mythological, historical or religious), Portraiture, Landscape Painting and Still-Life painting. At first sight, it would seem obvious to look for representations of labour solely in the so-called genre painting. However, the representation of labour is not restricted just to *genre* painting.

Representations of labour already pop up in history painting, *id est* narrative paintings, representing a *storia,* both in mythological scenes and in religious scenes. Thus, the oldest representations of labour predate the emergence of genre painting. When the genre painting emerged, in the sixteenth century, the representation of the

19. *See* section §3.06.
20. E. Buysen, 'From Peasant Stories to "Urbane or Elegant Modern": A Bird's Eye View of Genre Painting in the Mauritshuis', in A. Van Suchtelen & Q. Buvelot, *Genre Paintings in the Mauritshuis,* Zwolle, Waanders Publishing, 2016, 10-25; E. De Jongh, 'Inleiding', in S.H. Levie, *Tot lering en Vermaak,* Amsterdam, Rijksmuseum, 1976, 1-10, E. De Jongh, *Questions of Meaning. Theme and Motif in Dutch Seventeenth-Century Painting,* Leiden, Primavera Pers, 2000, 9-19; L. De Pauw-De Veen, *De begrippen 'schilder', 'schilderij' en 'schilderen' in de zeventiende eeuw,* Bruxelles, AWLSK, 1969, 167-179; J. DiFuria, 'Genre, Audience, Origins and Definitions', in A.J. DiFuria, *Genre Imagery,* London, Routledge, 2016, 14-19; P.C. Sutton, 'Masters of Dutch Genre Painting', in C. Sutton, *Masters of Seventeenth Century. Dutch Genre Painting,* Philadelphia Museum of Art, 1984, XIV-XV and S. Slive, *Dutch Painting. 1600-1800,* s.l., Yale University Press, 1995, 121-176.

daily life of the working class was biased and moralistic. These paintings are more revealing as far as the (mis)conceptions are concerned of the more dominating classes living in the cities about agricultural workers than the working conditions of these workers themselves. Genre painting evolved due to Gustave Courbet (1818-1877) who triggered a paradigm shift. In what has been called 'manifesto of realism', the painter reflects upon the label of realism that he was given by art critics.[21] He tries to explain what his real intentions were. He criticizes a tendency of his colleagues just to imitate or copy the works of ancient or more modern painters. Instead Courbet urges painters to look around and to try to catch the habits, the ideas and the visual culture ('les moeurs les idées, l'aspect') of their time. Courbet refers to 'living art' (*art vivant*). Courbet's paintings about working (class) people lack the bias of the classical age of genre painting. Furthermore, he uses the strategies and the visual language of history painting, applying it to scenes of working people. Thus, he opts for a horizontal frame, like in secular history painting. He monumentalizes his workers by the sheer size of his paintings and by the use of close-ups. Prior to Courbet, genre paintings were much smaller in size. A typical, albeit paradoxical example is the representation of a seventeenth-century dockworker by Adriaen Brouwer (1605-1638) (Figure 3.9). The dockworker is shown standing in a very noble pose, in a so-called contrapposto, from head to toe.[22] He is presented in a proud manner, in an individualized or anecdotal way. He gazes and defies the spectator, rather than being represented as a person who is being gazed at. Though such a position is more typical for the representation of an aristocrat, the small size of the painting (31, 5 cm × 19 cm) is typical for genre painting.

§3.05 LOOKING FOR LABOUR IN HISTORY PAINTING

[A] The Book of Prayers

Among the oldest representations of labour in Western art, many can be found in books of prayer dating back to the fifteenth century. Usually, these books of prayer which were produced both for the clergy as well for laymen, contained, a calendar informing for each month about the days dedicated to saints and important moments of the liturgical year. Some of these months were illustrated.[23] Usually, a scene specific not only to the kind of seasonal agricultural labour which was typical for the month concerned was used as a miniature but also the seasonal leisure of the rich and famous

21. https://www.atlasofplaces.com/painting/lart-vivant/.
    The so-called Manifesto is in fact a brief introduction to the exposition of works of Courbet in the Pavillon du Réalisme at the World exhibition of Paris (1855).
22. https://kmska.be/nl/meesterwerk/een-sjouwer.
    The Royal Museum of fine arts attributes this work to Adriaen Brouwer, whereas Annette De Vries attributes this work to a follower of Adriaen Brouwer. (A. De Vries, *Ingelijst Werk. De verbeelding van arbeid en beroep in de vroegmoderne Nederlanden*, Zwolle, Waanders Uitgevers, 2004, 189-192).
23. *See* M. Smeyers & J. Van der Stock, *Vlaamse miniaturen voor vorsten en burgers. 1475-1550*, Gent, Ludion, 1997, 58-71.

could be depicted, like the hunting season. In fact, the hunting season takes place when agricultural labour is at a standstill.

These representations clearly do not seek to convey a meaning to work as such. In view of the seasonal character of work in an agricultural society, it is safe to say that agricultural work is used as a metaphor for a circular vision of time. There is not a trace of a biased or moralistic approach to the working people who are being depicted.

Examples of these books are legion. Among the most well-known containing such calendars, there are *Les très riches heures du Duc de Berry* (Figure 3.10) from the Limbourg brothers, the *Breviarium Mayer vanden Bergh* (Figure 3.11) and the *Breviarium Grimani* (Figure 3.12).[24]

Examples of these illustrated calendars can be found from the fifteenth century to the start of the sixteenth century. When the printing industry emerged, these wonderfully illuminated manuscripts tended to disappear. However, the famous series of the seasons painted by Pieter Brueghel the Elder has often been linked to this Flemish tradition.[25] In 1565, Pieter Brueghel painted indeed six panels related to bi-monthly periods for the dining room of Nicolaes Jonghelinck of his country house *Hof Ter Beken*, just outside the city walls of Antwerp. One of these panels apparently got lost.[26] Only one of the remaining five panels represents the leisure of the rich (*Hunters in the snow*), although Bruegel does not depict hunting aristocrats, but their assistants and hunting dogs. The other scenes do relate to seasonal work:

- The Hay harvest (June-July).
- The Harvest (August-September).
- The Return of the Cattle (October-November).
- The Dark day (February-March).[27]

[B] The Mythology

Mythology has been a constant source of inspiration for artists ever since the Renaissance and the rise of humanism. In Mount Olympos, Hephaistos or Vulcanus operated as a smith in a forge. Rubens,[28] Cornelis Schut[29] and Velasquez (Figure 3.13) have all dedicated a painting to this God and took care to represent a contemporary

24. https://commons.wikimedia.org/wiki/Category:Brevarium_Grimani, M. Smeyers & J. Van der Stock, *Vlaamse miniaturen voor vorsten en burgers. 1475-1550*, Gent, Ludion, 1997, 58-71 and https://en.wikipedia.org/wiki/Tr%C3%A8s_Riches_Heures_du_Duc_de_Berry.
25. *See* in this respect the PhD thesis of B. Kaschek, *Weltzeit und Endzeit*, München, Willem Fink, 2012, 203-221.
26. *Contra*: R. Falkenburg, 'La série des saisons', in R. Falkenburg & M. Weemans, *Bruegel*, Paris, Hazan, 2018, 94-95. The author argues that the missing panel is not 'missing', but is the *Carrying of the Cross* of the Kunsthistorisches Museum of Vienna, known to be in the possession of Nicolas Jonghelinck.
27. The panel is in fact linked to the cutting of wood.
28. P.P. Rubens, *Vulcanus forging the rayes of Jupiter*, around 1,638, Oil on canvas, 182.5 × 99.5 cm, Madrid, Prado, Inv. P001676.
29. C. Schut, *Vulcanus in his forge*, not dated, Oil on oak, 61.5 × 86 cm, Munich, Alte Pinakothek, Inv. N° 2064.

forge. Another famous painting of Velasquez seems to show a contemporary Workshop of Tapestry Weavers (*Las Hilanderas)* (Figure 3.14). If given a closer look, this is just the setting of the narrative of the story of the weaver Arachne who defied the Gods and was (rightly so) transformed into a spider. Hence, there is no reason at all, to look for 'a meaning of work' in such a painting. The relation between the representation of labour and the narrative as well as the meaning of the mythos is accidental. However, in retrospect, these kind of paintings were important and prefigured to some extent Courbet's revolution. History painting indeed allowed to represent a working environment of a size unprecedented in genre painting.

[C] Genesis: Labour after the Fall of Sin

A much stronger and immediate link between the representation of Labour and the issue of its meaning is present in one of the foundational narratives of Christianity. I am referring to the infliction of Labour upon Men after the Fall of Sin. It is well known that the French word for labour (*travail*) is derived from an instrument of torture (*tripalium*).[30] In *Genesis,*[31] it is told that God punished humankind for having bitten the forbidden fruit, the apple of the three which stood in the middle of the Garden of Earthly Delight. The passage concerned is the following:

> [3:17] And to the man he said, 'Because you have listened to the voice of your wife, and have eaten of the tree about which I commanded you, "You shall not eat of it," cursed is the ground because of you; in toil you shall eat of it all the days of your life;
> [3:18] thorns and thistles it shall bring forth for you; and you shall eat the plants of the field.
> [3:19] By the sweat of your face you shall eat bread until you return to the ground, for out of it you were taken; you are dust, and to dust you shall return.'

Hence, the meaning of Labour is pretty clear. Contrary to the Garden of Earthly Delight, Humankind needs to perform labour in order to provide for its subsistence. Furthermore, labour requires effort. It will require toil and sweat.

Religious Art did focus on this fragment of the first book of the Bible. One of the oldest stained glass windows of Canterbury Cathedral shows precisely Adam delving into the earth as the first farmer of mankind (Figure 3.15). It dates back to the 1170s. In her unsurpassed PhD thesis, *Ingelijst Werk* (Framed Labour), Annette de Vries has demonstrated that the iconography changes[32] around the midst of the seventeenth century. Adam is indeed seen delving into the same soil, but the focus is much less on the idea of the Paradise Lost and much more on the positive valorization of labour. Thus, the benefits of Labour our Shown, rather than the focus on toil, sweat and effort. It is a representation of the narrative without the *thorns and thistles.* Such an approach is consistent with an emerging work ethic. Furthermore, it provides proof of an

30. *See* A. Supiot, *Critique du droit du travail,* Paris, PUF, 1994, footnote 6, p. 4.
31. *Genesis*, III, 17-19.
32. A. De Vries, *Ingelijst Werk. De verbeelding van arbeid en beroep in de vroegmoderne Nederlanden*, Zwolle, Waanders Uitgevers, 2004, 23-31.

approach to ethics which is less deontological and more in line with an idea of eudemonia (the good life in the Aristotelian meaning). The author demonstrates this evolution by means of a very idyllic version of Adam's labour by Jan Bruegel the Younger (Figure 3.16).

[D] The Land of Cockagne

This discourse on work ethics is at odds with a medieval Utopia, known as the Land of Cockagne. Representations of this subversive text paying a tribute to what were considered vices in medieval times are extremely rare.

This utopian dream was expressed over 750 years ago in the probably Picardian *Fabliau de Cocagne*. The French medievalist Jacques Le Goff did not hesitate to qualify this fable as 'la seule véritable utopie du Moyen Age'.[33] It is a utopia *avant la lettre,* since the term *Utopia* was introduced by Thomas More in his novel entitled as such (1516). The qualification was based on the fact that this fable describes the story of a man who discovers an unknown land in which the ideal social order is realized, in stark contrast to the feudal society of the time. The latter is thus indirectly subjected to criticism.[34] Since the etymology of the word U-topia refers both to a good place and a place which does not exist at all, it can also be construed as being projected in a distant future.

This land of Cockagne is not a widespread theme in iconography from the Middle Ages to the Renaissance. The only known *painting* that depicts this story is attributed without dispute to Pieter Bruegel the Elder. The panel on oak is signed in large capitals by PIETER BRUEGEL and dated in the Roman numerals MDLXXVII (1567). It measures 52 cm by 78 cm and has been in the *Alte Pinakothek* in Munich since 1917 (Figure 3.17).[35][36]

---

33. J. Le Goff, *L'utopie médiévale: Le Pays de Cocagne,* Revue européenne des sciences sociales, 1989, 276.
34. J. Le Goff, *L'utopie médiévale: Le Pays de Cocagne,* Revue européenne des sciences sociales, 1989, 276.
35. *See* in this connection, *inter alia*: R. Marijnissen, *Bruegel. Tout l'oeuvre peint et dessiné,* Antwerp, Mercatorfonds, 1988, 333-334; M. Sellink, *Bruegel, Het volledige werk,* Bruges, Ludion, 2011, No. 159. The following publications of the Alte Pinakothek also deserve mention: R. an der Heiden, *Pieter Bruegel der Altere. Das Schlaraffenland und der Studienkopf einer Bäuerin in der Alten Pinakothek,* Munich, Hirmer Verlag, 1985, 35p.; Mirjam Neumeisters' review in M. Neumeister, *Alte Pinakothek,* Hatje Cantz Verlag, Munich, 2009, 84 and Konrad Rengers' review in X., *Alte Pinakothek,* Pinakothek-Dumont, Munich, 2005, 68. Mention can also be made of an original contribution in which this panel was interpreted as a criticism of the Spanish occupation of the Netherlands. This reading, however, found little support and sometimes encountered explicit opposition. F.H. Ross, 'An Interpretation of the Land of Cockaigne (1567) by Pieter Bruegel the Elder', *Sixteenth Century Journal,* 1991, 299-329 https://doi.org/10.2307/2542737. Personally, I found the author's leap from a *goose* that appears on this panel to 'les geux' (the aristocrats who conducted the revolt) too audacious. It seems to me that the aristocracy is already represented by the knight adorned with the lance.
36. The analysis in this contribution is based upon a more extensive study which I published in a Liber Amicorum dedicated to Professor Willy Van Eeckhoutte: F. Dorssemont, 'Bruegels Luyeleckerlant (1567), een utopie van een maatschappij zonder arbeid of een dystopie ten

Among art historians, there is today a great consensus that Pieter Bruegel's composition of Cockaigne was inspired by an undated print bearing the monogram PB (*see* Figure 3.18).[37] Louis Lebeer, who discovered this print and acquired it for the Royal Print Room in Brussels, left a dissonant note in a study of 'Le Pays de Cocagne'.[38] He believed that this print was posterior to the painting. He identified the monogram as a reference to Pieter Baltens (1527-1584), an opinion that is widely shared.[39]

For a proper understanding of the intrinsic meaning of the performance, the legend seems relevant. As Lebeer has already remarked, this legend in no way betrays a moralistic undertone.[40]

In another engraving that is believed to have been made shortly after Pieter Bruegel's death, and which is attributed to the engraver Pieter Van der Heijden, the legend lacks any moralistic undertone (*see* Figure 3.19).[41] Once again, laziness as opposed to gluttony is the main theme (*Die daer luij en lacker sijt boer, crijsman oft clercken/Those who are lazy and comfortable, peasant, knight or clergymen)* This phrase clarifies that the three figures refer to the three classes, whereby the word 'clerck' is carefully used, which was ambiguous in Bruegel's time. It could refer to a member of the clergy or to a scribe.

As for the intrinsic meaning of Bruegel's painting, there are elements that point to both a moralizing message and a rather subversive one. Since the piece was not painted for any public space, a subversive message is far from inconceivable. A number of elements point to a classic moralizing message. For instance, it cannot be denied that the *Fabliau de Cocagne*, as well as the society within which it operated, had undergone a major transformation since the second half of the thirteenth century. The moralizing approach of the printed versions of the Story of Cockagne, *Schlaueraffenland* and the *Luyeleckerlandt* is evident. Nor can it be denied that social support for idleness, especially that attributed to beggars and vagrants, was diminishing in an increasingly secularized society. The Church increasingly faded into the background as an institution that organized the care of the poor and called on its sheep to recognize the figure of the Son of God in the person of beggars and vagabonds.

---

faveure van de arbeidsmoraal?', in X., *Liber Amicorum Willy van Eeckhoutte. De taal is gans het recht*, Mechelen, Kluwer, 2018, 393-428.

37. *See* W.S. Gibson, *Bruegel*, Amsterdam, Elsevier, 1977, 180; *See* J. Müller, 'Das Schlaraffenland', in I. Mössinger & J. Müller, *Pieter Bruegel d.A. und das Theater der Welt*, Munich, Deutsche Kunstverlag, 2014, 213, M. Sellink, *Bruegel, The Complete Work*, Bruges, Ludion, 2011, No. 159 and M. Bassens & J. Van Grieken, *Bruegel in zwart en wit*, Veurne, Hannibal, 2019, 252.
38. In his *Catalogue raisonnédes estampes de Bruegel l'ancien* Lebeer (1969, p. 153) does not express himself explicitly on the question of the anteriority or the posteriority of the print by Pieter Baltens. In the same sense (posteriority of the Baltens engraving) also: An der Heiden 1985, p. 28.
39. L. Lebeer, *Le pays de Cocagne*, Miscellanea Panofsky, Bulletin des Musées royaux des Beaux arts, 1955, 207 In his *Catalogue raisonné des estampes de Bruegel l'ancien* (Brussels, Bibliothèque royale Albert I, 1969, 153), Lebeer does not express himself explicitly on the question of the anteriority or the posteriority of the print by Pieter Baltens. In the same sense (posteriority of the Baltens engraving) also R. an der Heiden, *Pieter Bruegel der Altere. Das Schlaraffenland under der Studienkopf einer Bäuerin in der Alten Pinakothek*, Munich, Hirmer Verlag, 1985, 28.
40. L. Lebeer, *Le pays de Cocagne*, Miscellanea Panofsky, Bulletin des Musées royaux des Beaux arts, 1955, 205.
41. *See* M. Sellink, *Bruegel, Het volledige werk*, Bruges, Ludion, 2011, No. 160.

However, a number of elements argue against such an overly moralizing interpretation. It strikes me that the legends among the Baltens *inventor* and the Bruegel *inventor* prints contain no moralistic undertone, contrary to the written book. Since these prints were not subject to preventive censorship, this is relevant in my opinion.[42]

Above all, it is worth remembering the important nickname that van Mander gave to Bruegel. Despite van Mander's obsessive attention to the idea that Bruegel as a peasant among peasants, was called upon to imitate peasant life, Bruegel is above all 'den Drol'.[43] 'Il est drôle' in French means 'He is funny'. Bruegel is a master of humour. In his humour lies much 'amor'. In my opinion, it is wrong to see this painter as a moralist, who starts from a Manichean ethic based on a sharp contrast between virtues and vices. Also in his *Christ and the Adulteress,*[44] in the spirit of the Gospel passage, there is no question of a moralizing register. In fact, rather than an opposition between Christ and the moralizing woman, the central theme in this grisaille painting is an opposition between Christ and the scribes.[45] Perhaps Bruegel is aware of the folly of man, but this is never a source of indignation, but rather of a generous and understanding smile.[46] Bruegel in his paintings does not glorify labour, for there is also room for pleasure. When he glorifies labour, it is primarily about 'honest labour' as opposed to mercantile speculation. In my opinion, he is not an interpreter of an oppressive work ethic that is made subservient to the needs of that mercantile capitalism.

[E] Altarpieces for Corporations

Another example of religious paintings depicting a narrative which was closely related to the world of labour are the altarpieces commissioned by the arts and crafts in the Southern Netherlands after the iconoclast troubles of the sixties of the sixteenth century.

During the so-called *Ancien Régime*, the period running from the Middle Ages till the French Revolution, journeymen and their masters were organized in so-called Corporations (*Arts et Métiers, Zünfte*). These corporations organized at the municipal level were based upon a privilege granted by public authorities ensuring a monopoly to the members of the corporation. The only way to exercise the profession was to be admitted by the Corporation and to follow the training as an apprentice given by the journeymen. By limiting the number of people involved, the members of the profession

42. *See in extenso* J. Van der Stock, *Printing Images in Antwerp,* Rotterdam, Sound 1 Vision interactive, 1998, 43-56.
43. A.F. Mirande & G.S. Overdiep, *Het Schilderboek van Carel van Mander,* Amsterdam, Wereldbibliotheek, 1943, 258: 'There are therefore few of his works that a viewer can look at seriously, without laughing, no matter how stern, grim and dignified they may be'.
44. P. Bruegel the Elder, *Christ and the Woman taken in Adultery,* 1565, Oil on Oak, 24.1 × 34.4 cm, London, Courtauld Institute.
45. E.M. Kavaler, *Pieter Bruegel: Parables of Order and Enterprise,* Cambridge, Cambridge University Press, 1999, 13-15.
46. E.M. Kavaler, *Pieter Bruegel: Parables of Order and Enterprise,* Cambridge, Cambridge University Press, 1999, 13-15.

were able to earn a decent living. The corporations were no democratic or egalitarian structures. They were governed by the masters, the only people allowed to open a workshop and sell products and services at the market. The acquisition of the title of master was difficult and more expensive for journeymen coming from other cities and not being relatives of a master. Craftsmen worked in small workshops.

The veneration of a patron saint was crucial to fostering a professional identity, overcoming the fragmentation of the professional community within workshops and obscuring the inequality between journeymen and their masters.

But how to identify these saints fit for purpose? The choice seems to have been an autonomous one, exercised at the level of each municipality. Ideally, the patron saint was a person having exercised the craft himself. This quite often takes us back to times when a still clandestine Church could not fall back upon priests financed by the authorities or the Community. Priests combined their office with a profession. But just exercising the profession was not enough to be a role model for the future members of the profession. Neither was it enough to be canonized by the Church.

From a Christian perspective, being a role model as a craftsman meant being charitable and generous towards clients with poor incomes not able to afford the services provided. It could mean serving the people as a judge in an incorruptible way, being as just to the rich as to the poor widows and orphans. This is why Saint Yves became a patron saint of the lawyers.[47] For the Church, martyrdom for upholding one's religious convictions was definitely a bonus. In an ideal scenario, this martyrdom was strengthening the professional identity as well, insofar as the saints 'enjoyed' the 'privilege' to be martyred with the tools of the craftsmen's trade.

The works of art ordered by the corporations representing these patron saints were made to decorate their altars in the chapels of prestigious municipal churches. These chapels constituted the meeting place for communal services in honour of the patron saint or in honour of deceased members.

The Church and the Corporations had different agendas in view of the iconography of these altarpieces. Whereas the Church would insist on representing the martyrdom of the patron saint or better a scene of the life of Jesus which with some goodwill could be related to the craft at hand, the Corporations would prefer to represent their patron saint, if possible not while being martyred but while actually exercising his craft.

A number of patron saints who have been chosen for the just, charitable and generous exercise of their profession will be presented here. I will focus on the representation of these saints in the altarpieces of the corporations of the most prominent sixteenth-century city of the Low Countries: 'la preclara et famosa città d'Anversa', as Ludovico Guicciardini called the *Metropolis*. Indeed, one of the best-documented cases is the refurbishment of the altars of the arts and crafts in the Cathedral of Our Lady in Antwerp, after the Spanish rulers took over control in 1585.[48]

47. *See* G. Martyn, *Jacob Jordaens' Sint Ivo ..., patroon van niet alleen de advocaten*, Pro Memorie, 2010, 218-239.

48. *See, inter alia*, F. Prims, 'Altaarstudieën', in *Antwerpiensia*, 1938, 254-339; 1939, 278-447; N. Peeters, 'Diversité et originalité d'une expérience formelle de transition. Les triptyques des

Cosmas and Damian[49] were two brothers, who were known as physicians. Contrary to ordinary physicians, they systematically refused to be paid for their services. They are called for this reason the *anargyroi* (from the Greek Ανάργυροι, 'unmercenaries'). The two physicians were living in the Syrian city of Aegaea. Since they refused to sacrifice for pagan idols, they were together with three other brothers subjected to a series of attempts to put them to death, until the proconsul Lysias decided to behead all five brothers. This always works. This persecution took place during the reign of Emperor Diocletian (244-311). The most famous 'operation' which the brothers undertook, was a miracle they performed after their death. When they saw that the white guardian of a Basilica in Rome dedicated to both of them was suffering from bone cancer affecting one of his legs, they dropped by, amputated the leg and replaced it with the leg of a black man who had recently passed away. In the *Legenda Aurea*, Jacopo de Voragine tells us that the brothers took great care to put the cancerous leg in the tomb of the deceased black man.[50] There is no reason to assume that they send a bill to the patient who woke up with a healed leg.

This impressive story has been represented on the right wing panel of a triptych painted by Ambrosius Francken for the Altar of the Surgeons and the Barbers in the Antwerp Cathedral of our Lady (Figure 3.20). It is dated as finished in 1593.

Cosmas and Damian are also venerated in the Eastern Orthodox Church.[51] The Russian icons do not represent the narrative of their martyrdom or their miracles. Instead, they represent the saints in a devotional manner with the attributes of their medical profession. Such a more devotional iconography is not reserved to Russian icons. The back of both the left and the right wing panel of the Francken triptych show Cosmas and Damian in a non-narrative and devotional manner. Both saints are represented as statutes painted in grisaille against a dark background.[52] Their attributes refer both to their profession and to their martyrdom.

Crispinus and Crispinianus are the less well-known patron saints which the Corporation of the Antwerpian shoemakers and the leather makers have chosen.[53] Both saints have also been represented by Ambrosius Francken. The story of the two brothers is similar to that of Cosmas and Damian. Both of them were martyred under the reign of Emperor Maximinianus (250-311), the co-emperor of Diocletianus for their

corporations dans la cathédrale d'Anvers (1600)', in B. D'Hainaut-Zveny & R. De Koninck, *Machinae Spirituales*, Bruxelles, IRPA, 2014, 47-60; Th. Van Lérius, *Notre-Dame d' Anvers avant la seconde invasion française en 1794*, Anvers, Imprimerie de L.J. De Cort, 1841, 38 p. and J. Vervaet, *Catalogus van de altaarstukken uit de Onze-Lieve-Vrouwekerk te Antwerpen en bewaard in het Koninklijk Museum*, Jaarboek KMSK Antwerpen, 1976, 197-244. In a more general perspective, there is the seminal PhD thesis of D. Freedberg, *Iconoclasm and Painting in the Revolt of the Netherlands, 1566-1609*, Garland, 1988, 290 p.

49. *See* G. Duchet-Suchaux & M. Pastoureau, *La Bible et les Saints*, Paris, Flammarion, 2008, 84-85 and R. Giorgi, *Comment reconnaître les Saints*, Paris, Hazam, 2004, 96-99.
50. *See* J. De Voragine, *La légende dorée*, Paris, Les éditions du Seuil, 1998, 615-618.
51. *See* A. Tradigo, *Icons and Saints of the Eastern Orthodox Church*, Milano, Mondadori, 2004, 296.
52. The back of both panels are now covered with a cloath. But Prims witnessed the existence of these representations, while working on his contribution on the altarpieces (F. Prims, *Altaarstudiën in Antwerpiensia*, 1939, 392-393. A recent restauration of these side panels also confirmed that they were painted at the back.
53. G. Duchet-Suchaux & M. Pastoureau, *La Bible et les Saints*, Paris, Flammarion, 2008, 92-93.

religious convictions. After having been made subject to various attempts to put them to death, they were beheaded also. They also gave proof of distributive social justice, since they made shoes for free for poor people who could not afford them. The striking feature of one of the earliest triptychs painted for the Antwerp Cathedral by Ambrosius Francken (1589) in an attempt to restore the damages due to iconoclasm, is the fact that the interior of the wings and the central panel are entirely dedicated to the martyrdom. No narrative describing the good deeds of both Saints is being depicted. The exterior of both wings represents a representation of two statues of the saints. The focus on the martyrdom of both saints can be explained by the fact that the tools of their trade have been used in a failed attempt to skin their corpses.

One of the rare representations of Crispinus and Crispinianus in the *exercise* of their trade is painted by an anonymous artist at the back of the central panel of a triptych, representing the life of Saint Hubertus, attributed to the Dutch painter Pieter Pourbus (1524-1584) (Figure 3.25). The anonymous painting at the rear of the central panel was discovered by the curator of the Gouda City Museum at the aforementioned exhibition organed by the ILO in 1957 at an exhibition held in Geneva, entitled *Art et Travail.* The curator was able to acquire it from a private owner and it was moved to the museum. It represents both saints in a very profane way in their workshop.[54]

Not all patron saints were martyrs.[55] For those who were, the Church was very keen on showing their martyrdom for obvious reasons. They were martyred because of their refusal to adore pagan statues. In sum, these catholic saints were pioneers in the combating of idolatry. At times, when protestants were accusing the Catholic Church of idolatry, these saints were a reminder that the Catholics had no lessons to be taught.[56] This obsession with the debate about idolatry, unfortunately, constituted an obstacle in presenting these patron saints in the fulfilment of their craft. Saints who were not known to have died as martyrs could more easily be shown in the exercise of their craft. Despite the absence of a clear-cut rule imposing the depiction of a Christological scene on the central panel, there was a growing tendency to show a scene related to the New Testament on the central panel.[57] In case, the patron saint was indeed a person featured in the New Testament, no problem occurred. An example is the many paintings of Saint Luc painting the Madonna., ever since the prototype of Rogier Van der Weyden.[58] In such an exceptional scenario, it was able to pay a tribute

---

54. P. Huvenne, *Pieter Pourbus (1524-1584)*, Brussel, Gemeentekrediet, 1984, 191: 'Ware het niet dat het decorum van de keerzijde laat veronderstellen dat het hier om heiligen gaat, dan zou men de voorstelling net zo goed als een profaan beeld kunnen interpreteren'.
55. For the issue of martyrdom: J. De Voragine, *La Légende dorée*, Paris, Seuil, 1998, 846 p.; G. Duchet-Suchaux & M. Pastoureau, *La Bible et les Saints*, Paris, Flammarion, 2014, 317 p.; R. Giorgi, *Comment reconnaître les saints?*, Paris, Hazan, 2004, 383 p. and X., *Bibliotheca Sanctorum*, Roma, Pontificia Università Lateranense Istituto Giovanni XXIII, 1961-1987.
56. *See* on this issue: R. De Koninck, *Horreur sacré et sacrilège*, Bruxelles, Académie royale de Belgique, 2018, 96 p. and R. De Koninck, *Vidit et doluit, et trucidavit, et occidit. Violence de l'idole et l'image de la violence*, Littératures classiques, 2010, 41-53.
57. *See* in this respect: V. Herremans, *The legitimate use of images: depiction, retable and veneration in post-Tridentine Flanders*, Simiolus: The Netherlandish Quarterly for the History of Art, 2015-2016/3, 122-123.
58. Voir https://collections.mfa.org/objects/31035/saint-luke-drawing-the-virgin?ctx=8f3bd9e6-3153-461d-80c5-7816e9d6f579&idx=2; D. De Vos, *Rogier van der Weyden. The Complete works,*

to the Mother of God and to show the patron saint of the painters at work. Another example might be Saint Joseph, the patron saint of the carpenters. Usually, patron saints do not feature in the New Testament. Hence, it was a challenge to identify scenes of the life of Christ intertwined with the profession concerned.

The central panel of Ambroise Francken's Altarpiece of the Corporation of Schoolmasters by Ambroise Francken (1587) shows *Christ among the Pharisees* as 'a true teacher teaching the truth', relegating their patron saint Ambroise to the left (Figure 3.21). Marten de Vos depicted the *Marriage at Cana* around 1596 for the altarpiece of the Innkeepers (Figure 3.24) In 1598, Ambrosius Francken painted the *Multiplication of Breads* for the bakers' altarpiece (Figure 3.23).[59] The most ingenious example is the altarpiece of the Corporation of the Harquebusiers, painted by Peter Paul Rubens, which depicts the carrying of Christ, a reference to the etymology of their Patron Saint's name (Christophore, Christ-o-ferens).

In all these cases, the representation of the religious scenes whether related to the patron saints and/or the Christological scenes serves to create a common professional identity nourished by the rituals administered around the altarpiece.[60] This professional identity was useful in transcending obvious class distinctions between the journeymen and the masters, also taking into account that journeymen and masters were active in different workshops within the same city.

§3.06 THE NINETEENTH CENTURY

[A] Industrialization

The nineteenth century stands out as a golden age for the representation of labour in its own right. There was no need to resort to an alibi of a mythological or a religious narrative. The iconography of these works of art is rich. A lot of subjects are being represented.

In a number of works, there is a clear-cut fascination for the new industrial environment where workers are active. Workers appear subordinate to the infrastructure, but still their efforts are shown. These images are 'shot' at a distance, so the workers do not dominate the scene. The world of steel manufacturing inspired both Alfred Menzel's *Eisenwalzwerk* (1875) (Figure 3.24) and Meunier's *La Coulée de l'Acier à Seraing* (around 1880) (Figure 3.25).

New York, Harry N. Abrams, 1999, 203, H. Mund, 'De Heilige Lucas tekent de Madonna,' in L. Campbell & J. Van der Storck, *Rogier van der Weyden,* Leuven Davidsfonds, 2009, 399-402 and B. Ridderbos, *Schilderkunst in de Bourgondische Nederlanden,* Leuven, Davidsfonds, 2014, 112-113.

59. R. Fabri & N. Van Hout, *Van Quinten Metsijs tot Pieter-Paul Rubens,* Antwerpen, BAI publishers, 2009, 141-146 (analysis by S. Grieten).
60. A. Thijs, 'Religieuze rituelen in het emancipatieproces van Vlaamse en Brabantse handwerksgezellen (zestiende-negentiende eeuw)', in C. Lis en H. Soly, *Werken volgens de regels,* Brussel, VUBPRESS, 1994, 239 and F. Verleysen, *'Pretense confrerieën'? Devotie als communicatie in de Antwerpse corporatieve wereld na 1585,* Tijdschrift voor Sociale Geschiedenis, 2001, 160-166.

In other works, the *impetus* is more on their efforts, rather than on the environment. Workers are shown as heroes, sometimes in heroic (semi) nudity. In other works, there is a focus on the physical traces the toil and efforts have left on their bodies. These two approaches are not necessarily contradictory. They might both want to do justice to the dignity of the workforce. The first approach is based upon a kind of sublimation, whereas the second is more veristic or naturalist. The message is identical, but the first series of images might appear more acceptable. The second approach focuses on vulnerability. Both approaches demonstrate how labour cannot be dissociated from the human body.

[B] Work Accidents

This kind of vulnerability reaches a dramatic peak in a number of works representing work accidents. A number of branches were particularly sensitive to work accidents, like the construction sector, harbours, mining and fishing industries. Work accidents are the result of a hazard or a risk which is unfortunately materialized and provokes casualties and a sense of loss among relatives. Hence, the imagination of these work accidents is centred around a number of chronological stages. Some posters were even produced in order to raise awareness. Few works of art focus on the occurrence of the accident. Others focus on the dead corpses, others on those who survived. Some works of art focus on the identification of the dead victims (Figure 3.28)[61] or on the loss of mourning expressed by relatives or sweethearts (Figure 3.29).

In case of massive casualties, there was scope and a need for the establishment of monuments commemorating the victims. In fact, this need continues to be felt till the present day. The recent Monument for the casualties after the implosion of the Rana Plaza Factory is an example of the continuation of this tradition (Figure 3.30). These monuments are a transhistorical phenomenon. They qualify as monuments insofar as they commemorate events, without commemorating specific illustrious persons. Contrary to classical monuments aimed ideally to foster national identities[62] and to facilitate the identification of citizens with 'their' Nation State, these monuments do not tend to glorify anything. Instead, they tend to offer consolation to the relatives and the loved ones of the deceased.

The monuments commemorating work accidents are very different from the Monument to Labour by Constantin Meunier (1831-1905). This Monument has been construed to glorify Labour (Figure 3.33).[63] The Belgian State integrated the pieces

61. *See also* F. Dorssemont, ' Over de representatie van arbeidsongevallen in het oeuvre van Constantin Meunier', in I. De Wilde, P. Humblet & L. Janssens, *Brugge*, Die Keure, 2023, 83-101.
62. On the issue of identitarian monuments, *see* J. Wijnsouw, *National Identity and Nineteenth Century Franco-Belgian Sculpture*, New York and Routledge, 2018, 265 p.
63. *See* in this respect the seminal PhD thesis of Surah Levine (S. Levine, *Monumental Transformations: The Changing Status of Constantin Meunier's Monument to Labor*, Chicago, Illinois, 1996). In 2022, I had the occasion to dedicate the so-called Sinzheimer Lecture to Meunier's Monument to Labour (F. Dorssemont, *Das Monument au Travail von Constantin Meunier -alias Arbeit als Fundament der Nation*, Soziales Recht, 2023, 199-212). *See also* M. Jerome-Schotsmans, *Constantin Meunier. Sa vie, son œuvre*, s.l., Oliver Bertrand editions, 2011, 311-329.

designed by Meunier into a monument construed by an architect for the very first centennial (1930) of the Belgian State. The Monument to Labour of Meunier was erected in order to reconcile the anonymous working class with the Nation State. They are atypical monuments since they do not commemorate specific events or illustrious artists, poets, writers, military or politicians. The common denominator of classical monuments is that they helped to foster a national identity. The iconology of this Monument is profoundly anthropological. The reliefs in fact relate to the four elements, hence to Nature. Thus, the mining scene refers to the element earth, and the Harbour Scene to the element water. The agricultural scene refers to the air and the Glass Manufacturing scene to the element fire. Thus, Meunier indicates that labour constitutes a relation between humankind and nature, allowing any individual to regenerate him or herself. Labour provides them with an opportunity to ensure subsistence and livelihood. The Monument also focuses on the reproduction of mankind through procreation by a vertical axe between the Sewer who supersedes the relief and the maternity scene in front of the monument. Whereas labour ensures regeneration, maternity ensures procreation. The art of Meunier tends to pay a tribute to the dignity of the workers. This is abundantly clear while studying the three seated sculptures of the ancestor, and the aforementioned puddler and miner.

A common feature, of these representations, irrespective of the medium concerned, is that artists tend to opt for a strategy of sublimation. The dramatic moment of the accident is in fact rarely shown, as if it would be too sensational or inappropriate. Even when dead corpses are shown, they are rarely shown in a naturalist or mutilated way. From the point of view of gender, these representations are not deprived of some bias. Men are put in the position of victims, whereas women are put in the position of mothers or female partners deploring them (Figures 3.28 and 3.29).

[C] Leisure

Labour is not just an issue of vulnerability, efforts and work accidents, it can also be seen as the opposite of leisure. Leisure and Labour entertain a dialectical relation with one another. The non-working time constitutes a limit to the subordination of the worker. Leisure would be meaningless if could not be opposed to working time. Hence, the representation of leisure is *suo modo* a part of the representation of the world of labour. It is about the absence of work or the freedom from work in the life of the working men and women.

One of the oldest revindications of the labour movement is the reduction of the daily working time to eight hours. In fact, the Second International declared 1 May as an international day of combat to achieve this revindication in 1889. A famous image published in the French periodical l' *Assiette au Beurre* exemplifies this revindication in direct connection with 1 May (Figure 3.31).

This weekly French periodical not deprived of anarchistic tendencies published a cover on the occasion of 1 May 1908 designed by Jules Grandjouan (1876-1968). It represents three allegorical figures representing Work, Leisure and Sleep. The use of half-naked women representing these abstract concepts derogates from the classical option to represent abstract concepts by either men or women in the function of the *genus* of the noun. All concepts used here are actually masculine concepts (Le Travail, Le Loisir, Le sommeil). Hence, it seems clear that women are used to please the male gaze. The female working hero is represented as a female coalmine worker (*hiercheuse*), which can be identified by her scarf and a pickaxe. The latter is bizarre since a hiercheuse did not use a pickaxe reserved for their male colleagues. They used a shuffle to pick up the coals, harvested by their male comparators. The scarf constitutes a nice contrast with the representation of leisure by a woman, with loose hair. The woman representing 'sleep' is represented by a woman in a kind of pyjama trousers with a face which is obscured. In Belgium, in 1921, the *Commission Syndicale* of the *Parti ouvrier belge* which sought to federate the socialist trade unions published an article by Charles van Roose which has an iconography which is similar (Figure 3.32).[64] It also reflects a tripartite division of the day into eight hours of work, eight hours of leisure and eight hours of rest. There is however a major difference The people represented are not at all allegorical figures who are naked. They are figures fully clothed and hence situated in real time. They are representations of both men and women. Men are at work, and women are relegated to the domestic sphere. The idea of the man as the sole breadwinner is thus being portrayed. In fact, 1921 marks the year of the adoption of a Belgian law introducing the eight-hour daily work limit. Whereas the French cover represents an allegorical representation of aspiration in an undefined space, *id est* a utopia, the Belgian cover probably represents the acquisition of the right. Since the law was adopted on 14 June 1921, the poster (in French: *affiche*) should be dated a *posteriori* and has no connection to the 1 May celebrations. In France, the eight-hour daily limit was established by law in 1919.[65]

The issue of the limitation of the daily working hours needs to be distinguished from the issue of the weekly rest period. A potential candidate for a representation of the weekly daily rest period is two similar representations of people enjoying leisure during the day painted by Georges Seurat. The most famous painting is the *Dimanche à la Grande Jatte* (Figure 3.34) by Georges Seurat. It represents in essence middle-class bourgeois 'enjoying' a Sunday at the Grande Jatte, an island in the Seine River near a suburban locality situated at the northwest of Paris. This painting finished in 1886 was preceded by another painting situated in a location near the Grande Jatte, also in a municipality northwest of Paris: *Bathers at Asnières* (1884) (Figure 3.33).

Both paintings are similar in size. In fact, their size is monumental, each measuring more or less 2 meters (high) × 3 meters (wide). This horizontal as well as monumental size is fit for history painting dedicated to commemorating *uomini illustri* or historical events, whereas this is an example of genre painting representing daily life. In both paintings, Seurat introduces and perfections his neo-impressionist technique of pointillism. Both paintings have been primarily studied for these technical and stylistic innovations. Both paintings represent human beings in profiles, as if in a frieze.

64. *See* X., *Bread & Roses. Ue autre histoire des affiches syndicales*, Bruxelles, Editions Méta-Morphosis, 2015, 26-27.
65. I. Leray, 'La réduction du temps de travail pour tous: la loi du 23 avril 1919 sur les huit heures', in J.P. Lecrom, *Deux siècles de droit du travail*, Paris, Les éditions de l'atelier, 1998, 117-128.

They are represented as present-day people, but the profile prevents us from perceiving them as real individuals, *id est* as persons with an identity. These persons hardly relate to one another. Despite the apparent similarities, there are also huge divergencies between both paintings. The so-called *cadrage* (the zooming in) in the *Bathers* is much closer, whereas it is much more remote in *Dimanche à la Grande Jatte.* The painting of *Bathers at Asnières* is composed of lower-class people The horizon mirrors the world of work, with chimneys and bridges. In *Dimanche à la Grande Jatte* this world of work is rather absent. It is occupied by representatives of a more 'superior' class. They do not bathe, everything is more formal and less relaxed. Linda Nochlin referred to the latter painting as an anti-utopian painting. This qualification was based upon an analysis made by the very utopian Marxist philosopher Ernst Bloch in his *Das Prinzip Hoffnung.*[66] The German Philosopher only detects people being bored and idle and qualifies the image as a landscape of painted suicide. This spirit is clearly absent in the *Bathers.* The question arises to what extent *Bathers* could be seen as utopian, as a horizon of hope, to quote Bloch himself. It is obviously a scene situated in a specific place, which is even identified as an existing *topos.* It is situated in time, as a scene contemporary to the genesis of the painting with people dressed in contemporary fashion. However, how realistic was the fact that working heroes of the lower classes could enjoy such a weekly rest in 1884? This rather crucial legal issue is hardly taken on board by art historians. The French law instituting the weekly rest period on a Sunday was in fact only introduced more than twenty years later. Seurat never outlived that moment, since he died in 1891. The *Loi établissant le repos hebdomadaire pour les ouvriers et les employés* dates back to 13 July 1906.[67] The neighbouring country Belgium, was a source of inspiration since a similar law was adopted a year previously.[68] In the UK, the weekly rest period on Sunday was rooted in religious traditions, which gave rise to the continental notion of the *Dimanche anglaise.* Albeit, this tradition is also reflected by an older French law of 1814, an anti-clerical tide in France led to the abolition of that law in 1880. In this respect, the Belgian historian Nandrin referred to the institution of the weekly rest period as 'une utopie récupérée'.[69] Some other countries instituted the weekly rest period prior to France and Belgium, such as Germany and Austria (1895). The ILO Convention nr. 14 introduced a weekly rest period in 1921.[70]

Contrary to the Land of Cockagne, it needs to be stressed that this image of the *Bathers* is an atypical utopia. Indeed, in a classical utopian representation, the entire

66. L. Nochlin, *Seurat's Grande Jatte: An anti-Utopian Allegory,* Art Institute of Chicago Museum Studies, Vol. 14, No. 2, The Grande Jatte at 100, 1989, 133-142.
67. N. Chambelland-Liébault, 'Un repos dominical pour tous?', in J.P. Lecrom, *Deux siècles de droit du travail,* Paris, Les éditions de l'atelier, 1998, 105-116.
68. H. Willems, *De lijdensweg van een rustdag: de wet op de zondagsrust (1905)*, RBHC, XXXII, 2002, 73-116, https://www.journalbelgianhistory.be/nl/system/files/article_pdf/BTNG-RBHC%2C%2032%2C%202002%2C%201-2%2C%20pp%2073-118.pdf.
69. J. Nandrin, 'La laborieuse genèse du droit social belge: une utopie récupérée', in G. Kurganvan Hentenryk (ed.), *La question sociale en Belgique et au Canada,* Brussel, 1988, 123-135.
70. Thus, Art. 2 of this ILO Convention provides:

society is represented, and all classes are taken together. This is what makes Bruegel's painting so typical. It focuses on all orders of society.

[D] Conflictuality

Last but not least, a lot of works of art focus on conflictuality. Artists have shown all stages of the conflict, from the causes of the strikes to the failed attempts of bargaining to the deliberation in an assembly to have recourse to strike, to the strike itself and its consequences for those willing to strike and those unwilling to participate, but still losing their employment due to strike.[71] The choice of the episode usually reflects the position of the artist. Those focusing on the causes of the harsh military repression express sympathy. Those focusing on the non-participating workers confronted with unemployment seem to convey a different message, more hostile to strike.

§3.07 SOME CONCLUDING OBSERVATIONS RELATED TO THE 'MEANING OF WORK'

For obvious reasons, it has been impossible to provide within the context of this contribution a full *catalogue raisonné* of all the works of art representing labour in Western art from the Middle Ages to the present day. Instead, this paper sought to highlight a number of conceptual thresholds examining the question of whether artistic representations of labour can reveal the 'meaning of work' in a specific society at a specific moment. The first threshold to be overcome is the prejudice that labour has been represented *solely* in some nineteenth-century industrial past. The second prejudice might be to look for it solely in what is commonly called genre painting. Representations of labour have emerged in history painting and much prior to the nineteenth century.

It is also relevant to overcome the idea that the intrinsic meaning of a representation of labour is always related to the meaning of work. Thus, the book of prayers represents labour as a metaphor to represent time. In an agricultural society, work is per se seasonal work. Agriculture necessitates an awareness of time. As *Ecclasiasticus* admonishes us: *there is a time to plant and a time to uproot.*[72]

Article 2

> 1.The whole of the staff employed in any industrial undertaking, public or private, or in any branch thereof shall, except as otherwise provided for by the following Articles, enjoy in every period of seven days a period of rest comprising at least twenty-four consecutive hours.
>
> This Convention was complemented in 1957 by the C106 – Weekly Rest (Commerce and Offices) Convention.

71. *See* in this respect F. Dorssemont, 'Some Perspectives on the Representation of Industrial Disputes under the Shadow of Repression in European Art (1870-1914)', in F. Dorssemont, *On the (Artistic) Representation of Industrial Disputes in the Shadow of Repression in European Art (From 1870 till 1914 and beyond)*, Berlin, Springer Verlag, 2024, 5-49.
72. *Ecclesiasticus*, Chapter III, 1.

Although it is unthinkable to represent an abstract notion such as labour without having recourse to the representation of workers, a more abstract notion such as social justice has been represented in a purely allegorical way. Paradoxically, no recourse was made to what Courbet called a 'real allegory'[73] in order to represent 'social justice' in the first seat of the ILO.

Some religious representations of labour do have a profound anthropological dimension. This is particularly through for the representations showing Adam at work after the Fall of Sinn. However, the meaning of work in representations showing Adam at work has evolved from an admonishment of divine punishment to a more positive eudemonic message. The anthropological dimension of labour also builds a relation which has never been more poignant. Through Labour humankind construes a relation with nature itself. The genius of Meunier's Monument to Labour is that he represents this relation in a way which is not just specific to agricultural work. He is representing the four elements through the branches of agriculture, mining, dock work and glass manufacturing.

Representations of labour cannot be deprived of ideology. The word ideology has many meanings. N. Hadjinicolaou spoke about 'idéologies imagés' in a Marxist meaning.[74] Indeed, some works of art tend to conceal tensions between the classes, such as the images serving a cult of patron saints. Rituals tended to conceal conflicts between masters and journeymen. Modern representations of conflictuality tend to show tensions between classes. From a Marxist perspective, the latter are not ideological. They in fact demystify an ideology of class reconciliation.

One of the most basic anthropological intuitions might be that labour cannot be dissociated from corporality. It is impossible to represent labour, without representing workers, *id est* human bodies supposed to perform labour. This is a message for all seasons. Images showing fatigue, and efforts pay witness to that idea. In the case of work accidents, this message is unmistakable. However, these images go beyond a mere reflection of our physical condition. They also express another kind of vulnerability affecting those people who lost their beloved children or lovers due to work accidents.

Last but not least, some works show a world of leisure of working men. Labour can be present in its absence. Without the shadow of labour, leisure becomes meaningless. This message is central in Seurat's *Dimanche sur la Grande Jatte.*

73. The notion real allegory refers to Gustave Courbet's work L'Atelier du peintre. Allégorie Réelle déterminant une phase de sept années de ma vie artistique (et morale) (Paris, Musée d'Orsay).
74. N. Hadjinicolaou, *Histoire de l'art et lutte des classes,* Paris, F. Maspero, 1978, 29-30.

Illustrations[75]

Figure 3.1 Mural Painting, ca. 1279-1213 BC, Tomb of Ipy, Deir El-Medienh (Copy by Norman de Garis Davies (1865-1941), New York, Metropolitan Museum)

75. All the reproductions fall under public domain, unless indicated otherwise. Where possible I have given the name of the photographer. The author thanks the Royal Museum of Fine Arts for providing high quality reproductions of their works of art.

Figure 3.2 Palma the Younger, Justice and Peace, ca. 1620, Oil on Canvas, 208 × 210 cm, Modena, Gallerie Estense, Inv. n° R.C.G.E. 239 © Filip Dorssemont

Figure 3.3 Jacob De Backer, Justice and Peace, ca. 1555-1585, Oil on Canvas, 210,6 × 178,3 cm, Antwerp, KMSKA, Inv. n° 6. © Hugo Maertens, Collectie KMSKA – Vlaamse Gemeenschap (Public Domain)

Figure 3.4 Luc Jaggi, Peace and Justice, Helvetian Stone, Geneva, Centre William Rappard (Old Seat of the International Labour Office) © ILO

Figure 3.5 Albert Hahn, Preamble of the ILO Constitution, 1926, Tiles of Delft, Centre William Rappard (Old Seat of the International Labour Office), © ILO

Figure 3.6 Maurice Denis, The Dignity of Labour, 1931, Oil on Canvas, Centre William Rappard (Old Seat of the International Labour Office) © ILO

Figure 3.7 Constantin Meunier, The Puddler, ca. 1926-1930, Bronze, Geneva, Entrance of the Present ILO Building, © ILO

Figure 3.8 Constantin Meunier, Kneeling Miner, ca. 1926-1930, Bronze, Geneva, Entrance of the ILO building, © ILO

Figure 3.9 Adriaen Brouwer, Antwerpian Docker, ca. 1620-1650, Oil on Panel, 31,5 cm × 19 cm, Antwerp, KMSKA, Inv. N° 897, © Hugo Maertens, Collectie KMSKA – Vlaamse Gemeenschap (Public Domain)

Figure 3.10 Barthélemy d'Eyck, September in Les très riches heures du Duc de Berry, ca. 1440, tempera on parchment, Chantilly, Musée Condé

Figure 3.11 Maximilian Master, September in Breviarium Mayer van den Bergh, ca. 1500, Tempera on Parchment, Antwerpen, Museum Mayer van den Bergh

Figure 3.12 Anonymous, September in Breviarium Grimani, ca. 1510-1520, Tempera on Parchment, Venezia, Bibliotheca Marciana

Figure 3.13 Diego Velasquez, The Forge of Vulcanus, 1630, Oil on Canvas, 223 × 290 cm, Madrid, Prado Museum, Inv. N° P001171

Figure 3.14 Diego Velasquez, Las Hilanderas, 1660, Oil on Canvas, 220 × 289 cm, Madrid, Prado Museum, Inv. N° P001173 (Wikilmediacommons)

Figure 3.15 Adam Delving, ca. 1170, Stained Glass, Canterbury, Canterbury Cathedral

Figure 3.16 Jan Bruegel the Younger, Adam Delving, ca. 1650, Oil on Wood, Private Collection

Figure 3.17 Pieter Bruegel, Land of Cockaigne, 1567, Oil on Oak, 52 cm × 78 cm, Inv. Nr. 8940, München, Alte Pinakothek © Alte Pinakothek

Figure 3.18 Pieter Baltens, Land of Cockagne, Prior to 1567, 222 × 303 mm, Bruxelles, KBR, Inv. Nr. S.V. 85370

Figure 3.19 Pieter Van der Heijden, Land of Cockagne, after 1569, 209 × 277 mm, Bruxelles, KBR, Inv. Nr. S.I.8722

Figure 3.20 Ambroise Francken, Triptyque of the Corporation of the Surgeons and the Barbers, 1593, Oil on Oak, 237 × 89 cm, Antwerp, KMSKA, n° inv 146-149. © Hugo Maertens, Collectie KMSKA – Vlaamse Gemeenschap (Public Domain)

Figure 3.21 Ambrosius Franken, Central Panel of the Martyrdom of Saints Crispinus and Crispianus 1589, Oil on Oak, 269 × 217 cm, Antwerp, KMSKA, Inv. Nr 145. © Hugo Maertens, Collectie KMSKA – Vlaamse Gemeenschap (Public Domain)

Figure 3.22 Frans Francken I, Triptyque of the Corporation of the School Masters and the Soap Manufacturers, 1587, Oil on Oak, 250 × 220 cm (Central Panel) and 250 × 97 cm (Side Panels), Antwerp, Cathedral of Our Lady

Figure 3.23 Ambroise Francken, Multiplication of the Breads and the Fishes, 1589, Oil on Oak, 280 × 212 cm, Antwerp, KMSKA, Inv. Nr 135.

Figure 3.24 Marten de Vos, Triptyque of the Corporation of the Innkeepers, 1597, Oil on Canvas, 268 × 235 cm, Antwerp, Cathedral of Our Lady.

Figure 3.25 Anonyme, Saint Crépin et Saint Crépinien, ca. 1557-1572, Oil on Oak, 131,5 × 129, 6 cm, Gouda, City Museum, n° inv. 55.073

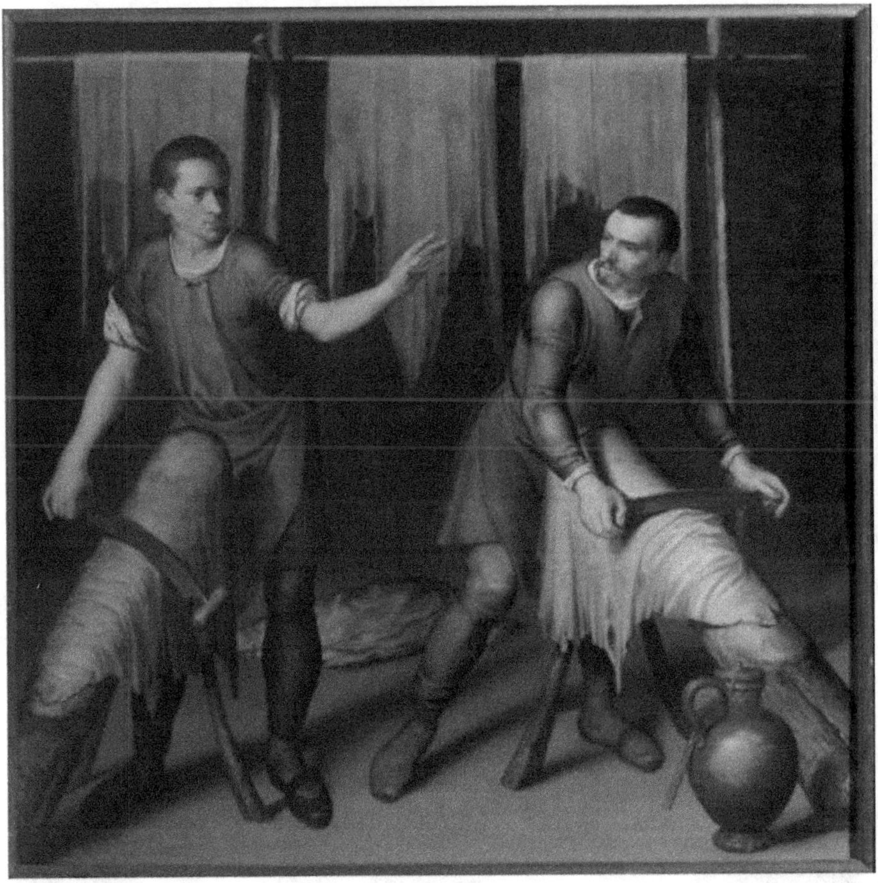

Figure 3.26 A. Menzel, Eisenwalzwerk, 1875, Oil on Canvas, 158 × 254 cm, Berlin, Alte Nationalgallerie, Inv. Nr A I 201, https://creativecommons.org/publicdomain/mark/1.0/

Figure 3.27 C. Meunier, La Coulée de l'Acier à Seraing, around 1880, 221 × 305 cm, Liège; Musée Bovery.(c) Wikimediacommons

Figure 3.28 Constantin Meunier, Le Griosu, 1890, Bronze, 151,5 × 212 × 108,5 cm, Brussels, KMSKB, Inv. 3200, © [Ektachroom (KMSKB)]: MM 472 – [Koninklijke Musea voor Schone Kunsten van België, Brussel/photo: Christophe Bouché, Brussel]

Figure 3.29 Anto-Carte, 1918, Piëta, Oil on Canvas, 94 × 112,5 cm, Mons, Collection du musée des Beaux-Arts (BAM), conservée à l'Artothèque, (photo: Atelier de l'Imagier), © Sabam Belgium 2023

Figure 3.30 Memorial of the Rana Plaza Collapse, 2013, Dakha

Figure 3.31 J. Grandjouan, Cover of the Assiette au Beurre of 18 April 1906 © BNF

Figure 3.32 Ch. Van Roose, Poster '888', 1921, Lithography

Figure 3.33 G. Seurat, Bathers at Asnières, 1884, Oil on Canvas, 201 × 300 cm London, National Gallery, Inv. nr. NG3908

Figure 3.34 G. Seurat, Dimanche sur la Grande Jatte, 1886, Oil on Canvas, 207,6 × 308 cm Chicago, The Art Institute, Inv. nr. 926.224

Figure 3.35 C. Meunier, Monument to Labour, 1930, Laeken, Rue Claessens. (CC BY 4.0 KIK-IRPA, Brussels)

CHAPTER 4

Smart and Autonomous Work: When Autonomy Reaches Subordination

Elena Gramano

§4.01 INTRODUCTION

The problem of the legal classification of working relationships has been an issue ever since a specific regulation of the employment relationship came into existence under different legal systems. Since the beginning of the twentieth century, in most jurisdictions, employment and social security systems followed a binary path, defining workers as either employees or autonomous workers (or self-employed contractors).[1]

The distinction between an employee and an autonomous worker became crucial at the point at which deeply different legal disciplines were built for and became applicable to each category.

At the very baseline of the distinction the assumption is, at least on paper, that while an employee exchanges her subordination to the employers for economic stability, granted for an indefinite period and via an almost armoured contract, an autonomous worker keeps bearing the risk of her economic activity in exchange for full autonomy in the organization of her work, outside any form of control, intrusion or power by the principal.

As a consequence, traditionally, only employees have been granted full protection under employment law regulations (protection during the employment relationship, at

1. In general, on this topic *see*: Mark Freedland (2003), *The Personal Employment Contract*, Oxford University Press; Mark Freedland & Nicola Countouris (2011), *The Legal Construction of Personal Work Relations*, Oxford University Press; Alain Supiot (2001), *Beyond Employment: Changes in Work and the Future of Labour Law in Europe*, Oxford University Press; Guy Davidov (2014), *The Goals of Regulating Work: Between Universalism and Selectivity*, University of Toronto Law Journal, 64, 1 https://doi.org/10.3138/utlj.0115; Adalberto Perulli (2020), *The Legal and Jurisprudential Evolution of the Notion of Employee*, European Labour Law Journal, 11(2), 117 https://doi.org/10.1177/2031952520905145.

the moment of termination and after termination), while autonomous workers have not known the same level of protection under employment law or, in the best case scenarios, have been covered by forms of protection that are a long way from the levels or models of protection granted to employees. In most cases, the employment contract has been the sole or main means of access to employment law protection granted by the law and by collective bargaining agreements.[2]

By building and defining the concepts of an employee and of an autonomous worker, lawmakers have taken the political responsibility for granting some subjects with a full set of safeguards and excluding a whole different group from any legal protection.[3] From that, the legal operation of the definition of the categories established by lawmakers and, at a later stage, the correct classification of the working relationship under the right juridical label followed by courts and interpreters are extremely important.

Under this scenario, there has always been a degree of uncertainty in the definitions of the categories of employees and autonomous workers provided by the law and by case law, which are inherently unable to represent the complexity of reality. Furthermore, the distinction between employees and autonomous workers has been challenged over the years by new forms of entrepreneurial organizations and new forms of work.[4]

Indeed, the development of new technologies and new ways of organizing businesses, the increases in persons' skills and qualifications, and even the increase in employees' autonomy in the organization of their own personal work have drastically blurred the distinction between employees and autonomous workers, which is no longer always tangible in economic relationships, leading lawmakers and labour lawyers, in general, to struggle with old categories and new phenomena. To add more complication to these problems, some kind of third categories have been introduced in some legal systems in the past decades (such as economically dependent work; quasi-subordination; work by projects, etc.), forcing judges and scholars to discuss the actual persistence and *raison d'être* of the traditional categories and whether it is possible or necessary to change, adapt or multiply them.[5]

While taking into consideration this context, only briefly depicted, the present contribution aims to offer a reflection on smart (or agile) work and autonomous work.

2. On this topic, *see* more in general Mark Freedland (2015), *The Segmentation of Workers' Rights and the Legal Analysis of Personal Work Relations: Redefining a Problem*, Comparative Labour law and Policy Journal, 36, 241-256.
3. Judy Fudge (2017), *The Future of the Standard Employment Relationship: Labour Law, New Institutional Economics and Old Power Resource Theory*, Journal of Industrial Relations, 59(3), 374-392 https://doi.org/10.1177/0022185617693877.
4. Katherine V.W. Stone (2006), *Rethinking Labor Law: Employment Protection for Boundaryless Workers*, in Guy Davidov & Brian Langille (eds), *Boundaries and Frontiers of Labour Law: Goals and Means in the Regulation of Work*, Oxford, UK and Portland, OR, 155-179.
5. Adalberto Perulli (2011), *Subordinate, Autonomous and Economically Dependent Work: A Comparative Analysis of Selected European Countries*, in Giuseppe Casale (ed.), *The Employment Relationship: A Comparative Overview*, Hart Publishing, 137-186; Pierluigi Di Gennaro (2020), *Subordination or Subjection? A Study About the Dividing Line Between Subordinate Work and Self-employment in Six European Legal Systems*, Labour & Law Issues, 6(1), 3-47.

By considering smart and autonomous work together, from a common perspective that will be described in the following paragraphs, we adopt and start from a hendiadys (included in the title of this contribution) that suggests a connection or at least a potential connection between the two terms that shall be considered under the umbrella of the general topic of this volume, which aims to *redefine work*, not just in reference to the notion of worker or the sole notion of subordination, but to redefine *work*, its concept, its meaning and its implications.

The aim of this contribution is to offer a reflection on the progressive autonomy in the organization of their working activity by traditional subordinate employees; and the specular and consequent need to rethink the notion of work and its legal labels, that – up to now – have been established mostly in order to relegate organisational autonomy solely to the sphere of self-employment.

In order to do that, it is important to start with a basic taxonomy. In fact, without going into the details of the separate legal notions of employees and autonomous workers adopted by different legal systems, we might begin by observing that most legal systems have a shared, at least partially common understanding of the notion of 'autonomous work' (or self-employment), at least in the sense that something that is not subordinate work is usually considered to be autonomous work; in this sense, autonomous work is that the second half of the sky populated by those workers who do not classify as subordinate employees. And for the purposes of this introduction, we could use this starting point as a general, a-technical, definition of autonomous work.

But what, however, is smart work? Do we all have a shared, at least partially common understanding of the concept of smart work? And first, and foremost, is it a legal notion?

§4.02 SMART WORK: NOTION AND MAIN FEATURES

When discussing smart work, we might start by saying that it is indeed not clear what smart work is from a legal standpoint. While the legal notions of subordinate work or autonomous work have often been defined not only by lawmakers but also further defined and elaborated by case law and scholars in the interpretation and application of the law, the concept of smart work is still relatively new.

Before being a legal concept, smart work is a new phenomenon that we can observe in the world of work and that shows that the new frontier of subordinate employment goes beyond the traditional boundaries of pre-defined working times and the physical location of the employer's premises. Low-cost information technology makes it possible and cost-effective to enable remote working performance. More and more people are moving towards an organizational models that involve remote work. Notwithstanding the fact that – at least at the current level of technology – not all work can be carried out remotely and that the potential pool for the use of smart work is mainly focused on clerical tasks, there are now many companies – including those in the manufacturing sector – that have started experimenting with remote work. The benefits, in fact, are well known: greater employee satisfaction, because employees can better manage their working time and the organization of their family life, and reduce home-work-home travelling times; the reduction in absenteeism; the increase in productivity per worked hour; and the reduction of energy, property and maintenance costs.

However, at least for the purposes of this chapter and without any intention to identify an exhaustive and all-encompassing definition, we believe that we cannot simply overlap the concept of smart work with that of remote work. Instead, we might define smart work as that form of subordinate work characterized by a certain margin of organizational autonomy of the employee in the performance of her working activities, under the umbrella of an employment contract and therefore under the regulation and the application of those rules provided for subordinate employees.

In this respect, the Italian legal system might serve as an example of a regulatory framework of a specific employment contract model where the legal subordination of the employee is deemed compatible with her autonomy in the organization of her working activities. Law No. 81, introduced in 2017, on what the Italian lawmaker called agile work or, indeed, smart work, provides a specific notion of this.[6]

While the purpose of this chapter is not to provide for a specific legal analysis of smart work under the Italian legal system, a very brief reference about the Italian legal regulation of smart work might serve as a basis for a more general reflection on smart and autonomous work (self-employment) and therefore to elucidate reflection on the contact and differences among these two types of work.

By means of Law No. 81 of 2017, a new regulation on smart work has been adopted in the Italian legal system, namely in order to 'increase the competitiveness and facilitate the reconciliation of working and private times' (Article 18, Law No. 81/2017).

This Law defines smart work as a *method of execution* of the subordinate employment contract that shall be regulated by a specific agreement between the employer and the employee. In particular, what distinguishes the 'smart' method of working from the 'regular' or standard one is the fact that the former is neither bound by specific time constraints (within the limits on the maximum duration of working time set out by the law or by collective bargaining agreements), nor by reference to a steady place of work, since the working activity might also be carried out outside the employer's premises, without a fixed location. To make this possible, the Law acknowledges the possibility of using technological tools to carry out the employee's activities.

6. Giuseppe Santoro Passarelli (2017), *Lavoro eterorganizzato, coordinato, agile e il telelavoro: un puzzle non facile da comporre in un'impresa in via di trasformazione*, WP CSDLE 'Massimo D'Antona'.IT – 327/2017; Michele Tiraboschi (2017), *Il lavoro agile tra legge e contrattazione collettiva: la tortuosa via italiana verso la modernizzazione del diritto del lavoro*, WP CSDLE 'Massimo D'Antona'.IT – 335/2017; Marco Lai & Leonardo Ricciardi (2016), *La nuova disciplina del lavoro agile, Diritto e pratica del lavoro* 707; Marco Manicastri (2017), *Lavoro agile: come cambia, Diritto e pratica del lavoro*, 88; Many contributions can be found in Gaetano Zilio Grandi & Marco Biasi (2018) (eds), *Commentario Breve allo Statuto del Lavoro Autonomo e del Lavoro Agile*, Wolters Kluver; and in Luigi Fiorillo & Adalberto Perulli (2018) (eds), *Il jobs act del lavoro autonomo e del lavoro agile*, Giappichelli.

It is important to underline that smart work does not constitute a new type of employment contract, but it is instead a method of performing the subordinate employment relationship.

In light of this definition, the key feature of smart work is the fact that it implies the presence of a regular employment contract, according to which the employee is subordinate to the employer, but the execution of the working activity is regulated according to the conditions set out by an agreement between the parties, that shall meet the requirements provided for by the Law. Therefore, it must be borne in mind that the worker is an employee and not an autonomous worker and that the employment contract that binds the parties is a regular one, which can be open-ended or fixed term.

In order to resort to smart work, the employee and the employer are supposed to sign a separate agreement, to be added to the employment contract that self-evidently remains in place; such separate agreement must be concluded in writing and is aimed at regulating several fundamental aspects of the smart relationship in order to safeguard the positions of both parties when the working activities are conducted remotely.

First of all, the agreement must regulate the type of activities that the employee might carry out remotely, i.e., outside of her usual workplace, and, specularly, also those which are supposed to be performed inside the usual workplace. In fact, Article 18 of Law No. 81/2017 implies that at least part of the working activity shall be executed inside the workplace. The Law does not require any minimum 'amount' of work to be performed inside the workplace and does not set any criteria in that respect, but leaves the decision to the parties to jointly identify those activities.

Second, the Law provides that the agreement shall also regulate the forms of exercise of the employer's directive power. More specifically, according to the Law, both the employer and the employee shall jointly establish *how* the employer is entitled to exercise her directive power. Some scholars have described such a situation as an oxymoron and interpreted the new Law as a significant modification of the traditional concept of subordination in so far as it restricts the unilateral exercise of the employer's directive power, which is what identifies subordinate work as such.

It can be assumed that the lawmaker ascertained the peculiarity of smart work and 'softened' the employer's prerogative to interfere with working activities – at least when performed outside the workplace – in order to balance the great flexibility granted by the Law in terms of time and place limits with the respect of the employee's private and personal sphere. Therefore, the Law recognizes the need to balance the employer's hierarchical position with the fact that working activities are carried out remotely and might, therefore, physiologically interfere with the employee's private life.

The Law goes even further by additionally requiring the agreement between the parties to regulate and therefore to limit the employer's power to control the duties carried out by the employees outside the company's premises, in compliance with general regulation on the monitoring power of the employer. Moreover, the agreement shall identify the behaviours connected with the execution of the work performed outside the company premises, which might give rise to the application of disciplinary sanctions.

Again, if in general the employer is entitled to exercise her managerial prerogatives within the limits exclusively provided for by the Law, with reference to the smart work then the employer is forced to bargain in order to establish the conditions of exercise of such prerogatives with the employee, i.e. with the same person who is subjected to those powers.

The agreement shall indicate the working tools used by the employee in order to perform her working activities. This is relevant since the employer is responsible for the safety of the technological tools assigned to the employees and such tools must be clearly distinguished from any personal tool the employee might be using.

Finally, the second main goal of the agreement is to regulate working time. As stated, the Law acknowledges that smart work is only subject to the limits of the maximum duration of working time set out by the Law and by collective bargaining agreements. Therefore, it is up to the parties to identify the employee's rest periods and to specify the technical and organizational measures aimed at ensuring the employee's right to disconnect from technological work equipment. While the Italian system might be among the first ones to provide for an extensive regulation of smart working, starting from its legal concept, the notion of smart work is directly or indirectly known, recognized and regulated by many other legal systems that still may not have adopted a specific legal definition or set of rules, but that recognize "self-organised-but yet subordinate" remote work as a form of employment fully compatible with the traditional model of subordinate work and with its regulation.

By taking the Italian law as an example, as it is the only one which formally regulated smart work among the European Union (EU) Member States, we could adopt, again for the sole purpose of the taxonomy of this chapter, a definition of smart work as that work that is still entirely subordinate work but is organized with a certain amount of autonomy by the employee herself.

More specifically, in the case of smart work, two aspects that traditionally belong to the archetypical notion of subordinate work are blurred: the *place* and the *time* of the working activity, as both might be largely organized directly and autonomously by the employee, with little or none interference from the employer.

§4.03 SMART WORK: AUTONOMY WITHIN SUBORDINATION

If we consider the perspective of the workplace, smart work does not necessarily mean remote work, or not entirely remote work anyway. However, smart work is characterized by the fact that some or most of the working activities can be performed outside the workplace, and therefore outside the physical perimeter of the place by definition owned and controlled by the employer.

The same goes for time: smart work is not necessarily performed within certain working hours, as long as the maximum limits of working time are respected.

I would like to focus on this specific perspective: the perspective of the workplace and time and the connected function of protection usually covered by labour law when work is performed inside or outside the workplace and within certain working hours.

If we go back to the roots of labour law, traditionally, labour law largely (not exclusively, but still largely) dealt with the primary and essential need to cover persons working inside a certain workplace, usually the employer's premises, in order to physically protect them from the intrusion and control of the employer. Progressively, labour laws were adopted and the whole axiological system of labour law was developed in order to separate the worker from the employer, keep the worker safe from the employer, and protect the worker's person, dignity, autonomy and self-determination.

Labour law was built on a concept of *work* that, beyond the specific legal definition of subordination, was still characterized by one aspect: work was performed physically within the employer's premises, inside a place that belonged to the employer and that, without any legislation or collective intervention, would have been entirely subject to the power and control and management of the employer. That is why, anything outside the workplace and outside the stipulated working hours was simply not considered work, or subordinate work, in legal terms.

Progressively, even inside the workplace and during working hours, workers conquered the space, with physical and moral protections designed to secure their liberty and freedom and dignity from the hands of the employer.

Given this context, the employment contract, on the one hand, and the workplace and the working time, on the other hand, ended up becoming inseparable, in the context of a vision of a complete protection of the weaker party within the employment relationship. In the past, again, the archetypical vision of the worker was someone who woke up every morning to walk to their workplace, which belonged and was run by someone else, i.e., the employer.

Today, in line with the goal of this Volume, we ask ourselves whether there is a need to *redefine the concept of work*; again, as stated above, not just to redefine the legal notion of a worker, nor solely the notion of subordination, but to redefine *work*, its concept, its meaning, its implications in the legal system as a whole.

We might pose this question on the redefinition of work by starting with a reflection on smart work.

Smart work is not just telework; it is not just remote work or home-work, but it is work without a place, it is work in a non-place of work. It is also work which is not bounded by time; it does not involve a specific definition of working hours.

Smart work is work where the employee is autonomous in the organization of her time and place of work; smart work is work that, substantially, extracts from the legal notion of subordination the dimension of the workplace and of working time, without challenging the fact that work performed outside the workplace and a particular time is and can definitely be subordinate work.

For this exact reason, smart work challenges an essential paradigm of labour protection and that is the co-essentiality of the protection of the working person through their protection in the workplace and time, and in particular through their protection against the possible intrusions/interferences of the employer.

The legal and sociological phenomenon of smart work places labour law scholars under obligation to understand whether and how the axes of protection that have settled over the decades on this assumption, which I would call the material *substratum* to which the labour law discipline applies, might have changed; it is not reasonable to avoid an overall rethinking of the very sense and rationale of labour law.

Redefine work, as the title of this volume suggests.

We could start with very practical examples, before moving to a more extended reasoning: first, and probably the easiest consideration relates to health and safety – what is the employer obliged to do when it comes to health and safety? How is the employer's obligation to guarantee safety at work actually expressed if there is no workplace at all? Does this imply that, for example, there shall be more space for the protection of the worker's personality and psychological, in addition, of course to her physical safety?

Second, we shall consider monitoring or control powers. Many scholars have already stressed that the employer is still in a position to monitor the employee even when the working activities are performed outside the workplace. So, how should the regulation on the monitoring power of the employer be updated in order to consider the specific perspective of smart work?

Third, and here we reach the core of our reasoning: in respect of the whole directive power and the constraints placed on the employer with regard to the inclusion of the worker in the organization, what happens when the physical place of work is not available anymore?

We could ask ourselves how does labour law apply when workers are placed outside the employer's premises, especially when their personal life is not clearly distinguished from their work. And what new protections might a smart worker need in order to embrace this new meaning of work? What's the function of labour law now that certain pillars are gone?

We might not have an exhaustive answer, and the question requires many facets to be taken into consideration.

However, what the phenomenon of smart work teaches us is that the regulatory focus of the concept of work shall now be moved to the *person* who works, their organizational autonomy, their dignity, and a broader dimension of work whereby the protections shall not be just about limiting employer prerogatives and powers (which is still essential). Instead, a new definition of work is required that overcomes the traditional boundaries in order to protect the new needs of the person who works autonomously *but within an employment relationship*.

I believe, essentially, that a new concept of work shall reshape or rather increase labour law protections, without neglecting the current set of protections for the worker, but rather taking into account new needs or interests that were simply not there when labour law was first developed, in a sort of circular manner according to which a new concept of work shall not only be used to broaden the scope of application of labour law but also its functions and goals.

And here, in conclusion, we shall come to the second term of the initial hendiadys that has been neglected so far: autonomous work (or self-employment).[7]

§4.04 AUTONOMOUS AND SMART WORK: A RECIPROCAL CONTAMINATION BETWEEN SELF-EMPLOYMENT AND SUBORDINATION

What is the connection between smart work and autonomous work, if any?

Autonomous workers have long been excluded from labour and social protections, on the assumption that precisely because self-employed, they were in a position to negotiate at market conditions and thus did not need any legislative or collective protection for their contractual standing.[8] Over the past few decades, scholars have started questioning the exclusion of a large number of autonomous workers from social protection on the basis of the abovementioned distinction, no longer considered effective in addressing emerging types of work and the new categories of workers that come with them.[9] The debate has thus focused on bogus self-employment and on new types of work, and more recently on platform work, to determine whether these workers may be brought under the umbrella of employment protection.[10]

The EU itself has focused its attention on fighting bogus self-employment by extending social protection to particularly vulnerable workers who fall outside the formal employment law's perimeter of protection. The European proposal for a directive on platform work is a recent example of this trend: through an unprecedented system that establishes a legal presumption of subordination, it seeks to extend social protection to platform workers.

However, social rights for genuinely self-employed workers have yet to become a priority at the EU as much as the national level.[11] Very little has been said about

7. Adalberto Perulli (2022), *A Critique of Self-Employment*, European Labour Law Journal, 13, 1 https://doi.org/10.1177/20319525221088604.
8. Maurizio Del Conte & Elena Gramano (2018), *Looking to the Other Side of the Bench: The New Legal Status of Independent Contractors under the Italian Legal System*, Comparative Labour Law and Policy Journal, 39, 579.
9. Adalberto Perulli (2020), *The Legal and Jurisprudential Evolution of the Notion of Employee*, European Labour Law Journal, 11(2), 117 https://doi.org/10.1177/2031952520905145; Miriam A. Cherry & Antonio Aloisi (2017), *'Dependent Contractors' in the Gig Economy: A Comparative Approach*, American University Law Review, 66, 635 https://doi.org/10.2139/ssrn.2847869.
10. On platform work, *see*: Jeremias Adams-Prassl (2018), *Humans as a Service: The Promise and Perils of Work in the Gig Economy*, Oxford University Press; Valerio De Stefano (2016), *The Rise of the Just-in-Time-Workforce: On-Demand Work, Crowdwork, and Labor Protection in the 'Gig-Economy'*, Comparative Labour Law and Policy Journal, 37, 471 https://doi.org/10.2139/ssrn.2682602; Antonio Aloisi (2016), *Commoditizied Workers: Case Study Research on Labour Law Issues Arising from a Set of 'On Demand/Gig Economy' Platforms*, Comparative Labour Law and Policy Journal, 37, 653. For a comprehensive account of national case law on how platform workers ought to be classified, *see* Christina Hiessl (2022), *The Classification of Platform Workers in Case Law: A Cross-European Comparative Analysis*, Comparative Labour Law and Policy Journal, 42 https://doi.org/10.2139/ssrn.3982738.
11. Luca Ratti (2020), *Self-Employment Matters: The EU's Response to the Lack of Social Protection for Independent Workers*, European Employment Law Cases, 3, 164 https://doi.org/10.5553/eelc/187791072020005003005; Chiara Garbuio (2021), *The Autonomous Workers and the*

ensuring social protection for genuine self-employed workers, who are often not immune to the need for social protection and economic support within the market, also in relation to principals in a dominant position.[12]

Under this acknowledgement, we might observe that the connection between autonomous and smart work relies on a sort of *paradox*: smart work is subordinate work performed autonomously by the worker. Smart work is subordinate work characterized by the autonomy and self-determination of the worker. On the opposite, autonomous work is often characterized by the weakness of the autonomous worker on the market and vis-à-vis its principal and also by her economical and organisational dependence on the principal.

Such basic observation not only requires, as we have already stated, the need to rethink the fundamental functions and goals of labour law in its axiological frame, but it also drives us to expand the very notion of subordinate work: work can be subordinate, and therefore protected by labour law, even when performed autonomously. However, also autonomous work is worthy of the legislator's attention not merely to avoid standard employment's stringent obligations being disregarded, but above all to issue ad hoc regulatory instruments for the benefit of genuine self-employed workers, specifically to their social citizenship and dignity.

The border between subordination and autonomy and the application of their respective sets of rules shall rely on the control of the organization to which the employee belongs: subordination is no longer or not exclusively work directed by an employer, performed under the punctual direction of an employer, but can be work performed autonomously in an organization owned and controlled by an employer. The control exercised by the employer is often no longer directed at specific working activities of the single employee, but rather at the overall organization in which each working activity is inserted.

Smart work is a clear proof of this shift of the border of subordination: smart workers organize their working activities autonomously, starting from the place and time of their work, but have no power or control whatsoever over the organization they belong to.

Smart work has indirectly but efficiently expanded the notion of subordination and its scope of application, without any changes in the legal definition of subordination, because the main feature of subordination still exists and is represented by the power that still belongs fully to the employer, that might be not exercised directly over the worker and her activities but rather over the organization as a whole.

Needed Responses of Social Protection Systems to Overcome Transitions, Italian Labour Law e-Journal, 14(2), 1-16; Venera Protopapa (2021), *The New Working (Poor) Class. Self-Employment and In-Work Poverty in the EU: A Supranational Regulatory Strategy*, Italian Labour Law e-Journal, 14, 41.

12. Adalberto Perulli (2022), *A Critique of Self-Employment*, European Labour Law Journal, 13, 1 https://doi.org/10.1177/20319525221088604. Please allow a reference to Elena Gramano (2022), *Self-Employment in the EU and Italian Legal Systems: Recent Trends and Missed Steps*, International Journal of Comparative Labour Law and Industrial Relations, 38(4), 453-472 https://doi.org/10.54648/ijcl2022020.

Rapid technological developments; new ways of offering services on the market through websites, digital platforms, and online providers; fragmentation of the employing entity into groups or nets of companies sharing decisions and processes often outside formal relationships of control or of capital sharing; mechanization of working activities; increased levels of workers' skills required by the labour market; all these factors seem to have thrown the traditional legal parameters of legal classification of work into crisis, thus challenging the dogmatic categories of subordinate and autonomous work themselves.[13]

However, the legal problems which have arisen due to technological and economic changes have always been looked at according to an external perspective: the labour market has been analysed by considering the different contractual models used by the economic subjects to exchange work and remuneration, from a point of view that has mainly remained outside the boundaries of the employment relationship.

Nevertheless, the very same factors shaping the labour market are currently influencing the employment relationship itself.[14] Even 'inside' the most regular and clearly subordinate employment contract, such factors are profoundly changing the way employers and employees are executing their contractual relationship. Therefore, these circumstances make it imperative to adjust the employment contract to the needs of organizational flexibility.

In the current rich theoretical debate, the need to adopt an approach aimed at focusing also on the core of the employment relationship has not been given much space, especially in the context of the growing mainstream idea that the overwhelming evolution of information technology would be expected to determine how to overcome the very concept of subordination and stable work.

The first aim of this chapter is to give evidence of the fact that subordination is not inconsistent with the changes that are deeply influencing our society and ways of living and working. Instead, it is our opinion that the employment contract was originally conceived and is still one of the most flexible legal tools among the regulations of contracts; a tool that has internalized organizational flexibility as a feature of the employment relationship.

From this perspective, reconsidering the employment contract and its relationship to the concept of organization and performance might be one of the keys to looking at the new forms of work as well.

In this context, smart work plays a central role, since it is bounded neither by specific time constraints nor reference to a steady place of work, since someone's working duties might also be carried out outside a company's premises, without a fixed location.

---

13. Miriam A. Cherry & Antonio Aloisi (2017), *'Dependent Contractors' in the Gig Economy: A Comparative Approach*, American University Law Review, 66, 635 https://doi.org/10.2139/ssrn.2847869.
14. Frank. Hendrickx (2018), *Regulating New Ways of Working: From the New 'Wow' to the New 'How'*, European Labour Law Journal, 9(2), 195-205 https://doi.org/10.1177/2031952518781449.

A new concept of organization is beginning to form: an organization that becomes part of the very assumption underlying the employment relationship, which does not only imply the exchange between a certain working activity for a remuneration but rather also the exchange of skills and flexibility to perform different duties for a remuneration.

A central role is still played by the employment contract as a tool to ensure the organizational needs of the company are met in the face of technological changes that are dramatically reshaping the ways of working. Put differently, labour law and its tools shall continue to fulfil their role as 'innovation facilitators', enabling social institutions to adjust and survive even chaotic revolutions.

At the same time, a fruitful debate on autonomous work should thus tackle self-employed workers' status as individuals in need of social protection and the criteria to identify the measures' addressees.

The challenge, indeed, is for the regulatory system to respond to transformations effectively thus achieving its protective aims and delivering legal certainty for trade.

CHAPTER 5

Telework and Right to Disconnect

Tania Bazzani

§5.01 INTRODUCTION

During the pandemic, telework proved to be a crucial solution for businesses to avoid temporary, or worse permanent, suspension of workforce from work activities while complying with social distance measures.

Although telework had already existed in all European Union (EU) Member States before the pandemic, the pandemic emergency enabled a change in attitude towards it by dampening the mental reservations and concerns of management, which was often oriented towards demanding face-to-face work.[1]

While the significant access to telework has highlighted its potential benefits for employees and employers, it has also highlighted its possible negative effects.

This contribution focuses on a problematic aspect that emerged during the pandemic because of the massive use of telework, and which relates to the increasing blurring of boundaries between working and rest time. In particular, the absence of a clear-cut demarcation between these spheres has often resulted in the encroachment of working time to the detriment of rest time. Organizations showed to be oriented towards demanding continuous availability for work, pushing employees to be online and ready to work even outside normal hours.[2]

This proves that transformations in the world of work need to go hand in hand with safeguarding rights so that the impact of technology can improve workers' conditions and not worsen them. In this regard, a right to disconnect should guarantee

1. Gálvez, A., Martínez, M.J. & Pérez, C. (2012), Telework and Work-Life Balance: Some Dimensions for Organisational Change, J. workplace Rights, vol. 16(3-4), 2012-2012 https://doi.org/10.2190/wr.16.3-4.b, http://triggered.stanford.clockss.org/ServeContent?url=http://baywood.stanford.clockss.org/BWWR/BAWOOD_BWWR_16_3/X41R44567W154226.pdf.
2. Chung, H. & Van der Horst, M. (2018), Women's Employment Patterns after Childbirth and the Perceived Access to and Use of Flexitime and Teleworking, Human Relations, vol. 71(1), 47-72 https://doi.org/10.1177/0018726717713828.

employees to disengage from work and not respond to work-related electronic communications, such as emails or other messages, during their rest time.

Within this picture, this article questions whether it is conceivable to find a solution at the EU level by adopting a directive for all the EU Member States and whether a fit-all solution or ad hoc solutions are preferable.

To address the aforementioned issues, this contribution will be structured in three parts.

The first part of this article will deal with the difficulty of disconnecting from working as a phenomenon that has emerged in the context of the pandemic, outlining the solutions put in place by the Member States in order to guarantee the enjoyment of rest time, without work interference. In this first part, two phenomena, made evident by the post-pandemic situation, will be highlighted: the dematerialization of the workplace and the flexibilization of working time, the latter being particularly relevant to our contribution.

In the second part of the article, the EU acquis in which the issue under consideration is situated will be illustrated, as well as the possible solutions to deal with it, which find at their core the discussion on the right to disconnect. This will highlight the key elements of the European framework, which are useful for the conceptualization of a right to disconnection.

Finally, based on the findings in the previous two parts, the third part will address the question initially posed, that is: Should a right to disconnect be embedded in an EU directive, and, if yes, should it propose a fit-all solution or create a framework for a possible different way of implementation?

§5.02 TELEWORK: POTENTIAL BENEFITS, POSSIBLE RISKS AND AN 'ALWAYS ON' CULTURE

The pandemic has accelerated the use of telework, easing employers' qualms about this form of work organization. But what do we mean by 'telework'? This chapter adopts the definition of telework found in the European Framework Agreement of Telework, signed by the social partners in 2002, according to which telework 'is a form of organising and/or performing work, using information technology, in the context of an employment contract/relationship, where work, which could also be performed at the employers premises, is carried out away from those premises on a regular basis' (Article 2).[3]

The main features of telework are therefore the use of ICT (information and communication technologies), to perform a work activity that, although it could be performed in the company, is performed outside its premises. Thus, the definition used in this article covers various forms of work outside the premises of the enterprise, which may have different definitions and regulations at the national level. An example is provided by the Italian system, in which 'telelavoro' is telework carried out according to the normal company's working time, and usually performed at home, and

3. European framework agreement on Telework (2002), https://resourcecentre.etuc.org/sites/default/files/2020-09/Telework%202002_Framework%20Agreement%20-%20EN.pdf.

'agile work', which is a form of organization extremely flexible in terms of both place and time. According to the definition here used, they both are telework.

Thus, telework at the European level indicates a conceptual umbrella capable of encompassing several cases, which may be characterized by different legal disciplines at the national level.

As is known, telework had an exponential increase during the pandemic, but in some Member States and sectors it was already in use before.

In July 2020, 48% of the employees who responded to the 2020 Eurofound e-survey of the same year declared to have worked at home at least some of the time during the pandemic.[4] It was also estimated that 39.6% of paid work by dependent employees was carried out at home during the pandemic.[5]

The use of telework in the EU-27 rose between 2019 and 2021 from 11% to 22%, practically doubling in two years.[6]

The prevalence of telework varied consistently across countries, sectors and types of works, with jobs 'teleworkable' (i.e., when work can be carried out in telework) and other non-teleworkable. For example, the higher share of telework can be highlighted before and after the pandemic in Sweden, Finland, and Denmark, with comparatively more employees than the other Member States working in knowledge- and ICT-intensive services.[7] Before the pandemic, the prevalence of telework was particularly high in the same sector across all the Member States. Indeed, 40% of workers in IT and other communication services already were working regularly in telework in 2018 in the EU-27.[8] Relatively high prevalence can be highlighted before the pandemic also for high-skilled professionals and managers.[9]

The lockdown has highlighted the benefits that teleworking can bring to employers and employees. In the former case, telework can result in greater employee engagement and increased employee productivity.[10] Furthermore, telework makes it possible to cut some of the fixed costs normally borne by organizations, such as electricity and heating costs, and at the same time, it allows accessing talent from different countries.[11] Moreover, in some realities, telework, if managed by the social

4. Eurofound (2020), *Living, Working and COVID-19*, COVID-19 series, Publications Office of the European Union, Luxembourg, 31, https://www.eurofound.europa.eu/en/publications/2020/living-working-and-covid-19.
5. *Ibid.*, p. 31, https://www.eurofound.europa.eu/en/publications/2020/living-working-and-covid-19.
6. Eurofound (2022), *The Rise in Telework: Impact on Working Conditions and Regulations*, Publications Office of the European Union, Luxembourg, 7 & 8, https://www.eurofound.europa.eu/en/publications/2022/rise-telework-impact-working-conditions-and-regulations.
7. European Commission (2020), *Telework in the EU Before and After the COVID-19: Where We Were, Where We Head to*, Science for Policy Briefs, 2, https://joint-research-centre.ec.europa.eu/document/download/1ccf7717-ab52-4215-b14a-08d74e9d44fc_en.
8. *Ibid.*, p. 2.
9. *Ibid.*
10. Eurofound (2022), *The Rise in Telework: Impact on Working Conditions and Regulations*, Publications Office of the European Union, Luxembourg, 7 & 8, https://www.eurofound.europa.eu/en/publications/2022/rise-telework-impact-working-conditions-and-regulations.
11. Messanger J.C. (2023), *Chapter 1, Some Reflections on the Experience of Telework During the Covid-19 Pandemic: A Paradigm Shift and Its Implications for the World of Work*, in (eds

partners at the company level, can foster the development of innovative organizational modalities, in which collaboration between team and team leader becomes a constant and periodic exchange and confrontation, with the aim of managing the organization of teleworking in step with the achievement of team objectives.[12]

For the employees, telework may prove to be strategic for the purpose of achieving a greater reconciliation of work time and personal time, which improves individual quality of life, and consequently also quality of work.

However, this is not automatic, as, for example, in the case of parents, where the positive impact of telework in terms of work-life balance can occur if supported by sharing care responsibilities between the parents and by equal access to telework. The pandemic, indeed, already showed the disproportionately negative impact on women under different perspectives: care responsibilities, unpaid jobs, difficulties in accessing telework in low-status and/or low-paid jobs, and limited career opportunities.[13]

Similarly, in the case of workers with disabilities, telework can be a valuable way to ensure their integration into the world of work,[14] provided that employers do not obstacle it by refusing this possibility unjustifiably and disproportionately. Further, the employer should guarantee – through the implementation of appropriate policies – that telework does not result in the isolation of workers with disabilities.

Telework can also save time needed to commute to work and reduce the influx of cars and other vehicles into cities, making them less stressful and less polluted.

But alongside these potential benefits, new risks have also been highlighted.

Telework is an organizational form of work, which is based on the necessary use of ICT: the risk of improper processing of employees' personal data, which does not comply with current legislation, is possible.[15]

Moreover, precisely because telework requires the use of ICT, health risks for workers must also be considered. The negative impact on health coming from radiation because of the use of technological devices is highlighted by the European Parliament.

Countouris, N., et al.), *The Future of Remote Work*, European Trade Union Institute, https://www.etui.org/sites/default/files/2023-05/The%20future%20of%20remote%20work_2023.pdf#page=21.

12. For example, in the case of Michelin Italia, https://www.filctemcgil.it/images/download/ACCORDI/gomma_plastica/2022/220107%20-GOMMAPLASTICA_MICHELIN-SAMI-VERBALE%20ACCORDO%20SMART%20WORKING.pdf.
13. Arabadjieva K. & Franklin P. (2023), *Chapter 4, Home-Based Telework, Gender and the Public-Private Divide*, in (eds Countouris, N., et al.), *The Future of Remote Work*, European Trade Union Institute, https://www.etui.org/sites/default/files/2023-05/The%20future%20of%20remote%20work_2023.pdf#page=21; Chung, H. (2022), *The Flexibility Paradox. Why Flexible Working Leads to (Self-)Exploitation*, Bristol University Press.
14. Taylor, H., et al. (2022), *The Changing Workplace: Enabling Disability-Inclusive Hybrid Working*, Work Foundation, https://www.lancaster.ac.uk/media/lancaster-university/content-assets/documents/lums/work-foundation/TheChangingWorkplace.pdf. Furthermore, Art. 5 of the Employment Equality Directive (2000/78/EC) provides that employers must provide 'reasonable accommodation' to workers with disabilities to enable them to access employment: telework can be a tool in this sense.
15. Rodríguez Ayuso, J.F. (2020), *Risk Assessment as a Fundamental Criterion for Extensive Interpretation in Determining the Suitability of Telework*, IUS ET SCIENTIA, vol. 6(2), https://web.archive.org/web/20210119215312id_/https://institucional.us.es/revistas/Ius_Et_Scientia/VOL6-2/Ius_et_Scientia_vol_6_n2_04_rodriguez_ayuso.pdf.

Indeed, according to the International Agency for Research on Cancer, radio-frequency radiation is considered a possible cause of carcinogenic effects. Pregnant women may therefore be particularly at risk in the event of exposure to radio-frequency radiation.[16]

Then, workers' physical health can be at risk as a result of muscular tensions and musculoskeletal disorders based on monotonous, repetitive operations and static posture maintained for long periods of time.[17]

Psychological health can also be damaged by using digital tools for prolonged periods: this may lead to reduced concentration and cognitive and emotional overload, as well as aggravate phenomena such as isolation, dependence on technology, sleep deprivation, emotional exhaustion, anxiety and burnout.[18]

The just mentioned health problems can be caused, or increased, by the interference between working time and rest time, when their respective boundaries are uncertain.

Confusion between working and rest time may also support the development of an 'always on' culture, in which the teleworker is always and everywhere reachable. This has a negative impact not 'only' on the psycho-physical health of workers but also on their other fundamental rights, including the right to fair remuneration (e.g., the employee works within her rest time, but she is not paid for), the limitation of working hours and work-life balance (the employee never disconnects and she is always available for working), and the right to equal treatment between men and women, given, as already mentioned, the disproportionate impact on women.[19]

§5.03 MEMBER STATES' RESPONSES DURING THE PANDEMIC

The responses of the EU Member States to the problem of the blurring of boundaries between working time and rest time, and the need to guarantee a right to disconnect, have been varied and multiform. Indeed, such responses have sometimes consisted of regulatory provisions in the form of laws, sometimes in the form of agreements, and sometimes as codes of practice.[20]

16. European Parliament resolution of 21 January 2021 with recommendations to the Commission on the right to disconnect (2019/2181(INL)) (2021/C 456/15), considering 'd', https://eur-lex.europa.eu/legal-content/EN/TXT/PDF/?uri=CELEX:52021IP0021.
17. *Ibid.*, considering 'd'.
18. Policy Department for Economic, Scientific and Quality of Life Policies, European Parliament (2021), *The Impact of Teleworking and Digital Work on Workers and Society. Special Focus on Surveillance and Monitoring, as well as on Mental Health of Workers*, April 2021, https://www.europarl.europa.eu/RegData/etudes/STUD/2021/662904/IPOL_STU(2021)662904_EN.pdf.
19. European Parliament resolution of 21 January 2021 with recommendations to the Commission on the right to disconnect (2019/2181(INL)) (2021/C 456/15), considering 'c', https://eur-lex.europa.eu/legal-content/EN/TXT/PDF/?uri=CELEX:52021IP0021.
20. European Commission (2024), Study exploring the social, economic and legal context and trends of telework and the right to disconnect, in the context of digitalisation and the future of work, during and beyond the COVID-19 pandemic, Final Report: Visionary Analytics: ilvinas Martinaitis, Audronė Sadauskaitė, Aurinta Garbašauskaitė, Olea Morris, Vainius Bartasevičius, Nini Gigani; Notus: Maria Caprile, Pablo Sanz, Juan Arasanz; European University Viadrina: Tania Bazzani: https://ec.europa.eu/social/BlobServlet?docId=27464&langId=en.

Furthermore, some Member States had already adopted regulations in the field of the right to disconnect before the pandemic, whereas others only on the occasion of the pandemic.

France, Belgium, Italy and Spain adopted provisions on the right to disconnect already from periods before the pandemic.

France was the first Member State which adopted a legislation setting a right to disconnect, in 2016, and now regulated by Article L.2242-17 of the Labour Code.[21] However, it is interesting to highlight that such a right, before being embedded in a piece of legislation, was recognized by a national cross-sectoral agreement of 2013[22] on quality of life at work with the aim of encouraging 'businesses to avoid any intrusion on employees' private lives by specifying periods when devices should be switched off'.[23]

Belgium adopted the Law on strengthening economic growth and social cohesion in 2018, according to which companies with more than fifty employees must consult and negotiate with their workplace health and safety committees (*comité pour la prévention et la protection au travail*) about the use of digital communication tools and disconnection from work.[24] However, in the case they don't reach an agreement, the company is not obliged to adopt a right to disconnect. Further, in Belgium, universally applicable sectoral collective agreements and company agreements set a right to disconnect and cover beyond the 47% of workers employed in companies with more than fifty employees.[25]

From February 2022 civil servants in Belgium are allowed to switch off work emails and phone calls out of working hours.[26] Then, a new piece of legislation, adopted in October 2022, sets the obligation for employers in the private sector with twenty employees or more to implement a right to disconnect in a collective bargaining agreement (CBA) or through organizations' work rules.[27]

In Italy, the right to disconnect was mentioned by Law No. 81/2017, regulating agile work. However, such a law does not establish a guaranteed and equal disconnection time for all workers and refers its regulation to negotiation between the parties. Law No. 81/2017 provides that the right to disconnect should be embedded in an agreement which identifies the worker's rest time as well as the technical and organizational measures necessary to ensure the worker's disconnection from the

21. https://www.legifrance.gouv.fr/codes/article_lc/LEGIARTI000043893940.
22. Turland F. (2014), *France: A Legal Right to Switch Off from Work*, Eurofound, 18 December 2014, https://www.eurofound.europa.eu/fr/resources/article/2014/france-legal-right-switch-work.
23. *Ibid.*
24. Eurofound (2021), *Right to Disconnect: Exploring Company Practices*, Publications Office of the European Union, Luxembourg, 18.
25. *Ibid.*
26. Wood, J. & Shine, I. (2023), *Right to Disconnect: The Countries Passing Laws to Stop Employees Working Out of Hours, Centre for the New Economy and Society*, World Economic Forum, 3 February 2023, https://www.weforum.org/agenda/2023/02/belgium-right-to-disconnect-from-work/.
27. Bouciqué, W. & Vets, E. (2023), *The Right to Disconnect: Which Countries Have Legislated?*, Global HR Lawyers, 26 July 2023, https://iuslaboris.com/insights/the-right-to-disconnect-which-countries-have-legislated/.

work technological instruments. But the law does not explicitly require an agreement resulting from collective bargaining, leaving the employee in a weak bargaining position with respect to her/his employers if collective bargaining is not used.

In Spain, Article 88 Organic Law 3/2018 regulates the right to disconnect: employees shall have the right to switch off devices in order to guarantee that their time off, leave and holidays are respected, together with their personal and family privacy. Within this picture, collective bargaining between employees' representatives and employers shall be implemented by developing adequate internal policies.[28]

More recently, the Royal Decree Law 28/2020, of 22 September on remote work, provides explicitly a right to digital disconnection in case of 'teleworking' in Spain.

In contrast to the above examples, in other cases – such as Greece, Portugal and Slovakia – the right to disconnect was introduced on the occasion of the pandemic (in 2021), and not previously.[29] Croatia, instead, introduced a right to disconnect more recently, in 2022 (in force in 2023), and Luxembourg did it in 2023.[30]

In addition to legislative interventions, a code of Practice was adopted by Ireland in 2021: such a code, although not legally binding, can however be used by courts when deciding on the merits of a case.[31]

The heterogeneous solutions put in place by the Member States can partly be traced back to their own industrial relations systems, where countries with a strong collective bargaining tradition have preferred to address the problem through collective agreements between the social partners at various levels, territorial and/or sectoral rather than by law (or through a combination between law and collective agreements).

Indeed, in countries, where a right to disconnect is not set by law, collective bargaining can play an important role. In Germany, for example, the right to disconnect has been implemented in relevant company agreements, such as in the case of Volkswagen (since 2011), BMW, Daimler, Deutsche Telekom and Evonik.[32]

The responses of the EU Member States to the need to guarantee a right to disconnect vary not only in the way they provide for a right to disconnect (law, collective bargaining, code of practice) but also in their content, outlining different possible ways to implement the right to disconnect: switching off communication media outside normal working hours, not answering employer's calls, not receiving calls, etc.

A 'soft' implementation involves common responsibility by workers and managers for guaranteeing the right to disconnect through different actions, such as 'awareness raising of the risks of constant connection, training and the management of

---

28. Lerouge, L. & Trujillo Pons, F. (2022), Contribution to the Study on the 'Right to Disconnect' from Work: Are France and Spain Examples for Other Countries and EU Law?, European Labour Law Journal, vol. 13(3), 450-465 https://doi.org/10.1177/20319525221105102.
29. Eurofound (2023), *Right to Disconnect: Implementation and Impact at Company Level,* Publications Office of the European Union, Luxembourg, 7, https://www.eurofound.europa.eu/en/publications/2023/right-disconnect-implementation-and-impact-company-level.
30. *Ibid.*
31. *Ibid.*
32. Eurofound (2021), *Right to Disconnect: Exploring Company Practices,* Publications Office of the European Union, Luxembourg, 17, https://www.eurofound.europa.eu/en/publications/2021/right-disconnect-exploring-company-practices.

out-of-hours communication (such as through regular reminders that messages do not require an answer outside of working hours)'.[33] A 'hard' approach, instead, based on the exclusive employer's responsibility, is to stop all the work communications with her/his employees during rest time.[34] The hard approach has the advantage of being more protective, considering the disbalance contractual position between employee and employer; however, it is more rigid, and this can be a problem for both the employee and the employer.

An example of a hard approach to the right to disconnect is that one of Volkswagen, which shutdowns (through a disconnection of its server) all the work communications with its employees within a specific time range (disabled between 18:15 and 07:00), with the exception of cases of specific projects. However, such exceptions must be prior agreed with the works council.[35] In this case, therefore, the rigidity of a hard approach is addressed through possibilities to introduce agreed exceptions.

An example of a soft approach is one of the Belgian 'Solvay' (agreement at company level, 2017).[36] In this case, the implementation of the right to disconnect focuses on supporting responsible use of email while promoting a culture according to which availability outside working hours and during holidays should not be requested or expected. Such policies should be developed on the basis of training and actions supporting employees' own responsibility for disconnection.[37]

The different ways of implementing the right to disconnection also intersect with the variations of telework, which can consist of work totally carried out in telework, or can alternatively be hybrid, implying an alternation with work in the employer's premises.[38]

§5.04 DEMATERIALIZATION OF THE WORKPLACE AND FLEXIBILIZATION OF WORKING TIME

Teleworking, and in general the use of new technologies at work, have highlighted two phenomena that are having a rapid and considerable impact on the world of work.

First, we can speak about 'dematerialisation' of the workplace in the case new technologies make it possible to work outside the company premises, basically from wherever one wishes. Of course, only in the case in which the type of job allows it (i.e., when it is 'teleworkable').

33. *Ibid.*, p. 2.
34. *Ibid.*, p. 1.
35. *Ibid.*, p. 50 and p. 33.
36. *Ibid.*, p. 33.
37. *Ibid.*
38. Eurofound (2023), *The Future of Telework and Hybrid Work*, Publications Office of the European Union, Luxembourg, https://www.eurofound.europa.eu/en/publications/2023/future-telework-and-hybrid-work.

Working from wherever implies the need to adapt the chosen workplace/s to the current changes in society.[39]

Indeed, the possibility of working in any place to carry out a job entails several pending issues. An example is provided by the case of accidents while working in telework. In this regard, during the pandemic, the German Federal Social Court[40] recognized an accident during home working as an 'accident at work' based on the principle of equal treatment between employees who work from home and those who work in the company. Nevertheless, such clarity is not present in all the Member States. But how would the matter have been decided if the work had taken place in a park? This issue represents a new challenge for the world of work, which national and EU institutions need to address.

In order to understand the phenomenon 'dematerialisation' of the workplace in case of telework, it is relevant to highlight that in case of telework, the Directive on the minimum safety and health requirements for the workplace does not apply. Such directive, indeed, refers to a definition of 'workplace', which is confined within the physical premises of the undertaking and/or establishment: telework is therefore excluded from its application. However, telework falls under the application of the Safety and Health Framework Directive,[41] which does not include a specific definition of workplace: the concept of workplace in this directive is instead interpreted in a broad sense.[42]

Although this article will not address the typical issues arising from the dematerialization of the workplace, such a phenomenon is relevant in combination with other phenomena, particularly relevant for the issue addressed in this chapter: the flexibilization of working time.

Flexibilization of working time means the possibility of not strictly adhering to a fixed working time. This entails a certain degree of autonomy to decide when to work. The flexibilization can be combined with the dematerialization of the workplace when the employee can decide not only when working but also where s/he works.

According to Chung (2022),[43] the flexibilization of working time based on the choice of employees is fundamental for achieving good results in terms of work-life balance or well-being.

However, although working in a way that is 'independent of time and place has the advantage that, thanks to ICT, workers can organise their work (including their

39. COM(2021) 323 final, Communication from the Commission to the European Parliament, The Council, the European Economic and Social Committee, and the Committee of the Regions, EU strategic framework on health and safety at work 2021-2027. Occupational safety and health in a changing world of work {SWD(2021) 148 final} – {SWD(2021) 149 final}, 5, https://eur-lex.europa.eu/legal-content/EN/TXT/PDF/?uri=CELEX:52021DC0323&from=EN.
40. German Federal Social Court (*Bundessozialgericht Verhandlung* B2 U 4/21 R).
41. Council Directive 89/391/EEC of 12 June 1989 on the introduction of measures to encourage improvements in the safety and health of workers at work.
42. Popma, J. (2013), *The Janus Face of the 'New Ways of Work': Rise, Risks and Regulation of Nomadic Work*, ETUI Working Paper, July 2013. https://papers.ssrn.com/sol3/papers.cfm?abstract_id=2376713.
43. Chung, H. (2022), *The Flexibility Paradox: Why Flexible Working Leads to (Self-) Exploitation*, Bristol University Press.

working time) themselves based on their individual situation, there is also an inherent danger that there will no longer be respect for the boundaries between paid work and private life' (Eurofound and International Labour Organization (ILO), 2017:49).[44]

Thus, the flexibilization of working time can create obstacles in monitoring compliance with the limitations to working hours, which are necessary to guarantee the health and safety of workers.[45]

This phenomenon amplifies its impact in combination with the dematerialization of the workplace: if the employee can choose when to work and where to work, and s/he decides to work in a non-typical working environment, such as a park, for example, the personal perception of the distinction between her/his working time and rest time will be particularly difficult to frame. Or, faced again with the possibility of choosing when and where to work, my colleagues and/or my employer may be convinced that I must be always available, affecting the frequency and the demand to be contacted at all times, blurring the distinction between rest and work time.

This can result in difficulties to 'disconnect' from work, difficulties in disengaging from work, long working hours, lack of respect for rest period and holidays, stress and even burnout (Eurofound and ILO, 2017).[46]

Hence telework seems to require on the one hand a certain clarity in the management of working time, and on the other hand mutual trust and reliability, between employer and employee, to guarantee compliance with legal obligations.[47]

A working relationship centred on clarity and trust potentially fosters new ways of organizing work, in which it is possible to remotely measure team performance and the degree of team coordination.

§5.05 EU ACQUIS AND DISCONNECTION

The problem of ensuring a right to disconnect has been particularly discussed in the last few years, also because of an increasing use of ICT at work.

It is precisely the use of such technologies, which has accelerated the process of blurring rest and working time in a context of dematerialization of workplace and flexibilization of working time.

44. Eurofound and the International Labour Office (2017), *Working Anytime, Anywhere: The Effects on the World of Work*, Publications Office of the European Union, Luxembourg, and the International Labour Office, Geneva, https://www.eurofound.europa.eu/en/publications/2017/working-anytime-anywhere-effects-world-work.
45. An extreme flexibilization of working hours blurs the boundaries between work time and rest time, making it more challenging to delineate these periods clearly. Additionally, it raises issues related to accurately quantifying hours worked. *See* for example Order of the Court (Eighth Chamber) of 22 April 2020, Case C-692/19, *B v. Yodel Delivery Network Ltd*: the CJEU was asked on the criteria for quantifying the hours of a platform worker: 'For the purposes of [Article 2(1)] of Directive [2003/88] how is a worker's working time to be calculated in circumstances where the individual claimant is not required to work fixed hours but is free to determine his own working hours within certain parameters e.g. between the hours of 7.30 and 21.00?' The Court did not answer as the worker was classified as self-employed.
46. *Ibid.*
47. Sewell, G. & Taskin, L. (2015), Out of Sight, Out of Mind in a New World of Work? Autonomy, Control and Spatiotemporal Scaling in Telework, Organization Studies, vol. 36(11), 1507-1529.

Within this constellation, the CJEU case law provides relevant elements to clarify the compatibility between rest time and working time. The significant case law regards especially stand-by time.

Although there is no definition of stand-by time at the European level, it is possible to understand it as a situation in which the employee can be contacted by the employer to perform work, even during his or her rest time.

The European Court of Justice has admitted, within certain limits, the possibility of requesting - and performing - work during rest time from work, in the case of stand-by time. This is admissible as long as work during the rest time does not prejudice the guarantee of health protection.

The Court of Justice clarifies this aspect referring to the relationship between the Working Time Directive[48] and the Safety and Health Framework Directive.[49]

[A] Relationship Between Working Time Directive and Safety and Health Framework Directive

The Working Time Directive lays down minimum health and safety requirements for the organization of working time, setting minimum standards for daily rest, weekly rest, and annual leave, as well as maximum weekly working time. According to this directive, 'working time is any period during which the worker is working, at the employer's disposal and carrying out his activity or duties, in accordance with national laws and/or practice' (Article 2). Rest time, however, is any time that is not working time. This directive therefore provides a binary, dichotomous definition of working time and rest time.[50]

The Safety and Health Framework Directive concerns the implementation of measures to encourage improvements in the safety and health of workers at work and lays down general principles concerning the prevention and protection of workers against occupational accidents and diseases.

The CJEU provides important indications about the relationship between the two mentioned directives in case of stand-by periods, i.e., those rest periods in which the employee can be contacted by the employer and asked to perform a working activity.

According to the CJEU, the classification of a standby period as a 'rest period' for the purposes of the application of Directive 2003/88 does not affect the duty of employers to comply with specific obligations to ensure the health and safety of their workers. These obligations are specifically formalized in Articles 5 and 6 of Directive

48. Directive 2003/88/EC of the European Parliament and of the Council of 4 November 2003 concerning certain aspects of the organization of working time.
49. Council Directive 89/391/EEC of 12 June 1989 on the introduction of measures to encourage improvements in the safety and health of workers at work.
50. Mitrus, L. (2022), *Defining Working Time Versus Rest Time: An Analysis of the Recent CJEU Case-Law on Stand-by Time*, A Thematic Working Paper for the Annual Conference of the European Centre of Expertise (ECE) in the field of labour law, employment and labour market policies: Regulating working time in times of digital and agile work, March 2022.

89/391. It follows that employers may not establish standby periods so long or so frequent that they constitute a risk to the safety or health of workers, regardless of whether these periods are classified as 'rest periods' within the meaning of Article 2 of Directive 2003/88. It is up to the Member States to define in their national law how this obligation is to be implemented.[51]

Therefore, in any case, stand-by time or not – the worker must normally be able to benefit from an effective rest period, in order to guarantee effective protection of her/his safety and health (*see*, among others, Case C-350/06 and C-520/06 *Schultz-Hoff and Others* [2009] ECR I-350/06 and C-520/06 EU:C:2009:18, paragraph 23).

This aspect highlights that, although compatibility between rest time and work performance can be allowed – subject to specific conditions set out by the Court of Justice – this must always be understood in compliance with the fundamental principles of the regulation protecting workers' health and safety.

[B] Compatibility Between Work and Rest Time

The Working Time Directive conceptualises work time and rest time as mutually exclusive, with one being defined in opposition to the other.[52] However, this dichotomy is mitigated by the CJEU through its case law. Consequently, the CJEU recognizes a certain degree of compatibility between rest time and work performance in case of stand-by time, which is rest time in which the worker can be called by the employer to work. In the case law regarding stand-by time, the rest time within which the employee can be asked to perform the work is called 'waiting time', and during this time s/he can receive the call.

In the stand-by time case law, it is crucial to understand whether waiting time – the time in which the employee can receive the employer's call to work – is rest time or should instead be considered working time.

In the case, waiting time is actually rest time, working time is only the time in which the work activity is effectively performed (as, for example, in the *Simap*, *Dellas* and *Jaeger* cases, *D.J. v. Radiotelevizija Slovenija*, Case C-344/19).

However, to understand whether waiting time is actually rest time, according to the CJEU, it is necessary to consider the specific circumstances on a case-by-case basis.

---

51. Judgment of the Court (Grand Chamber) of 9 March 2021, *D.J. v. Radiotelevizijia Slovenija*, case C–344/19, para. 65; Judgment of the Court (Grand Chamber) of 9 March 2021, *Stadt Offenbach am Main (Période d'astreinte d'un pompier)*, case C-580/19, para. 60; Judgment of the Court (Fifth Chamber) of 11 November 2021, *M.G. v. Dublin City Council*, case C-214/20, para. 47.
52. Judgment of the Court of 9 September 2021, *XR v. Dopravní podnik hl. m. Prahy, akciová společnost*, Case C-107/19, ECLI:EU:C:2021:722; Judgment of the Court (Grand Chamber) of 9 March 2021, *D.J. v. Radiotelevizijia Slovenija*, Case C–344/19, ECLI:EU:C:2021:182; Judgment of the Court of 3 October 2000, *Sindicato de Médicos de Asistencia Pública (Simap) v. Conselleria de Sanidad y Consumo de la Generalidad Valenciana*, Case C-303/98, EU:C:2000:528; Judgment of the Court of 9 September 2003, *Landeshauptstadt Kiel v. Norbert Jäger*, Case C-151/02, EU:C:2003:437.

For example, the CJEU explained that in the case of an obligation to remain at the workplace during waiting time, such time is considered working time,[53] irrespective of the work actually performed by the persons concerned.[54]

Further, in order to understand whether waiting time is working time, according to the Court attention must be paid to the nature and intensity of the constraints imposed on the employee during the stand-by time, such as, for example, the time within which the employee is expected to react.

In Matzak,[55] the employee was expected to respond to the employer's calls in only eight minutes, setting in this way constraints on his rest time of both temporal and geographical nature: eight minutes to respond implied a limitation of Matzak's rest time that was excessive and affected his ability to enjoy his free time. According to the CJEU, 'the obligation to remain physically present at the place determined by the employer and the geographical and temporal constraints resulting from the requirement to reach his place of work within eight minutes are such as to objectively limit the opportunities which a worker in Mr Matzak's circumstances has to devote himself to his personal and social interests'.[56] Therefore, in this case, the waiting time was considered working time.

In contrast, the reaction time in *D.J. v. Radiotelevizija Slovenija*[57] was one hour and, given the circumstances of the case, the conditions of stand-by time were considered to be compatible with management of rest time: in this case, 'the worker is not subject, during those periods, to constraints such that his or her ability to pursue his or her own private interests is objectively or very significantly affected'.[58]

The constraints on the employee reached such intensity to consider stand-by time as working time also in the case *RJ v. Stadt Offenbach am Main*.[59] The worker had to be able to reach the town boundary of his workplace within a twenty minute-response-time, in uniform, with the service vehicle made available to him by the employer. The specific circumstances of the case, overall assessed, proved that the waiting time could be considered 'working time', since 'the constraints imposed on that worker during that period are of such a nature as to constrain objectively and very significantly the ability that he (or she) has to freely manage, during the same period, the time during which his (or her) professional services are not required and to devote that time to his or her own interests'.[60]

53. Judgment of the Court of 3 October 2000, Case C-303/98, *Sindicato de Médicos de Asistencia Pública (Simap) v. Conselleria de Sanidad y Consumo de la Generalidad Valenciana*, para. 48.
54. Judgment of 9 September 2003, case C-151/02 *Landeshauptstadt Kiel v. Norbert Jäger*, ECLI: EU:C:2003:437.
55. Judgment of 21 February 2018 in case C-518/15, *Ville de Nivelles v. Rudy Matzak*, ECLI: EU:C:2018:82.
56. *Ibid.*, para. 63.
57. Judgment of the Court (Grand Chamber) of 9 March 202, *D.J. v. Radiotelevizijia Slovenija*, case C–344/19, ECLI:EU:C:2021:182.
58. *Ibid.*, para. 50.
59. Judgment of the Court (Grand Chamber) of 9 March 2021, *RJ v. Stadt Offenbach am Main* (Période d'astreinte d'un pompier), case C-580/19, ECLI:EU:C:2021:183.
60. *Ibid.*, para. 61.

Even in *XR v. Dopravní podnik,*[61] the constraints imposed on the employee were so strong as to dissuade him from planning any kind of recreational activity, even for a short duration. In this case, among other circumstances, the employee was allowed to go to the factory canteen, situated 200 meters from his workstation, but he has to be equipped with a transmitter alerting him, and, if necessary, be ready within two minutes, in front of the factory canteen, to be picked up by the service vehicle. In this case, stand-by time is considered working time.

Substantially different is instead the case *MG v. Dublin City Council,*[62] in which the employee could choose not to respond to some of the employer's calls and was allowed to perform other paid activities in the stand-by period.

Although the CJEU provides important criteria for determining whether the waiting period can be considered working time or rest time, it is up to the national courts to assess whether the working arrangements in the specific case objectively and in a very significant way limit the worker's opportunities to pursue other activities.[63]

It is relevant to note at this point that, although the EU case law admits a certain degree of compatibility between work and rest time, it admits such compatibility – under the already mentioned circumstances – only in the case of stand-by time. Therefore, outside the stand-by time cases, compatibility between rest time and working time must be excluded in light of EU law.

[C] Recording of Working Time

To ensure compliance with working time limitations, it is particularly important to set up an appropriate working time recording system. Therefore, the implementation of a right to disconnect intertwines with the obligation of companies to register working hours.

In *Federación de Servicios de Comisiones Obreras (CCOO) v. Deutsche Bank* (ECJ Judgment, 14 May 2019, C-55/18), the CJEU ruled that 'the Member States must require employers to set up an objective, reliable and accessible system enabling the duration of time worked each day by each worker to be measured' (paragraph 60).

Nevertheless, according to paragraph 63 of the judgment, Member States may exercise their discretion to determine the specific arrangements for implementing the system for recording working time.[64] In doing this, they should have regard for 'the specific arrangements for implementing such a system, in particular the form that it

61. Judgment of the Court (Tenth Chamber) of 9 September 2021, *XR v. Dopravní podnik hl. m. Prahy, akciová společnost*, case C-107/19, para. 35. Aspect also mentioned in *D.J. v. Radiotelevizija Slovenija*, para. 37.
62. Judgment of the Court (Fifth Chamber) of 11 November 2021, *MG v. Dublin City Council*, case C-214/20.
63. Mitrus, L. (2022), *Defining Working Time Versus Rest Time: An Analysis of the Recent CJEU Case-Law on Stand-by Time*, A Thematic Working Paper for the Annual Conference of the European Centre of Expertise (ECE) in the field of labour law, employment and labour market policies: Regulating working time in times of digital and agile work, March 2022.
64. Judgment of the Court (Grand Chamber) of 14 May 2019, *Federación de Servicios de Comisiones Obreras (CCOO) v. Deutsche Bank SAE*, Case C-55/18, para. 63.

must take, having regard, as necessary, to the particular characteristics of each sector of activity concerned, or the specific characteristics of certain undertakings concerning, inter alia, their size'.[65] In this sense, the implementation of such a system should always guarantee the possibility for Member States to derogate, *inter alia*, from Articles 3 to 6 of the WTD 'when, on account of the specific characteristics of the activity concerned, the duration of the working time is not measured and/or predetermined or can be determined by the workers themselves'.[66] Even in cases of derogation, Member States should still maintain due regard for the general principles of the protection of the safety and health of workers.[67]

The system recording working time not only ensures compliance with working time limitations and provides 'the organisation and means necessary for the protection of the safety and health of workers' (paragraph 63) but also guarantees the determination of overtime,[68] allows effective control by the relevant institutions such as labour inspectorates,[69] and creates the conditions for an effective exercise of the role of workers' representatives according to Article 11(3) WTD.[70]

§5.06 DISCONNECTION: A DIRECTIVE?

In its Resolution of 21 January 2021 with recommendations to the Commission on the right to disconnect,[71] the European Parliament reiterates the need to ensure respect for working time and its predictability as an essential aspect to ensure the health and safety of workers and their families.

According to the European Parliament, disconnection from work must be guaranteed not only through the recognition of a right to disconnect but also thanks to awareness-raising, information, and training campaigns on working time and the right to disconnect in order to promote a reasonable use of digital tools to protect the mental and physical health of workers.[72] For this reason, on the one hand, employers should not require workers to be available or reachable outside working hours and, on the other hand, workers should refrain from contacting their colleagues for work purposes outside the agreed working hours.[73]

---

65. *Ibid.*
66. *Ibid.*
67. Leccese, V. (2022), *Monitoring Working Time and Working Time Directive 2003/88/EC: A Purposive Approach*, A Thematic Working Paper for the Annual Conference of the European Centre of Expertise (ECE) in the field of labour law, employment and labour market policies: Regulating working time in times of digital and agile work, March 2022.
68. Judgment of the Court (Grand Chamber) of 14 May 2019, *Federación de Servicios de Comisiones Obreras (CCOO) v. Deutsche Bank SAE*, Case C-55/18, para. 47.
69. *Federación de Servicios de Comisiones Obreras (CCOO) v. Deutsche Bank*, para. 56.
70. *Ibid.*, para. 62.
71. European Parliament resolution of 21 January 2021 with recommendations to the Commission on the right to disconnect (2019/2181(INL)), https://eur-lex.europa.eu/legal-content/EN/TXT/?uri=CELEX%3A52021IP0021.
72. *Ibid.*, Art. 4 of the proposal of directive, https://eur-lex.europa.eu/legal-content/EN/TXT/?uri=CELEX%3A52021IP0021.
73. *Ibid.*, considering n. 20.

The social partners at the EU level attempt to reach a framework agreement to recognize a right to disconnect. After the impossibility of signing an agreement, European Trade Union Confederation (ETUC) called the Commission to initiate legislative action,[74] while BusinessEurope seemed to prefer to intervene through soft law.[75]

On Tuesday 12 December 2023, the Commissioner for Jobs and Social Rights, Nicolas Schmit, affirmed that the Commission would follow up the commitments to legislate on the right to disconnect.[76]

Although, as we have analysed, the Safety and Health directive, the Working Time directive and the EU case law imply that a right to disconnect has to be guaranteed by the Member States, a directive could be useful to raise awareness in the field and to make sure the right of disconnect is implemented in all the Member States.

But should a possible directive on the right to disconnect include a one-size-fits-all solution, based on the options that seem to better work within the Member States? Could such a directive make use of the EU case law and its criteria?

While it is important to introduce rules that can ensure a right to disconnect, it seems difficult to adopt a solution that can fit all Member States and all organizations.

Member States have different industrial relations systems and different legal cultures. In some countries, a solution based on the law seems to prevail, in others a solution based on collective bargaining seems preferable, and in still others a solution is adopted in which these two aspects are integrated.

The management of teleworking then depends very much on the structure of the organization in which teleworking is adopted and, on the work, to be performed. The corporate culture and the level of trust between the parties may also condition the choice between a soft or hard approach. Teleworking itself may also be hybrid or total, and this difference can also play a role in implementing a right to disconnect.

How then to create a basic common ground, to be ensured in each Member State, without imposing a specific solution?

In this respect, the EU case law can be particularly useful.

The general rule remains the need to ensure compliance with the regulation guaranteeing rest periods and time limitations. In *Federación de Servicios de Comisiones Obreras (CCOO) v. Deutsche Bank*, not only the importance of a working time recording

---

74. ETUC (2023), *Telework: Legislative Action Needed by the EU Commission*, https://www.etuc.org/en/pressrelease/telework-legislative-action-needed-eu-commission.
75. BusinessEurope on the Declaration of the Belgian Presidency on the Future of Social Europe claims that 'In our views, such declaration should be based on shared political and strategic priorities for the future European Social Agenda, rather than proposals for further legislation.' Written Input Towards La Hulpe Declaration on the Future of Social Europe and Comments on the Belgian Presidency. Discussion Note on the European Pillar of Social Rights, November 2023 https://www.businesseurope.eu/sites/buseur/files/media/position_papers/social/2023-11-03_eu_cross-industry_employers_written_input_la_hulpe.pdf. *See also* Golden, D. (2003), *Just a Matter of Time? The 'Right to Disconnect'*, Social Europe, 12 December 2003, https://www.socialeurope.eu/just-a-matter-of-time-the-right-to-disconnect.
76. Rapporteur of the EU Parliament, Agius Saliba, A. (2024), *The Right to Disconnect in 'A Europe Fit for the Digital Age'*, 20 January 2024, https://www.europarl.europa.eu/legislative-train/theme-a-europe-fit-for-the-digital-age/file-al-legislative-proposal-to-the-commission-on-the-right-to-disconnect.

system was highlighted but also its possible derogations. The system to be adopted – whatever it may be – should prove to comply with the general rule, i.e., ensuring compliance with the regulation guaranteeing rest periods and time limitations, and it should also: (i) prove to comply with the rules on safety and health of workers; (ii) guarantee the determination of overtime;[77] (iii) allow effective control by the relevant institutions such as labour inspectorates;[78] (iv) create the conditions for an effective exercise of the role of workers' representatives.[79]

Another relevant aspect is that the CJEU admits a degree of compatibility between work activity and the right to rest exclusively in stand-by cases, and only under certain conditions, but health and safety at work should be guaranteed.

The idea that compatibility between working and rest time is admissible within a certain degree only in the case of stand-by time needs to be considered in conjunction with the content of the Transparent and Predictable Working Conditions Directive.[80] According to this directive, both in case of entirely or mostly predictable and unpredictable patterns, the employer has the duty to inform the employee on fundamental elements of the working time. This certainly includes the modalities and conditions of the stand-by time.

In other words, if a certain compatibility between work performance and rest time is only possible in the case of stand-by time, this can only be achieved if the conditions of stand-by time are clearly indicated in the information embedded in the employment contract. And such conditions should be set within the limits and according to the criteria indicated by the CJEU and mentioned in section §5.02.

Whether it is the law on which the employment contract is based, or collective bargaining, depends on the choice of each Member State. Inappropriate, however, would seem to leave the matter of the right to disconnect to the total freedom of the parties to the individual relationship, given the different bargaining power positions between employer and employee.

§5.07 CONCLUSION

The use of technology is becoming increasingly predominant in the world of work, highlighting new challenges for the meaning of the work debate.

The pandemic led to a relevant increase in the use of teleworking: the use of technology makes it possible to work from any place and at any time, leading to a dematerialization of the workplace and a flexibilization of working time. This can bring not only many potential benefits but also possible risks.

77. Judgment of the Court (Grand Chamber) of 14 May 2019, *Federación de Servicios de Comisiones Obreras (CCOO) v. Deutsche Bank SAE*, Case C-55/18, para. 47.
78. *Ibid.*, para. 56.
79. *Ibid.*, para. 62.
80. Directive (EU) 2019/1152 of the European Parliament and of the Council of 20 June 2019 on transparent and predictable working conditions in the EU.

One of these risks concerns the blurring between working and rest time. This can be fostered by an always-on culture, according to which workers must always be online and respond to their employers' requests, at all times.

Some of the Member States have tried in various ways to address this problem and to ensure a right to disconnect. The responses have been varied and multifaceted in content, form, and timing of implementation.

Adopting a common ground of rights for all the employees in all the Member States seems to be a condition for technology to have a favourable impact on labour, within a fair competition domestic market.

The EU legal acquis, and particularly the CJEU case law, already provides important elements, which imply the recognition of a right to disconnect. However, an EU directive would help establish clear minimum standards across all Member States regarding the right to disconnect, while also encouraging responsible technology use and increasing awareness of this issue, effectively serving as a catalyst for attention among the public.

CHAPTER 6

Work-Life Balance: Well-Balanced with Equal Opportunity Goals?

Christina Hiessl

§6.01 INTRODUCTION

Indications that the quality of life and work is under strain in the twenty-first century have been on the rise in the recent past. Eurofound's most recent survey on risks to workers' well-being[1] finds that two out of five workers in the European Union (EU) report high work intensity, and about the same share works 'unsocial' work hours. The OECD[2] finds that almost one in two workers report suffering or struggling with life, whereby the share is lower rather than higher among those who are in full-time regular employment. Clearly, whereas demanding and unpredictable work schedules and expectations to work overtime when needed are a challenge and a potential risk to psychosocial well-being for every worker, these issues are exacerbated for workers shouldering responsibilities also outside the context of paid work. And while it would be an oversimplification to reduce work-life balance (WLB) needs to issues of family care, it is clear that being in charge of the care of family or household members has always and will continue to be the most prevalent and systemic reason for WLB difficulties.

In late 2022, the European care strategy[3] was published. Unsurprisingly, it confirms that care needs are and will be increasing over the foreseeable future, while

1. Eurofound (2023), Psychosocial Risks to Workers' Well-being: Lessons from the COVID-19 Pandemic, European Working Conditions Telephone Survey 2021 series, Publications Office of the European Union, Luxembourg.
2. Devaux, M. & Piatrova, A. (2022), Health and Well-Being of the Workforce. In: OECD, Promoting Health and Well-Being at Work: Policy and Practices, OECD Health Policy Studies, OECD Publishing, Paris, https://doi.org/10.1787/e179b2a5-en.
3. *See* Commission Communication on the European care strategy, 7 September 2022, COM(2022) 440 final.

the available pool of possible carers is shrinking. Put bluntly, the increase in life expectancy,[4] which is not paired with an equivalent increase in *healthy* life expectancy,[5] means that the post-retirement generation is gradually moving from being a major *source* of care (e.g., for their grandchildren) to being a major group of care recipients over possibly the major share of their post-retirement years. On average, already today, more than a quarter of people aged 65 or over, and two-fifths of people aged 75 and over living at home need long-term care (LTC). The number of people needing LTC is projected to increase from somewhat more than 30 million today to over 38 million by 2050.[6]

While the EU's approach clearly pleads for an expansion of affordable and available professional care,[7] it seems clear that, with a view to the already present crippling staff shortages in the care sector,[8] informal care by relatives will remain a key source of care in the foreseeable future. And whereas notably care for the elderly is currently often provided by spouses who are retired and thus not facing issues of WLB, this may be subject to change with a view to rising retirement ages and an increase in the share of people living alone or with a spouse who is themselves in need of care.

In other words, despite the gradual decrease and eventual stagnation of fertility rates in the EU at a rather low level,[9] the reconciliation of work and private or family life is by no means losing importance; if anything, its relevance is on the rise. Note that adult LTC needs are not only less 'schedulable' than the birth of the child but also have a less predictable trajectory, with needs likely to increase rather than decrease over time. They also tend to confront workers at a later point in their career – a time which frequently overlaps with what could be the most productive and well-paid period of labour market participation for women with a childcare-related career break (and/or prolonged part-time work) in their thirties.

The last-mentioned aspect immediately connects with a key concern to be addressed in the present article: workers are confronted with demands to provide

4. Which temporarily dropped due to COVID-19, but has since rebounded and reached a new all-time high of almost 79 years for men and more than 84 years for women in 2023. *See* Eurostat, Life Expectancy by Age and Sex, https://doi.org/10.2908/demo_mlexpec.
5. Which has barely increased since measurements started in 2004. In 2021, it still stood at just over 63 years for males and just over 64 years for females. *See* Eurostat, Healthy life years by sex, https://doi.org/10.2908/hlth_hlye.
6. Commission Communication on the European care strategy, *supra* n. 3, p. 4.
7. Cf. notably the Council Recommendation of 8 December 2022 on access to affordable high-quality long-term care (2022/C 476/01).
8. The Commission's Communication on the European care strategy (*supra* n. 3, p. 11) estimates that more than 1.6 million LTC workers would have to be added by 2050 to keep LTC coverage at the same level as in 2022. Note that 'same level' means upholding a situation in which many are not able to use professional care to the extent they would want to. 13 % of parents do not make use of any paid childcare for financial reasons, and the same is true for a third of households with LTC needs, with many more not using professional services to the preferred extent. Disabled children are even cared for exclusively by their parents in half of all cases (*Ibid.*, p. 2). Thus, paradoxically, even a large-scale increase in the public financial means devoted to the affordability of care would only be effective if paired with an unprecedented successful recruitment of care personnel – at times when staff shortages are rising also in many other sectors of the economy.
9. Around a level of 1.5 live births per woman: *see* Eurostat, Fertility Indicators, https://doi.org/10.2908/demo_find.

unpaid care for others (mostly family members) in a highly unequal manner, and this inequality has an unmissable gender component. Women in all countries still have (partly significantly) lower employment rates and lower average hours spent in paid work, but – with the exception of six OECD countries[10] – more hours spent on *paid and unpaid* work combined.[11] This gendered participation in work and care, which will be explored in somewhat more depth in section §6.02, will be a guiding pillar for attempts made in the present chapter to evaluate existing WLB policies and the potential of legislative innovation. For this purpose, section §6.03 explores – with reference to the status quo in national and EU law – how legal policies could and should be designed when aiming for a proper balance between WLB and equal opportunity goals. Section §6.04 concludes.

§6.02 WLB OPPORTUNITIES: REINFORCING GENDERED PARTICIPATION IN WORK AND CARE(?)

Policies to help workers reconcile work and family life exist in virtually all countries.[12] At the EU level, the relatively narrow focus of the Parental Leave Directive[13] has been largely replaced (as of August 2022) by the WLB Directive,[14] which effectively sums up the most important types of WLB policies related to family care – including paternity leave (Article 4), parental leave (Article 5), carer's leave (Article 6), force majeure leave (Article 7), and requests for flexible working arrangements (Article 9). The broad and open formulation of the last-mentioned aspect allows it to work as a catch-all provision that might cover arrangements which in some countries would be designed as specific rights – such as parental part-time or leave for terminally ill relatives.[15] The minimalistic design of most of the concrete types of rights at the European level means that all EU states have put in place (either in their law or in widely applicable collective agreements) policies that go beyond the compulsory minimum harmonization in at least some aspects.[16] This can include the granting of concrete rights to arrangements that under the WLB Directive would only fall under the 'right to request' (*see also infra* at §6.03[D]), but more notably of longer leave durations (including for maternity leave

10. Denmark, Italy, Mexico, the Netherlands, New Zealand, Norway.
11. OECD, Social Protection and Well-being Database: Time Spent in Paid and Unpaid Work, by Sex.
12. Cf. the OECD Family Database, many aspects of which will be cited below.
13. Council Directive 2010/18/EU of 8 March 2010 implementing the revised Framework Agreement on parental leave concluded by BUSINESSEUROPE, UEAPME, CEEP and ETUC and repealing Directive 96/34/EC.
14. Directive (EU) 2019/1158 of the European Parliament and of the Council of 20 June 2019 on WLB for parents and carers and repealing Council Directive 2010/18/EU.
15. For a more in-depth overview *see* Berger, L. M. & Carlson, M.J. (2020), Family Policy and Complex Contemporary Families: A Decade in Review and Implications for the Next Decade of Research and Policy Practice. Journal of Marriage and Family, 82(1), 478-507 https://doi.org/10.1111/jomf.12650.
16. *Ibid.*

– *see* subsection §6.03[A] on their questionable classification as WLB rights) and/or better payment than prescribed by the Directive.[17]

In stark contrast to other aspects of national labour law that 'top up' the minimum standards harmonized at the EU level, more generous rights to interrupt or reduce work for reasons connected to family care tend to receive criticism notably for their impact on gender equality. At first sight, this may appear counter-intuitive, as notably rights to take leave for family reasons and return to the same position are, indisputably, a vital element to prevent women from dropping out of the labour market due to family care. Yet, at the same time, even when leave rights are formulated in a gender-neutral way, research has consistently pointed out just how strongly the take-up of such rights is still influenced by traditional gender models. Accordingly, the more generous the system, the larger the gender gap in terms of labour market participation.

Eurostat's labour force survey Ad hoc module of 2018 demonstrates that when asked if and how childcare responsibilities influenced their current work situation, close to 80% of men answered that there was no such influence. Around or less than 2% each affirmed that they had made any changes in their job to increase income, changed their job or employer, transferred to less demanding tasks in their job, were currently on family leave or reduced working time. Another 6% affirmed not further specified 'other changes'; the rest did not answer the question. The numbers for all these forms of changes were higher (mostly at least twice as high) for female workers, with notably the share of those currently working reduced hours (15.5%) being more than six times larger than for male working parents. Regarding the impacts of childcare obligations in the past, respondents were asked exclusively whether they had interrupted their work for a significant duration (at least six months) for childcare reasons. This was affirmed by barely 6.5% and expressly negated by 89% of men, whereas almost 62% of women confirmed (and 31% negated). Additionally, 3.5% of women versus 0% of men indicated that they had never worked due to childcare obligations.[18] Responsibilities for the care of incapacitated relatives had overall less impact on the respondents' current work participation, but gender differences were obvious also here – with 4% of men versus 10% of women indicating that they had interrupted their work for this purpose for a significant duration and less than 2.5% of men versus 4% of women affirming a reduction of working hours.[19]

17. Which requires a minimum of ten days of paternity leave, paid at sick pay level; four months of parental leave, two of which are to be paid at a level so as 'to facilitate the take-up of parental leave by both parents' (Art. 8(3)); five days of carers' leave per year, which may be unpaid; force majeure leave with neither a minimum duration nor payment prescribed; and flexible working arrangements without any further specifications, which may also be rejected entirely by the employer (*see infra* at §6.03[D]).
18. Eurostat, Persons in Employment with Childcare Responsibilities by Effect on Employment and Educational Attainment Level, https://doi.org/10.2908/lfso_18ceffed; and Population by effects of childcare on employment and educational attainment level, https://doi.org/10.2908/lfso_18stwked; both customized for age group 25-64, and for the second dataset excluding respondents indicating they had never had children or were out of work for reasons other than childcare.
19. Eurostat, Persons in Employment or with Previous Employment Experience by Effects of Care of Incapacitated Relatives on Employment and Educational Attainment Level, https://doi.org/10.

Specifically for the take-up of parental leave, OECD data[20] show that a clear majority of European men are still not taking any of it, with women being about three times more likely to use any parental leave entitlements for their children. Where men do take leave, the duration tends to be a fraction of that taken by women – with the male average constituting less than a third of the female even in Norway and Sweden as the 'most equal' countries in this respect.[21]

All in all, these data leave no doubt about the fact that WLB rights that are formulated in a gender-neutral fashion are taken up in a highly gender-specific way. It is not the purpose of the present contribution to delve into the difficult question of the 'why' of these features – i.e., the degree to which they are due to actual immediate financial concerns (note that the gender wage gap is actually small for young couples *before* they have children),[22] longer-term financial considerations (in the sense that couples would consider the male parent's career opportunities more promising or more likely to be harmed by an extended period of leave), or general gender role perceptions – which may facilitate both a workplace culture that treats men who appear to prioritize their family over their work with suspicion and a lack of confidence in men's caring skills (both by themselves and their partners).

The question is much rather if and how the law can have an impact in this regard – whereby the 'if' can quite unambiguously be affirmed. Not only is there abundant evidence that parents do adjust their work and care arrangements to the legal system in place to a considerable degree (*see* next section for one aspect of this) but it is also indicated that such adaptions can have a lasting impact on gender norms over generations. The best example of this is Germany, where, more than thirty years after the country's reunification, empirical research still finds significant differences in the degree to which young parents' work and care arrangements conform to the male breadwinner model.[23] In other words, the fact that the East German legal (and political) regime promoted gender equality and women's main role as workers rather than homemakers much earlier and much more pronouncedly than in the West apparently still has an impact on generations that have mostly grown up post-reunification.

As to the 'how', it is important, as a starting point, to acknowledge the regulatory dilemma of policies aiming to promote WLB and equality in work and care at the same time. The significant cross-country differences present in all datasets[24] indicate that,

---

2908/lfso_18redsted; customized for age group 25-64 and excluding respondents indicating they had never had relevant care responsibilities.

20. OECD Family Database: PF2.2: Parents' use of childbirth-related leave. Data for 2021 were available for just about half of OECD Member States.
21. *Ibid.*, Charts PF2.2.C and PF2.2.E, pp. 5 and 7. Note that comparable data on leave duration by gender is available only for a minority of countries.
22. Even negative in some countries (meaning that women have a higher average income) for workers below age 25. *See* Eurostat, Gender Pay Gap in Unadjusted Form by Age: NACE Rev. 2 Activity (B-S Except O), Structure of Earnings Survey Methodology, https://doi.org/10.2908/earn_gr_gpgr2ag.
23. Ziegler, Y., et al. (2022), Working Mothers in East and West Germany: A Cluster Analysis Using a Three-Stage Approach. Gender in Management: An International Journal, 37(3), 423-437 https://doi.org/10.1108/gm-10-2020-0318.
24. For a cross-country overview of entitlements in 2023, *see* Table PF2.1.D of OECD Family Database: Parental leave systems, p. 9.

overall, countries stipulating particularly generous rights and failing to instal strong elements to counter adverse gender impacts (*see* next subsection) exhibit larger gender gaps. At the same time, it is clear that, without tools to enable the combination of work and care, many of the women using them in current reality might feel forced to make choices that cannot be considered socially desirable – such as abandoning their current employment, abandoning a wish to have children, leaving a care-dependent person without appropriate care, or opting for care arrangements that either bring the family in financial difficulties or are of dubious legality (such as the use of live-in carers, most of whom are severely underpaid and subject to precarious working conditions).[25]

In light of all these regulatory challenges, the next section will explore which regulatory strategies would be apt to address them, and to what degree these strategies are already present in current EU-level legislation and case law.

§6.03 WLB REGULATION: WHAT WORKS FOR EQUALITY?

To assess which regulatory strategies might achieve a proper balance between the aims of WLB and equality, it seems expedient to distinguish between policies focusing on maternity, parenting, and other forms of family care, respectively.

[A] Maternity

For maternity leave, the regulatory way forward in light of equality aims seems rather straightforward: as a type of leave that is reserved for female parents exclusively, it should be limited to what is necessary from a health and safety perspective – leaving the pursuit of childcare and WLB aims to other, gender-neutral instruments. At the same time, insofar as taking this leave *is* necessary in light of health and safety concerns, it should be well-paid, so as to avoid any incentive not to take it. In this sense, the choice made by Article 11 of the Maternity Directive[26] to tie maternity leave pay to the sick pay level seems problematic, as the latter is regularly determined, *inter alia*, with a view to avoiding fraudulent absenteeism – a risk which should arguably be of little relevance for maternity leave. Whereas the CJEU has confirmed this legislative decision and found that denying full pay during maternity leave does not amount to gender discrimination,[27] a broader understanding of equality might indicate that only full pay would effectively neutralize the financial disadvantage of a group which is exclusively female. Finally, in line with Article 6(8) of the International Labour Organization (ILO) Maternity Protection Convention (No. 183, 2000), individual employers should never be burdened with the costs of wage replacement during the

25. *See* Hiessl, C. (2022), Labour Rights for Live-In Care Workers: The Long and Bumpy Road Ahead. Social Sciences, MDPI, 11(12), 1-21 https://doi.org/10.3390/socsci11120547.
26. Council Directive 92/85/EEC of 19 October 1992, on the introduction of measures to encourage improvements in the safety and health at work of pregnant workers and workers who have recently given birth or are breastfeeding.
27. *See, e.g.*, CJEU, 14 July 2016, Case C-335/15 (*Ornano*).

leave period, as this would bear a risk of discrimination against young women in hiring.

In practice, this 'ideal' combination of elements does not seem to be applied in any country[28] – notably as the duration of maternity leave is generally not determined in the individual case in order to cover exactly the (possibly highly individual) medically necessary period of leave for each worker. Much rather, maternity leave systems depart from a concretely defined legal standard duration. This is understandable when considering that individual developments in relation to a particular pregnancy or birth are regularly not predictable in the beginning – so that doctors would usually start from a standardized duration anyway, while additional individualized leave for complications can be prescribed also when the standard duration is set by law.[29]

This begs the question of what would be an adequate standardized leave duration – whereby national lawmakers could hardly diverge more widely in their assessment. In 2023, paid maternity leave entitlements in the EU ranged from six weeks in Portugal to almost sixty weeks in Bulgaria.[30] At the EU level, Article 8 Maternity Directive requires Member States to grant workers a right to fourteen weeks of maternity leave, two of which are compulsory.[31]

The CJEU has repeatedly been confronted with questions concerning national systems granting much longer periods of maternity leave, notably in Spain (prior to a reform in 2021) and more recently in a French collective agreement.[32] The most recent of these cases, *Syndicat CFTC*, makes it painfully clear that, in late 2020, the Court is still struggling to embrace equality aims in relation to pregnancy – and/or reluctant to openly reverse its own case law, regardless of how questionable it appears in light of the general principle of equal treatment, the fundamental nature of which has been stressed over and over in the case law of the same Court. This specifically concerns the much-criticized[33] idea that, as the CJEU found forty years ago in the case of *Hofmann*,[34] maternity leave legislation should be allowed to protect not only the mother's biological condition but also the 'special relationship' between the mother and her newborn after childbirth. Never once has the Court explained what precisely should be the content of such a 'special relationship', why and to what degree it should be more worthy of protection than the child's relationship with its father, whether any of these

28. At least not in the OECD, for which an overview of the different national rules is contained in Table PF2.1.C of the OECD Family Database: Parental leave systems, p. 13.
29. *See*, at the EU level, Art. 5 Maternity Directive.
30. Chart PF2.1.A of OECD Family Database: Parental leave systems, p. 5.
31. Note that the fact that Portugal, Finland and Sweden have shorter maternity leave durations does not violate the directive, as long as women in these countries can effectively take at least fourteen weeks of paid leave (which is in practice ensured by generous parental leave rights).
32. Cases *Roca Álvarez* (CJEU, 30 September 2010, Case C-104/09), *Betriu Montull* (CJEU, 19 September 2013, Case C-5/12), *Syndicat CFTC* (CJEU, 18 November 2020, Case C-463/19).
33. *See, e.g.*, Suk, J.C. (2010), Are Gender Stereotypes Bad for Women? Rethinking Antidiscrimination Law and Work-Family Conflict. Columbia Law Review, 110(1), 1-69, p. 51; Robeyns, I. (2012), Should Maternity Leave Be Expanded?. Ethics and Social Welfare, 6(2), 206-212, p. 208 https://doi.org/10.1080/17496535.2012.682508.
34. CJEU, 12 July 1984, Case C-184/83.

assumptions are based on scientific findings (rather than simply the societal norms that guided the Court's case law in the early 1980s), or why it does not see a need to reassess this case law in light of Article 28 Recast Directive, which clearly allows for a justification of direct gender discrimination exclusively for 'the protection of women, particularly as regards pregnancy and maternity'. The assumption that the protection of a 'special relationship' can be equated with the protection of the woman herself would seem at least worthy of an explanation. Rather than addressing these questions upfront, the CJEU in *Syndicat CFTC* (just as in the earlier cases) reiterates the mantra of the special relationship, just to then seek ways to nonetheless find the specific discrimination at issue unjustified – *in casu* because the extra leave was not unconditionally granted to all women and could thus not credibly be claimed to be based on considerations of the protection of a special relationship that should be the same for all women. The conclusion *e contrario* that extra leave for all women beyond fourteen weeks could be justified without any apparent limits is not commented on further by the Court. Had the Court found that, in line with the logic just set out, the time needed to protect said special relationship should indeed be the same for *all women*, the conclusion would arguably be that this duration should be determinable at the EU level. Had the Court then found that the duration of fourteen weeks (which appears rather generous from a health and safety perspective – *see* next paragraph) should be sufficient, then any female-specific leave entitlements beyond that would arguably not fulfil the criterion of necessity to justify direct discrimination. Thereby, the decision would have come down as a bombshell judgment, considering that only four EU countries do not envisage a standard duration of maternity leave longer than fourteen weeks.[35]

When abandoning the ominous 'special relationship' concept and viewing maternity leave exclusively as a health and safety tool, the pertinent literature suggests, based on medical experience concerning the typical course of a pregnancy, that the approach to be followed is the Portuguese: a pregnancy that features no complications generally does not necessitate any leave before childbirth, and the recovery from childbirth generally takes up to six, exceptionally eight weeks. Accordingly, in the legal literature, it has been suggested that an equality-based review of the EU's approach to maternity should lead to a reduction of the fourteen-week entitlement to six weeks[36] or six to eight weeks.[37] At times, this is complemented by a proposal to increase parental leave by the same duration by which maternity leave is shortened, so the EU-level minimum total leave entitlement for women would not be shortened, while men's entitlement to parental leave would triple.

35. Portugal, Finland, Sweden and Germany. *See* Chart PF2.1.A of OECD Family Database: Parental leave systems, p. 5.
36. De la Corte Rodíguez, M. (2018), EU Directives on Maternity Leave: A Misleading Social Risk Approach and Its Unsatisfactory Effects on Both Mothers and Fathers. European Labour Law Journal, 9(2), 171-194, pp. 191 et seqq. https://doi.org/10.1177/2031952518780057.
37. Foubert, P. (2017), Child Care Leave 2.0: Suggestions for the Improvement of the EU Maternity and Parental Leave Directives from a Rights Perspective. Maastricht Journal of European and Comparative Law, 24(2), 245-263, p. 259 https://doi.org/10.1177/1023263x17709751.

Whereas such an approach would certainly be more distinctly inspired by equality aims, it seems to fall short of addressing the underlying issues from both a health and safety and an equality perspective. These issues start from the fact that the idea of a *voluntary* leave for health and safety reasons is, as such, questionable. OSH law is generally not voluntary – as this would risk that vulnerable workers who are exposed to pressure from employers are likely to forego entitlements. A worker cannot waive any of the rights given to them by any of the other OSH directives in the narrower sense[38] – nor by other directives with an OSH purpose, such as the Working Time Directive.[39] From this perspective, the level of protection granted by Article 8 Maternity Directive actually seems insufficient, as women could be subject to pressure to return to work after as little as two weeks – with most Member States having similarly short terms of compulsory leave.[40] As a result, to stay true to the health and safety purpose of maternity leave while minimizing gendered effects, maternity leave should ideally be designed as a portion of a female worker's overall childbirth-related leave entitlement that compulsorily needs to be taken in the first six to eight weeks after birth. Exceptions might be allowed based on a medical certificate that, in the individual case, rebuts the presumption that returning to work after a shorter time would not be responsible from an OSH point of view. At the same time, equality considerations indicate that this compulsory leave should not be given *in addition* to parental leave. If one accepts that men and women should be treated equally in terms of leave rights after childbirth, and birth mothers are on leave to be with the child during the first six to eight weeks already, there does not seem to be a reason *not* to deduct this period from her overall leave entitlement – or, vice versa, add an equivalent period of six to eight weeks to the entitlement of the second parent in the form of paternity leave or additional parental leave.

Regarding wages, less than half of the EU's Member States[41] provided for a 100% replacement rate during maternity leave in 2023. In some others, the replacement rate when taking the maximum period of leave could be as low as 22.6% (in Ireland).[42] As concerns, finally, the question of whether the employer is (partly) burdened with the cost of wage replacement during leave and might thus have a general disincentive to hire (younger) women, it seems difficult to assess the situation in the Member States, considering that the pertinent regulation is often found in collective agreements which – as the one at issue in *Syndicat CFTC* – may grant women considerable rights beyond the legal minimum at the cost of the employer.

All in all, the legislative status quo in this area is generally far (and in some countries very far) from what would be implied by the aims of health and safety as well as equality-based WLB.

38. The OSH Framework Directive 89/391/EEC and the individual directive in the sense of its Art. 16 – one of which is basically the Maternity Directive.
39. Directive 2003/88/EC of the European Parliament and of the Council of 4 November 2003 concerning certain aspects of the organization of working time.
40. De la Corte Rodíguez, *supra* n. 36, 181.
41. Austria, Croatia, Estonia, France, Germany, Hungary, Luxembourg, the Netherlands, Poland, Portugal and Slovenia.
42. Chart PF2.1.A of OECD Family Database: Parental leave systems, p. 5.

[B] Parental Leave

The most well-established and most researched aspect of WLB rights clearly concerns leave rights for workers to enable them to personally look after their children. Also in this regard, the regulatory direction when aiming to promote WLB and equality in work and care at the same time seems rather straightforward with a view to the regulatory dilemma mentioned in the introduction: as generous leave rights are clearly in the interest of better WLB but tend to worsen equality outcomes, the focus needs to be on incentivizing equal uptake of leave by male and female workers.

As a preliminary note, the present section does not contain a separate part on paternity leave, which is too vaguely defined to constitute an abstract concept to be distinguished from parental leave. Note, in particular, that also parental leave rights may – and actually *must* in the EU, according to Articles 4 and 10 WLB Directive – be (partially) paid *and* non-transferably reserved for one parent. In practice, paternity rights may differ from 'regular' parental leave in that they are more likely to be well-paid (even fully paid) and can be exercised while the other parent is also on leave[43] – yet both apply also to parental leave in several Member States. The OECD accordingly includes all forms of 'paid leave earmarked for fathers' under one heading.[44] Following this approach, this subsection discusses all leave rights meant to enable childcare together. This should not imply that it cannot be useful to have paternity leave as a separate category: in line with what has been argued in the previous subsection, this may be particularly useful if, under national law, the conditions for maternity leave differ from those for parental leave (e.g., in the sense that maternity leave is better paid) – so that having a separate category for paternity leave provides an opportunity to instal an equivalent form of 'privileged leave' for second parents.

While equality regarding such short and often most well-paid parts of the overall leave entitlement may be an important first step, it is unlikely to affect the main drivers of the 'motherhood penalty' in present-day labour markets.[45] After all, the latter notably has to do with the fact that – as described in the introduction, women tend to take many months, often years of parental leave, while most men do not take any. This is despite the fact that empirical research basically has an unambiguous answer as to how parental leave systems would need to be designed in order to stimulate male uptake.

In their study 'How Well Do European Child-Related Leave Policies Support the Caring Role of Fathers?', Bartova and Keizer[46] comprehensively reviewed the development of men's 'leave behaviour' in relation to the features of the legal system. They

43. Which some countries allow only to a limited extent or not at all for parental leave – in order to ensure the entitlement is actually used for childcare purposes.
44. Chart PF2.1.C of the OECD Family Database: Parental leave systems, p. 8.
45. First described in Budig, M.J. & England, P. (2001), The Wage Penalty for Motherhood. American Sociological Review, 66(2), 204-225 https://doi.org/10.2307/2657415.
46. Bartova, A. & Keizer, R. (2020), How Well Do European Child-Related Leave Policies Support the Caring Role of Fathers?. In: Nieuwenhuis/Van Lancker, The Palgrave Handbook of Family Policy, 369-396.

investigated rights to parental leave, paternity leave or transferred maternity leave, which men could use to stay at home with their children, compared this to the share of men making use of these rights, and arrived at an astonishingly clear conclusion: while women are found to take low- or even unpaid leave to care for their children in large numbers and for long durations in virtually all countries, fathers overwhelmingly take leave *if* and *exactly as long as* it is non-transferable and well-paid. Both criteria need to be fulfilled cumulatively. Accordingly, in the study, leave rights that secured at least two-thirds of a worker's wage *and* could not be transferred to the other parent were taken up by a clear majority of men in all countries.[47] What's more, the average duration for which men took leave was remarkably close to the exact maximum duration of the part that was well-paid and non-transferable.[48] Equally remarkable seems the finding that, where legal entitlements to well-paid leave were limited, significant shares of men reported taking annual leave (which is, per definition, non-transferable and fully paid)[49] in order to care for their children.[50] The numbers are very different for types of leave fulfilling only one of the two criteria. Un- or low-paid leave entitlements (which could be part of the same parental leave system, if the right to payment varies over the leave duration) were found to be taken up by just a negligible share of men throughout countries – even when they were reserved for fathers.[51] The share of fathers taking any of the parents' shared leave entitlements was somewhat higher, particularly when these were well-paid;[52] yet, the vast majority of men would still leave all of the sharable entitlement to their partner.

These strikingly clear results are very much in line with findings in other studies – including the most recent OECD data, which shows that even (the generally rather short) paternity leave entitlements are barely taken up when paid poorly (with the share of fathers claiming it as low as 16% in Austria), while 90% or more of fathers take up paternity leave in Luxembourg, the Netherlands and Slovenia, where it is fully paid.[53] Luxembourg additionally grants full pay for the first four to six months of its non-transferable parental leave entitlement and has thereby become the first and only country in which men are actually more likely than women to take up parental leave.

47. Short-term leave entitlements (often designed as paternity leave) were used by 62% of fathers in France (entitlement of more than two weeks), 74% in Spain (more than four weeks) and the UK (one week), and even 83% in the Netherlands (three days). Non-transferable and well-paid rights to longer leave, as they existed virtually exclusively in the Nordic countries at the time the research was conducted, were taken up by 70%-90% of fathers in Norway (ten weeks), by 81% in Iceland (thirteen weeks), and even 88% in Sweden (twenty weeks).
48. Cf., e.g., the numbers in Poland (14 days maximum, 12.6 days taken on average), Norway (10 weeks maximum, 9.8 weeks taken on average), Iceland (13 versus 17.6 weeks), and Sweden (20 versus 21.2 weeks).
49. *See* Art. 7 Working Time Directive.
50. Reported, e.g., by 43% of fathers in the UK and 60% in the Netherlands.
51. In the Netherlands, despite the very short duration of fully paid paternity leave, only 11% took additional unpaid parental leave. In the UK, 7% of fathers took unpaid, another 6% partly paid leave, and in the Czech Republic and Poland the total share amounts to 1%-2%. Among all parents taking un- or low-paid leave, the female share was reported to constitute 93% in Spain and even 96% in France.
52. E.g., 13% in Iceland and 7% in Slovakia.
53. *See* Chart PF2.2.B of OECD Family Database: Parents' use of childbirth-related leave, p. 3.

This compares to Poland, where (before the implementation of the WLB Directive in 2023) paid parental leave was fully transferable, resulting in men making up just 1% of those taking parental leave.[54] The finding that changes in male parental leave take-up are mainly dependent on the legal system (rather than general societal developments) are also reflected in the widely divergent national-level developments: between 2010 and 2021, take-up has more than quadrupled in countries such as Estonia and Lithuania, whereas it has even fallen in Austria, which started from a very similar low level as the former two countries in 2010.[55]

There is thus basically no room for doubts as to what childcare-related leave entitlements should ideally look like in order to promote WLB and stimulate male take-up. This ideal is of course a costly one for the public budget, so many countries may not be prepared to grant long and fully paid non-transferable leave to both parents of each child – which would ensure that both parents are enabled and incentivized to shoulder caring responsibilities for a substantial duration. Yet, even if the overall amount states decide to transfer to young families is not increased at all, a decisive difference for gender equality could be made by transferring these amounts not in the form of low benefits paid for a possibly very long duration of parental leave (which will in practice be taken up almost exclusively by women), but as non-transferable and well-paid benefits, granted for a shorter time. This will be unlikely to reach equality in practice (as, after the expiry of both parents' short maximum benefit duration, women are likely to take unpaid leave), but still, ensure that most fathers will assume the primary responsibility for childcare at least for a non-negligible period of time. In this regard, it should be noted that the degree to which fathers' involvement in the framework of parental leave rights has lasting *long-term* positive results is assessed somewhat more ambiguously in the pertinent empirical literature, compared to the very clear results regarding the take-up described above. Yet, various studies find that it does have an impact on the father's involvement in care tasks when the child is older,[56] on the relationship between the partners[57] and the gender role perception of the children.[58] Notably the last of these aspects may be considered particularly crucial for the pursuit of equality in the long term.

In practice, national parental and paternity leave systems vary widely in respect of all aspects just identified as crucial.[59] Spain has recently become the first and only EU

54. *Ibid.*, Chart PF2.2.C, p. 5.
55. *Ibid.*, Chart PF2.2.D, p. 6.
56. E.g., Cabrera, N.J., et al. (2008), Explaining the Long Reach of Fathers' Prenatal Involvement on Later Paternal Engagement. Journal of Marriage and Family, 70(5), 1094-1107 https://doi.org/10.1111/j.1741-3737.2008.00551.x.
57. Carlson, D.L., et al. (2016), The Division of Child Care, Sexual Intimacy, and Relationship Quality in Couples. Gender & Society, 30(3), 442-466 https://doi.org/10.1177/0891243215626709.
58. Keizer, R., et al. (2019), Perceived Quality of the Mother-Adolescent and Father-Adolescent Attachment Relationship and Adolescents' Self-Esteem. Journal of Youth and Adolescence, 48, 1203-1217 https://doi.org/10.1007/s10964-019-01007-0.
59. Chart PF2.1.C of the OECD Family Database: Parental leave systems, p. 8. Paid leave earmarked for fathers ranged from just two weeks in Cyprus and Czechia to thirty-one weeks in France. The average wage replacement rate when taking the full earmarked period ranged from 21.1% in Hungary to 100% in Estonia, Slovenia and Spain. Departing from the information in this study,

country where paid leave rights are exclusively non-transferable and fully paid, with no additional female-specific period for maternity (*see* next subsection), whereas Ireland still does not envisage any well-paid and non-transferable leave for fathers. The minimum requirement at the EU level, whose financial component will need to be fully transposed by August 2024, requires ten days of paternity leave paid at sick pay level, plus at least two out of a minimum of four months of parental leave to be paid at a level so as 'to facilitate the take-up of parental leave by both parents' (Article 8(3) WLB Directive). If this formulation is interpreted in line with the empirical evidence just presented (which indicates that parental leave entitlements replacing less than two-thirds of the wage are taken up only by a very small minority of men, while those replacing the full wage are taken up by nine out of ten working fathers), this payment would need to be set at a rather significant level.

[C] Single Parents

All that has been said in the previous subsections about the preferability of non-transferable rights needs to be put into perspective in relation to single parents. The CJEU has found in the past (case *Chatzi*)[60] that family situations that strongly deviate from the 'standard assumptions' on the basis of which parental leave rights are determined need to be assessed in light of the general principle of equal treatment. While this judgment concerned the case of multiple births, a much more widespread phenomenon is that of single-parent families[61] – the household type with the (by far) highest poverty rate,[62] with many more kept above the poverty line essentially due to family and childcare-related benefits.[63]

When analysing the consequences of the design of leave systems on the situation of single parents,[64] two things are immediately obvious. First, single fathers are, in

Bulgaria, Cyprus, Czechia and Estonia seem to have failed to implement the WLB Directive in time – seeing as it requires ten days of paid paternity leave plus a paid earmarked part of parental leave. Of the latter, only the implementation of the last two weeks could be postponed to August 2024 in accordance with Art. 20 WLB Directive, so that a total of fifty-seven days of earmarked paid leave for fathers should have been ensured already in 2023.

60. CJEU, 16 September 2010, Case C-149/10.
61. A relatively stable share of 17%-18% of children have lived in single-parent families in OECD countries in recent decades: *see* Chart SF1.2.B of OECD Family Database, Children in Families, p. 3. In 2023, 5.4% of adult women and 0.9% of adult men aged 25-54 were single parents with children. Eurostat, Number of persons by sex, age groups, household composition and working status (1,000), https://doi.org/10.2908/lfst_hhindws.
62. Forty-six per cent of single parent households (versus 20% of couple households) are at risk of poverty under the EU definition (less than 60% of the median income); 31% (versus 9% of couple households) are even income poor according to the OECD definition (less than 50% of median income).
63. Maldonado, L.C. & Nieuwenhuis, R. (2020), Dual-Earner Family Policies at Work for Single-Parent Families. In: Nieuwenhuis/Van Lancker, The Palgrave Handbook of Family Policy, 303-330, p. 312.
64. *See* Jou, J., et al. (2020), Paid Parental Leave Policies for Single-Parent Households: An Examination of Legislative Approaches in Thirty-Four OECD Countries. Community, Work & Family, 23(2), 184-200, https://doi.org/10.1080/13668803.2018.1517083; notably Table 1 and Figure 2 on pp. 190 et seq.

almost all systems, the group most severely penalized by systems created with biparental households in mind. Regarding maternity protection, this just reconfirms the adverse equality effects of long maternity leave entitlements, which are lost entirely if, for whatever reason, the child's biological mother is not staying with the child for the respective period after childbirth. Including the situation of single fathers is thus just one more reason to call for a design of leave systems where maternity leave has no impact on the total length of leave available to the parents (*see supra* at §6.03[A]). Second, the exact opposite is true for parental leave entitlements. Here, it is precisely the models that have been identified in the last subsection as most conducive to equality aims in the case of couple households that have the most penalizing effects for single parents. After all, when stipulating exclusively individual, non-transferable rights, the overall duration of parental leave available per child is halved if said child is raised by a single parent. In the data relating to 2016, which were used for the seemingly most recent comprehensive comparative study,[65] the non-transferable part of parental leave was in fact simply lost in case of single-parent families in almost all countries.

This outcome is highly problematic both from a WLB and an equality perspective – given that, as mentioned, the vast majority of single parents are female. When relying on non-transferable rights for couple households for the reasons set out in subsection §6.03[B], it would thus be vital to have special measures in place for single parents.

As for the nature of such special measures, it seems clear that simply doubling the single parent's child-related leave entitlements has the potential to increase gender gaps (as it ensures particularly long leave rights for a predominately female subgroup of the working population). Arguably, such a measure might seem justified to avoid increasing the often already severe financial strains and WLB difficulties faced by single parents. This dilemma could, however, be avoided by a policy approach which, instead of allocating excessive leave rights with potential negative long-term effects on the single parent's career, gives them a right to guaranteed (and ideally flexibly usable) professional childcare for a number of hours comparable to the leave entitlements of the lacking second parent.

Whether the continued lack of such targeted measures in the current legislative reality constitutes a violation of non-discrimination EU law has not yet been clarified. A preliminary request relating to the situation in Spain (the only EU country which, as mentioned, grants exclusively non-transferable and fully paid leave rights) has recently been declared inadmissible by the CJEU.[66] The main uncertainty in this regard relates to the fact that the essence of the discriminatory effect is regularly located in the area of social security rather than labour law. Under the Spanish system, parents such as the applicant *in casu* have a right to *unpaid* parental leave for up to three years until the child reaches the age of 3 – meaning that a single parent does not have less leave rights vis-à-vis their employer than a couple household would have combined. The difference – which is of paramount importance for households having an increased risk of poverty

65. *Ibid.*
66. CJEU, 16 May 2024, Case C-673/22 (*INSS*).

– is that the share of leave which is (fully) paid by social security is cut at sixteen weeks per parent. The situation thus presents itself primarily as an indirect discrimination under social security law, as the predominantly female group of single parents needs to fall back on entirely unpaid parental care after sixteen weeks, whereas thirty-two weeks are paid for a child with two working parents. However, Article 3(2) of Directive 79/7/EC on equal treatment in social security expressly excludes family benefits from that Directive's scope. Consequently, the question remains whether the CJEU would still see a violation of EU law in the fact that parental leave, which as such falls under EU law as it is regulated in its labour rights-related aspect, is granted under circumstances that are arguably not in line with Article 21 of the Charter of Fundamental Rights and the general principle of equal treatment. Equally unclear is whether the fact that, contrary to the old Parental Leave Directive, the WLB Directive requires at least a short period of parental leave to be *paid* makes a difference in this respect – as one might argue that only the latter brings the financial side of parental leave under EU law (even if this payment is generally arranged as a social security entitlement rather than continued wage pay by the employer).

Given these uncertainties, it currently seems largely left to national law to remedy the discrimination of a particularly vulnerable group in terms of parental leave rights.

[D] Flexible Working Arrangements

All of the above shows that, in relation to the care for small children for a rather short amount of time, regulatory tools have the potential to achieve high levels of equality and WLB simultaneously. At the same time, it has been mentioned already that the 'motherhood penalty' is less about short-term differences and much more about structural choices and changes that land women with children in a durably less favourable labour market position – compared to both women without and men with children. The pertinent research[67] indicates that this is most significantly connected to the choice of job and profession (either by – consciously or not – choosing a 'typically female' profession with usually child-friendly work hours from the start, or by transfers once the family is established) as well as the limitation of work experience due to long periods of leave and/or part-time work. It has also been shown repeatedly that, while a reduction of work hours for WLB reasons tends to have a significant effect on a worker's career, it is still clearly less detrimental compared to full-time leave, which effectively cuts the worker off from developments in their professional environment.

The last-mentioned aspect is, to a certain degree, also palpable in CJEU case law – considering that the Court even departs from an assumption that seniority-related wage increases (which work to the disadvantage of workers with [full-time] career

67. E.g., Dominguez-Folgueras, M., et al. (2022), The Motherhood Penalty in Spain: The Effect of Full- and Part-Time Parental Leave on Women's Earnings. Social Politics: International Studies in Gender, State & Society, 29(1), 164-189, https://doi.org/10.1093/sp/jxab046; Kahn J.R., et al. (2014), The Motherhood Penalty at Midlife: Long-Term Effects of Children on Women's Careers. Journal of Marriage and Family, 76(1), 56-72. https://doi.org/10.1111/jomf.12086.

breaks) are justified by differences in work experience.[68] By contrast, when part-time work experience is not or only partially taken into account for seniority-based pay (case *Nimz*),[69] company pensions (case *Bilka*),[70] access to employment (case *Kording*)[71] or promotion (case *Gerster*),[72] the CJEU requires a concrete justification with regard to all circumstances of the case.

It is thus clear that reducing WLB entitlements to a right to full-time leave is counterproductive if a proper balancing of work and family life can be achieved in different ways that are less likely to have negative long-term effects on women's labour market participation. In this sense, the WLB Directive introduced the notion of *flexible work arrangements*, defined as 'the possibility for workers to adjust their working patterns, including through the use of remote working arrangements, flexible working schedules, or reduced working hours' in Article 3(1)(f). The very nature of this broad, open concept implies that a concrete right to such agreements for all employees would not necessarily be realistic. Accordingly, EU law has chosen to instal a 'right to request' flexible work arrangements, thus permitting a reasoned refusal by the employer (Article 9).

The practical experience with this kind of broad and abstract provision, which aims to entitle employees to flexible arrangements if and to the extent to which this is possible without causing difficulties for the undertaking, seems to be very limited. No large-scale comparative analysis has been conducted on whether these kinds of norms existed prior to the implementation of the WLB Directive (which seems to have been the case in only a minority of countries) and whether they are effective in practice, given their rather vague formulation. At the EU level, it seems highly unclear to what degree employers should be obliged to prove an objectively important reason when rejecting requests for flexible work agreements. The formulation ('taking into account the needs of both the employer and the worker') certainly indicates that the right is somewhat weaker than, e.g., that of a disabled person to request 'reasonable accommodation' under Article 5 of Directive 2000/78.[73]

What does exist in a number of countries is what the WLB Directive designates as an option to 'take leave in flexible ways' (Articles 4(1) and 5(6)). While the pertinent OECD dataset[74] does not assess this aspect specifically, it is clear that in 2023 at least twelve countries[75] entitled parents to take parental part-time instead of full-time leave

68. CJEU, 17 October 1989, Case 109/88 (*Danfoss*). Note, however, that the judgment in *Cadman* (CJEU, 3 October 2006, Case C-17/05) clarifies that where an employee brings evidence 'capable of giving rise to serious doubts' that, in the individual case at issue, experience would significantly increase an employee's added value for the undertaking, the burden of proof shifts to the employer.
69. CJEU, 7 February 1991, Case C-184/89.
70. CJEU, 13 May 1986, Case 170/84.
71. CJEU, 2 October 1997, Case C-100/95.
72. CJEU, 2 October 1997, Case C-1/95.
73. *See, e.g.*, CJEU, 18 January 2024, Case C-631/22 (*Ca Na Negreta*).
74. Table PF2.1.D of OECD Family Database: Parental leave systems, p. 9.
75. Belgium, Denmark, Estonia, Finland, France, Germany, Italy, Korea, Luxembourg, Poland, Slovenia, Sweden. For a small number of countries, it is expressly stated that leave must be full-time; for the rest, this point is not expressly addressed.

– with or without a corresponding extension of the maximum period. Even less information is available on systems which consciously incentivize the take-up of part-time rather than full-time leave, and/or an improvement of the gender balance of take-up. An example would be the German 'partnership bonus', which rewards parents with an extra four months each of parental leave if both partners are reducing their work hours in parallel, to the effect that both are working between twenty-four and thirty-two hours per week. The bonus, introduced in 2014, has been taken up widely in practice according to the competent ministry.[76]

Clearly, when the entitlement to flexible arrangements is conceptualized as a right to receive (not just request), this considerably increases its likelihood of being taken up (including by employees with a weak bargaining position and/or consciousness of their rights). What is more, if the duration is quantified, equal sharing between the parents can be encouraged by the same methods as have been described for parental leave in subsection §6.03[B]. And while granting concrete rights by law may be difficult for aspects of flexible working such as remote work, which is clearly not realistic for all types of jobs and companies, there seems no reason why notably part-time leave should be considered unacceptable for any company that, under current law, is already forced to grant full-time parental leave when the conditions are fulfilled.

[E] Family Care Other Than Childcare

Whereas, as demonstrated in the preceding subsections, comparative information on the uptake of leave schemes focusing on children is systematically collected and analysed by the OECD, the same does not apply to other forms of informal care provision to family or household members. An overview of the existing leave schemes is, however, hidden at the very end of the data sheet on 'Additional leave entitlements for working parents'.[77] It illustrates the variety of paid and unpaid schemes for short-term leave entitlements (meant for immediate relief in case of unexpected care dependence), long-term leave or part-time, or adjustment of work hours. Some of these schemes are focused on specific situations (e.g., disability of the worker's own child, or terminal illness of a relative); others can be used for all situations featuring a defined severity of care needs and a sufficient connection between the worker and the care-dependent person.

None of these schemes seem to feature targeted measures to improve the gender balance of the uptake of these rights. This is logical whenever the person cared for is not the worker's child, so there is no standard assumption as to how many potential carers would be available in the household or family, whether they are of working age, and what would be their gender. For the same reason, these rights are generally not

76. In some German States, up to 42.2% of parents who share parental leave opt for this system. BMFSFJ, Elterngeld, https://www.bmfsfj.de/bmfsfj/themen/familie/familienleistungen/elterngeld/elterngeld-73752.
77. OECD Family database, Table PF2.3.B: Summary of leave entitlements to care for sick or ill family members, p. 5.

transferable, leading to an 'unintended' incentive to share them more equally than child-related leave rights that can be freely transferred between the parents (as they still exist in most countries).

However, compared to childcare-related leave types, WLB rights to enable the care of sick or disabled family members seem much more likely to be poorly paid or entirely unpaid. At the EU level, the WLB Directive does not require any payment to be provided for employees taking up 'carers' leave' under Article 6 and/or 'force majeure leave' under Article 7. In accordance with what has been set out above, this can be assumed to both decrease the likelihood of gender-balanced uptake very significantly and additionally indicate a significant financial impact for those (usually women) taking them up for a substantial period. Accordingly, it seems significant that at least fourteen OECD countries[78] have installed certain types or (often short) periods of fully paid leave, and another eight offer leave types with a wage replacement rate of more than two-thirds.[79] At the same time, it seems clear that long-term, well-paid leave entitlements may be difficult to finance in a context where care dependency is on the rise. Information on whether leave entitlements can be taken up part-time, and whether this increases the maximum duration accordingly, has not been systematically collected; the fact that a part-time option is mentioned spontaneously only for the Netherlands may indicate that most leave schemes are exclusively designed for full-time leave.

In a context where professional care for the frail and disabled is often insufficiently available and affordable, cases of care dependency in the family thus constitute a major risk for (mostly) women to drop out of the labour market or see their income reduced to a level that indicates financial hardship. Unless the system ensures that social security rights are maintained and continuously accrued throughout the period at issue (including by actual or fictitious payments to pension insurance schemes), the consequences could also be long-term and put the individual at a significant risk of poverty in later life.

Social security is, more generally, the elephant in the room when it comes to family care beyond childcare. Basically, from a workers' rights point of view, the suggestions to promote WLB and equality would be quite similar for childcare and LTC, in the sense that, in both cases, rights should encourage care participation by men and women while avoiding excessive limitation of labour market participation for individual (in practice usually female) workers. However, only for childcare needs is there a predictable trajectory of an initially intensive need for parental care to be gradually reduced once the child starts attending fully or partly subsidized nurseries and schools. For LTC, there is generally no such trajectory, and the care provided or financed by the state is insufficiently available in many countries.[80] In such a context, needless to say,

78. Australia, Austria, Chile, Croatia, Greece, Ireland, Israel, Italy, Latvia, Luxembourg, New Zealand, Norway, Spain, Switzerland.
79. Bulgaria, Estonia, Germany, the Netherlands, Poland, Romania, Slovenia, Sweden.
80. Cf. the preamble to the Council Recommendation of 8 December 2022 on access to affordable high-quality long-term care (2022/C 476/01).

even in the rare case that WLB rights are consciously designed as well-paid, individualized, non-transferable rights that encourage shared part-time take-up, neither WLB nor equality aims are likely to be achieved due to the sheer overwhelming care burden placed on families.

§6.04 CONCLUSIONS

This book explores the *meaning of work* from a legal perspective. In this regard, WLB has a rather peculiar role to play, as work is arguably a key part of most people's life and self-perception, while at the same time, there is a danger that work-related concerns come to dominate an individual's life to an extent that undermines their autonomy to make choices and potentially also their health and wellbeing. In this sense, choices to interrupt, reduce or alter participation in the labour market for 'private' reasons must be respected and protected. This has to do, for one thing, with the protection of genuine personal preferences to devote time to the care for a worker's loved ones – which tends to be overlooked in perspectives that reduce family care to a necessity caused by a lack of available and affordable professional care.[81] More than anything, the existence of such preferences is evidenced by the situation in countries such as Sweden, where parents, despite enjoying a universal right to affordable public childcare, tend to use their generous parental leave rights to stay at home with their children for a comparatively long time. For another thing, the current situation as described in the introduction makes it clear that it would be unrealistic to expect society to be able to stop relying on informal care to a substantial degree in the foreseeable future. Enabling family care as a core concern of WLB thus constitutes both an empowerment of employees and a societal necessity.

WLB should ideally be about more than just the possibility of *somehow* reconciling work and family life without risking either the loss of opportunities in professional life, or insufficient care provision for a loved one, financial hardship, or a combined care-work burden that threatens the worker's health and well-being. Much rather, a conscious design, which pays due attention to empirical insights, could and should strive to ensure that WLB measures effectively achieve a more equal distribution of paid and unpaid work in society. While the present contribution has mainly focused on intra-family inequality (i.e., gender imbalances), poorly paid parental leave systems also contribute to inter-family inequality – as, in a situation of scarcity of affordable professional care options (which is an issue in virtually all countries), high-income families are still likely to find paid care solutions for their loved ones, whereas unpaid family care may be the only option for low-income families.

As this contribution has argued, notably for improving gender equality without compromising WLB aims, a number of very clear policy directions can be indicated with a view to key aspects of existing WLB rights – concerning the conceptualization of maternity leave, the design of parental and other forms of childcare-related leave, or

81. Arguably a pitfall for academic observers, whose perception of the place that work should take in life may differ from that of other workers.

the stimulation of part-time rather than full-time uptake. However, it has become clear that the formula of 'well paid and non-transferable', which yields astonishing results notably for parental leave rights, has its limits when it comes to flexible working conditions (which are often not designed as a 'quantified' and thus sharable right) and notably family care beyond care for own children. These limitations underline the necessity of a long-term policy approach to WLB and equality: while there is ample proof that legal norms have a crucial impact on societal (including gender) norms, this is a gradual process, parts of which may take a generation to manifest. This is most notably true for the finding that children who experience both their parents as primary carers at least to some degree (which, as described, can be very effectively stimulated by legal incentives) experience a 'normalisation' of shared care responsibilities, which may be expected to influence their later choices in family life – also in respect of aspects that can hardly be directly influenced by legal stimuli.

A system working towards the 'normalisation' of choices which reduces or adapts work participation at certain points in a worker's life for family reasons for both men and women would potentially benefit all stakeholders. This very much includes employers, which could expect a more even distribution of work-related absences over the workforce, avoiding individual workers losing much of their professional potential due to prolonged leave, unexpected need for absences, and potentially reduced performance due to the overwhelming combined work-care burden. This would, as a side effect, reduce incentives for gender discrimination in hiring. Also, an increased uptake of WLB rights among workers in high-skilled, well-paying positions would frequently conform to these workers' personal preferences but is currently discouraged by a competitive workplace culture that favours 'male patterns' in relation to work and care. If combined with social security systems which ensure that at least a significant part of care needs is covered by available and affordable professional care, so as to avoid as much as possible that prolonged periods of full-time leave from work constitute a sheer necessity for financial reasons, such measures could gradually put society on track towards a healthy balance between work and family life.

CHAPTER 7
Privacy and Labour Law Traditions*

David Mangan

§7.01 INTRODUCTION

'Innovation' has been a totem for governments in this time of digitalization.[1] As a term used by governments, it denotes modernization. Labour law, however, does not garner such epithets. One of the paradoxical aspects of the rapid growth in use of information technologies within the work context is the continued reliance upon labour law frameworks that are not themselves necessarily updated. Labour law retains its orthodox form, without also taking the further step of updating these concepts where needed. While there are new regulatory instruments, such as the Platform Work Directive, these new efforts retain the traditional framework. Hesitation to update labour law betrays a view of it as an impediment to innovation. If the decision is to retain the traditional framework, then some form of updating must arise therein. Privacy offers one topic through which labour law may be modernized.[2]

---

* My gratitude to Frank Hendrickx and the Institute for Labour Law for the invitation to and hosting of the Third International Conference in Commemoration of Roger Blanpain.

1. *See*, for example, Sir John Whittingdale's (then Minister of State for Data and Digital Infrastructure) comment on the UK's amendments to its Data Protection Act (termed the UK GDPR) – 'The current one-size-fits-all, top-down approach to data protection that we inherited from the European Union has led to public confusion, which has impeded the effective use of personal data to drive growth and competition, and to support key innovations. The Bill seizes on a post-Brexit opportunity to build on our existing foundations and create an innovative, flexible and risk-based data protection regime': Data Protection and Digital Information Bill, Vol 741, 29 November 2023, Col 871 https://hansard.parliament.uk/Commons/2023-11-29/debates/46EF0AA6-C729-4751-A3DA-6A3683EB8B87/DataProtectionAndDigitalInformationBill?highlight=%22innovation%22%20%22economy%22%20%22employment%22#contribution-EF5AA12B-BA97-4F1C-980D-FFB5037988A6.
2. The concept of privacy discussed in this chapter is broad as a result of the current state of case law. While it is not explored in detail here, privacy and data protection overlap and are

§7.02 THE EMPLOYMENT RELATIONSHIP DIMINISHES A RIGHT TO PRIVACY

'Worker' means that an individual surrenders the scope of their right to privacy. A strenuous argument against this proposition is anticipated. Jean Savatier[3] argued that subordination does not encompass the entirety of a worker's life. Lord Wedderburn stated that a worker makes no offer to the employer of 'control over his entire private life, thereby giving up his civil liberties to the master.'[4] With twenty-first-century information technologies, have we not travelled some ways down this path, even if we have not reached the threshold of entirety identified by these authors? The argument here is that we have done so because the identification of someone as a worker limits their autonomy.[5] Although the concept of subordination has been a fixture of labour law, the various ways in which subordination has been extended as a result of information technologies render the concept more comprehensive. Innovations in information technologies have extended the scope of this intrusion into personal privacy.[6]

Here, there is an opportunity to revise labour law, particularly the familiar concept of subordination. Employers have an advantage over workers as a result of the latter's subordination to employers who can deploy workers as they think best for the enterprise. Information technologies have added to this situation.

This section explores how the architecture of workplaces, since factories, have been designed to facilitate surveillance. It also considers the implications of information technologies enabling employers to carry out more thorough surveillance of the workforce. Faced with such significant change, labour law must also adapt, or perhaps more correctly be allowed to adapt.

---

inter-related: Frank Hendrickx, *Protection of Worker's Personal Data: General Principles,* International Labour Organization Working Papers no.62 (5 May 2022), 7. The interconnections and distinctions between these two concepts may develop in a more clear and certain manner.

3. Jean Savatier, 'La liberté dans le travail' (1990) *Droit Social* 49. Gerard Lyon-Caen, drawing from Savatier, wrote: 'le 'salarie' qui conclut un contrat de travail, consent a la subordination pour la seule exécution de la prestation de travail; dans le reste de sa vie il demeure libre': Gerard Lyon-Caen, *Les libertés publiques et l'emploi,* Rapport au ministre du Travail de l'Emploi et de la Formation professionnelle (Paris, 1992), 154.
4. Lord Wedderburn, 'Labour Law and the Individual: Convergence or Diversity' in Lord Wedderburn, *Labour Law and Freedom: Further Essays in Labour Law* (London: Lawrence & Wishart, 1995), 313.
5. Limitations of autonomy may be found in discussions in other legal disciplines. Angela Daly has argued that the gaps in the regulatory framework for the flow of information on the internet 'exist because the system does not promote autonomy for users': Angela Daly, *Private Power, Online Information Flows and EU Law: Mind the Gap* (Oxford: Hart Publishing, 2016), 10.
6. Frank Hendrickx & Aline Van Bever, 'Article 8 ECHR: Judicial Patterns of Employment Privacy Protection' in Filip Dorssemont, Klaus Lörcher & Isabel Schönmann (eds), *The European Convention on Human Rights and the Employment Relation* (Oxford: Hart Publishing, 2013), 183–208, 185 wrote of the employment relationship as a facilitator of the limitations on rights.

[A] The Architecture of Workforce Surveillance

Workplace surveillance has existed in some form for a lengthy period. Human physical oversight has been an orthodox form of monitoring the workforce.[7] Compared to its contemporary form, human in-person monitoring was facilitated by workplace architecture[8] and limited to a human's time and attention in watching workers. Factories, for example, would have a walkway above the factory floor from which the entire workplace could be viewed. With a move to service industries, offices have removed the upper portion of the walls of offices to reveal interconnected cubicles whose occupants may be seen when a manager stands upright. The architecture of both types of workplaces provides management with opportune vantage points from which to monitor the workplaces.[9] In the later twentieth century, technology offered employers other means by which to oversee the workforce with phone call monitoring and video surveillance.[10] We also had the key card which granted employees access through doors. These cards were an early facilitator of the more minute data that is now routinely collected. Not only are times of arrival and departure documented electronically but also are movements within an office, whether attending a meeting in another department or simply using the restroom. In the twenty-first century, email and internet usage monitoring, global positioning system (GPS) tracking, electronic time clocks, and wearable technologies[11] add to a remarkable array of tools for workplace surveillance, whose capabilities include expansive data collection and processing.

This brief overview of the architecture of workplace surveillance tells of a movement away from a physical workspace to an expansive form of monitoring unencumbered by location, and without employers losing oversight of their workers. This 'privacy paradox'[12] reveals a change in workforce management in the early

7. Since the end of the COVID-19 pandemic, increasing numbers of employers are requiring their workforces to cut down or cease remote work, and to return to the physical office. It is notable that some of these employers are the same businesses that are said to embody innovation. *See*, for example, Joanna Partridge, 'Two-thirds of CEOs Think Staff Will Return to Office Five Days a Week, Survey Finds' *The Guardian* (5 October 2023) https://www.theguardian.com/money/2023/oct/05/two-thirds-ceos-think-staff-return-to-office-five-days-a-week-survey-finds.
8. The discussion of architecture in the context of the use of technology recalls Lawrence Lessig's four modalities in the regulation of human activity. Aside from architecture, laws, market, and norms comprise the remaining three: Lawrence Lessig, *Code Version 2.0* (New York: Basic Books, 2006). The argument pursued here is that the norms relating to the regulation of privacy at work seem to lack neutrality in relation to a balance of interests.
9. On the architecture and layout of the office, *see* the discussion in Nikil Saval, *Cubed: A Secret History of the Workplace* (New York: Anchor Books, 2015).
10. *See* the resulting litigation in cases such as those before the ECtHR *Malone v. UK*, Series A, no. 82 (1984) 7 EHRR 14, *Halford v. UK*, [1997] ECHR 32, and *Copland v. UK*, [2007] ECHR 253.
11. It seems workers acquiesce to some extent to the capacities of these technologies. There remain important matters for consideration with these technologies. *See*, for example, the arguments around wearable technologies and access to this data in Philippa Collins & Stefania Marassi, 'Is That Lawful? Data Privacy and Fitness Trackers in the Workplace' (2021) 37 *International Journal of Comparative Labour Law and Industrial Relations* 65.
12. As it has been called in Frank Hendrickx, 'From Digits to Robots: The Privacy-Autonomy Nexus in New Labour Law Machinery' (2019) 40 *Comparative Labor Law and Policy Journal* 365.

twenty-first century. Surveillance had been of a fixed location in the orthodox workplace. Technologies facilitate surveillance of a massive area in the early twenty-first century. Moreover, digitalization of work has not only extended the scope of the managerial gaze but has also expanded the type of information collected. The spectrum includes workers' conduct at the place of business as well as their off-duty activities, existing simultaneously in the physical and online spaces. Surveillance has moved from being of the workplace to the being of the workforce.[13] For this reason, it is argued that the scope of intrusion into workers' privacy has been extended by the classification of employment. Information technologies do not only blur the boundary between work and private life, but they also question the right to privacy when in an employment relationship.

What role does monitoring of the workforce fulfil? Is the workforce the reason for surveillance? Or, is the running of a business a reason for surveillance, with the workforce being one facet of a business? Workplace architecture suggests a Taylorist[14] response to the aforementioned questions: the workforce must be relentlessly watched in order to effect the most efficient level of productivity. This view of the workforce can be found among the United Kingdom business leaders,[15] as well as now former cabinet members of the British Government. Echoing Frederick Winslow Taylor's own negative assessment of the industrial workforce,[16] a group of these former ministers offered the following assessment: 'Once they enter the workplace, the British are among the worst idlers in the world.'[17] The increased capabilities of information technologies applied to the work setting may be driven by the approach these quotations outline. It must be noted, though, that this is a remarkably dire view of workers. Negativity has been capitalized by information technologies that enable not only the kind of detailed surveillance of workers that may be desired, but these technologies also accommodate another facet of this approach, that workforce efficiency can be 'datafied'. It is self-affirming that these technologies ostensibly provide the information to support this view. In response to the two earlier questions posed, a workforce necessitates surveillance, as opposed to surveillance being incidental to it.

13. David Mangan, 'From Monitoring of the Workplace to Surveillance of the Workforce' in Tamás Gyulavári & Emanuele Menegatti (eds), *Decent work in the digital age: European and Comparative Perspectives* (Oxford: Hart/Bloomsbury Publishing, 2022).
14. Frederick Winslow Taylor, *The Principles of Scientific Management* (New York: Harper Brothers, 1919).
15. The British worker's lethargy has been a galvanizing topics for some time: Alan Sugar, 'Lazy Brits should be ashamed' *Evening Standard* (10 June 2005) https://www.standard.co.uk/hp/front/lazy-brits-should-be-ashamed-7203218.html. The topic has re-emerged in the UK after Brexit in 2021 since there have been shortages of workers in key areas affecting the supply of goods.
16. Taylor called 'underworking' the 'greatest evil with which working-people in both America and England were afflicted': Frederick Winslow Taylor, *The Principles of Scientific Management* (New York: Harper Brothers, 1919), 13-14.
17. Kwasi Karteng et al., *Britannia Unchained: Global Lessons for Growth and Prosperity* (Basingstoke: Palgrave Macmillan, 2012), 61.

[B] The Case Law's Wayward Guidance

The case law of the European Court of Human Rights (ECtHR) does little to direct someone away from the idea that surveillance of the workforce is necessary.[18] Instead, these decisions recognize a procedural right to privacy only. This approach cedes the prima facie right to privacy at work, replacing it instead with a procedural requirement for employers to notify of surveillance (there are exceptions to this notification obligation). As long as workers know about surveillance, it seems permissible for it to be conducted. How much better off are workers for this knowledge? If this is the extent of transparency (instead of anything more like the purpose of surveillance, or a time limit to the duration of monitoring), it may be more important to ask what is the right to privacy at work?

The decisions discussed here have been selected for their recency, relevance to privacy at work, and as examples of the ECtHR's approach to privacy at work. This is not intended to be a comprehensive examination of ECtHR decisions on the topic.

The Grand Chamber's decision in *Bărbulescu v. Romania*[19] has been widely discussed.[20] These commentaries cannot overlook the fact that the court permitted the monitoring of correspondence and other communications, on social media accounts. Bărbulescu's employer required him to have a Yahoo! Messenger account for work reasons. He also had a personal account on the same platform. Bărbulescu's use of his Yahoo! Messenger accounts for personal reasons during work hours while on the premises formed the basis of the employer's decision to terminate him. Although the applicant knew of these regulations (having signed a confirming document), there appeared to be a question as to whether he had been notified that the employer was monitoring him, and the consequences of what the employer observed. The Grand Chamber reiterated that 'it is in the course of their working lives that the majority of people have a significant, if not the greatest, opportunity to develop relationships with the outside world'.[21] In doing so they ruled that there is a prerequisite for employers to inform employees 'in advance of the extent and nature of ... monitoring activities, or of the possibility that the employer might have access to the actual contents of his communications'.[22] When the court writes that workplace privacy cannot be reduced to zero,[23] it has a rhetorical flourish, but its meaning raises further questions. For

18. 'Monitoring of communication is often seen as a logical part of the general employer's right to control the workers': Frank Hendrickx, 'Privacy@work: A Systemic Introduction' in Frank Hendrickx, David Mangan & Elena Gramano (eds), *Privacy@Work* (Deventer: Wolters Kluwer, 2023), 39.
19. *Bărbulescu v. Romania* (ECtHR, Judgment 5 September 2017).
20. *See*, for example, Joe Atkinson, 'Workplace Monitoring and the Right to Private Life at Work' (2018) 81 *Modern Law Review* 688 and Adalberto Perulli & Elena Sychenko, 'Recent Jurisprudence of the European Court of Human Rights Relevant to Employment Law' (2018) 9 *European Labour Law Journal* 287, 294 ff. Note also Perulli and Sychenko express concern about the Court's approach to workplace privacy in this decision.
21. *Bărbulescu, supra* n. 19, [70]. This passage repeats parts of the earlier decision of *Niemietz v. Germany* (16 December 1992) [29], Series A no. 251-B.
22. *Bărbulescu, supra* n. 19, [78].
23. 'An employer's instructions cannot reduce private social life in the workplace to zero. Respect for private life and for the privacy of correspondence continues to exist, even if these may be

example, are the laws in Czechia, where employers have few restrictions on monitoring internet usage,[24] or Hungary, where the Labour Code prohibits employees from using employer-provided facilities for personal reasons without the employer's consent, unlawful?[25] The Grand Chamber identified further factors in assessing that proportionality and procedural guarantees against arbitrariness are met:

- the extent of monitoring where a distinction is made between the flow of communications and their content;
- whether the employer has provided legitimate reasons to justify monitoring and accessing the content of communications (where the latter is a more intrusive act warranting greater justification);
- whether monitoring could be achieved by less intrusive means than directly accessing the content of employees' communications, with consideration being given to the employer's aim in monitoring this content;
- the consequences of monitoring for employees, and whether the use of the results of monitoring met the employer's stated aim;
- whether the employee had been provided with adequate safeguards, such as an employer notifying employees about accessing the content of communications; and finally;
- that employees have access to a remedy.[26]

It is unclear to what extent these points have been followed.[27] For example, a distinction between monitoring the flow of communications as compared to their content seems to be far from uniformly applied. Moreover, a justification for monitoring seems to be a factor which has been inconsistently considered.

To this point, consider the reasoning in *López Ribalda and Others v. Spain.*[28] In this decision, the Grand Chamber recognized that surveillance for a legitimate purpose (theft of the employer's goods in this case) can be justified. To address losses due to theft, a supermarket installed both visible and hidden cameras. The visible cameras were aimed at the entrance/exit areas, targeting customers. Employees were told of the visible but not the hidden cameras. Functional for a ten-day period, both sets of cameras continuously recorded all individuals that passed within their view. Concealed surveillance recorded the dismissed applicants and others stealing (helping co-workers and customers to do so, as well as committing this act themselves) and

---

restricted in so far as necessary': *Baarbulescu, supra* n. 19, [80].

24. Martin Stefko, 'Privacy at Work in the Czech Republic' in Frank Hendrickx, David Mangan & Elena Gramano (eds), *Privacy@Work* (Deventer: Wolters Kluwer, 2023), 153.
25. Tamas Gyulavari, 'Privacy at Work in Hungary' in Frank Hendrickx, David Mangan & Elena Gramano (eds), *Privacy@Work* (Deventer: Wolters Kluwer, 2023), 297.
26. *Baarbulescu, supra* n. 19, [121]-[122].
27. *See* generally the Member State chapters in Frank Hendrickx, David Mangan & Elena Gramano (eds), *Privacy@Work* (Deventer: Wolters Kluwer, 2023).
28. ECtHR, Judgment 17 October 2019.

were terminated. While the court was troubled by the failure to inform employees about covert surveillance, the employer's conduct was found to be proportionate in the circumstances considering the degree of intrusion into employees' privacy factored together with the 'legitimate reasons'[29] justifying the deployment of surreptitious surveillance technology. *López Ribalda* suggests there may need to be a justification for surveillance.[30] In this case, the employer's decision was premised upon a 'reasonable suspicion that serious misconduct has been committed and the extent of the losses identified in the present case may appear to constitute weighty justification.'[31]

If we accept that the employer's actions in *López Ribalda* were proportionate, where does that leave the right to privacy at work? Common positions may be found in extreme examples, such as theft or excessive use of employer resources including at-work wifi connections.[32] The European Data Protection Working Party wrote in *Opinion 2/2017*: 'monitoring every online activity of the employees is a disproportionate response and an interference with the right to secrecy of communications. The employer should first investigate other, less invasive, means to protect the confidentiality of customer data and the security of the network'.[33] *Bărbulescu* did not display much adherence to this guidance. The possibility of surveying all activity draws attention to technologies that are capable of facilitating such ongoing monitoring. GPS, being one example, is the technology in question in the next decision.

The applicant in *Florindo de Almeida Vasconcelos Gramaxo v. Portugal*[34] had a company car for his work as a medical representative. The vehicle was available for both personal and work purposes. Kilometres outside normal working hours had to be reimbursed to the company. Originally, Florindo reported extra kilometres via an internal management system. Reporting then moved to GPS as an additional verification system on all company cars; though notification of the purposes of the GPS tracking was given after installation. These included the calculation of kilometres travelled during and after work, as well as the monitoring of discrepancies between declared travel and the GPS. The Portuguese Labour Code bans surveillance of work

29. *Ibid* [134].
30. Discussion of a justification for monitoring was absent in *Barbulescu*. Is this attributable to the fact that in *Barbulescu* there was a contract clause pertaining to at work private messages?.
31. *Ibid*. *See also* the factors in assessing the proportionality of video surveillance at *López Ribalda and Others v. Spain*. ECtHR, Judgment 17 October 2019, [116]. *López Ribalda* is consistent with *Köpke v. Germany* (ECtHR, Judgment 5 October 2010) where covert surveillance was permissible because it had been limited to 2 weeks in duration and targeted two employees who had been suspected prior to monitoring being put in place.
32. On the latter point, *see* the Czechia Supreme Court Decision 16 August 2012, file number 21 Cdo 1771/2011 which upheld an employee's dismissal for gross misconduct. *See* further discussion of this case in context in Martin Stefko, 'Privacy at Work in the Czech Republic' in Frank Hendrickx, David Mangan & Elena Gramano (eds), *Privacy@Work* (Deventer: Wolters Kluwer, 2023), 154.
33. Article 29 Data Protection Working Party, *Opinion 2/2017 on data processing at work* WP 249 (8 June 2017), 14.
34. *Florindo De Almeida Vasconcelos Gramaxo v. Portugal* (2022) App no. 26968/16 (ECtHR 13 December 2022).

performance, except for security reasons relating to individuals or company assets. This surveillance was also subject to authorization by the Data Protection Authority, which had been notified and positively assessed the system. Sometime later, a second GPS system was installed in Florindo's car. This system was hidden from the applicant. The employer subsequently found that the GPS system of which Florindo was aware had been tampered with. As a result, a cross-check of data entered by Florindo and the hidden GPS disclosed a discrepancy, with Florindo reporting fewer kilometres than the hidden GPS recorded. Florindo was terminated for these reasons.

The Fourth Section of the ECtHR found no violation of Florindo's Article 8 right. He had been notified of the monitoring. And so, he knew that his movements were being tracked by the company and that disciplinary measures could have been taken against him. The reasoning suggests that Florindo had no reasonable expectation of privacy regarding GPS monitoring, and the absence of a reasonable expectation justified the employer's decision to withhold from him the fact of the second GPS for investigative purposes. We view the majority's reasoning as an example of reasonable expectations being questioned as technologies create a greater sense of openness and transparency, particularly through monitoring technologies.[35] Applying the test developed in *Bărbulescu*, the applicant's right to private life had been proportionately reduced to safeguard the employer's right to control his expenses. The majority of judges supported the Court of first instance's conclusion that less invasive surveillance tools[36] than 24/7 GPS for three years of implementation were unavailable to investigate inconsistencies in the effective kilometres.

These recent cases offer some factors for further consideration. The Grand Chamber wrote in *Bărbulescu* that workplace privacy cannot be reduced to zero. *López Ribalda* indicated that there would need to be a justification for the use of the intrusive technologies. *Florindo* suggests that 'some technologies that are deemed necessary to protect an employer's interests are beyond scrutiny.'[37] As a group of cases from which to draw instruction to advise parties, these decisions are incongruent with the simple threshold of notice and consent to monitoring. A right to workplace privacy as set out in decisions such as *Niemietz*[38] challenges the guidance from *Bărbulescu*. Simple notification is a low threshold. It has questionable compliance with the prohibition on reducing an employee's privacy at work to zero. Technologies steer the scope of surveillance. Employers may additionally find support when monitoring is set within a context of ensuring employees are properly using work tools.[39] This sampling of decisions indicates that technology can be a significant driver of the law; that is, there

35. Frank Hendrickx, 'From Digits to Robots: The Privacy-Autonomy Nexus in New Labor Law Machinery' (2019) 40 *Comparative Labor Law & Policy Journal* 365.
36. Note this is another one of the points identified in *Bărbulescu, supra* n. 19.
37. Michele Mole & David Mangan, '"Just more surveillance": The ECtHR and workplace monitoring' (2023) 14 *European Labour Law Journal* 694.
38. Niemietz *v.* Germany (ECtHR, Judgment 16 December 1992).
39. *See* the approach in Poland to monitoring of internet usage and email where 'monitoring of the employee's business e-mail is acceptable, if it is necessary both to ensure proper organisation of work (allowing full use of the working time), as well as for the proper use of the work tools made available to the employee': Marta Otto, 'Privacy at Work in Poland' in Frank Hendrickx, David Mangan & Elena Gramano (eds), *Privacy@Work* (Wolters Kluwer: Deventer, 2023), 407.

are instances in which laws can be steered by technologies, especially when employees have been notified of the use of these technologies.

[C] Subordination in the Twenty-First Century: Information Asymmetry

As demonstrated by the case law of the ECtHR, the fact of being in an employment relationship attenuates the right to privacy at work. This section puts forward the argument that the worker's subordinate position as a result of the employment relationship forms the basis of an attenuated right to privacy which extends past the workplace. In some ways, this may be viewed as a settled proposition.[40] Yet, accepting the limitations imposed on employees as a result of the employment relationship casually overlooks that these technologies have facilitated not only intrusive monitoring but also the unprecedented extent of this surveillance and data collection. This chapter has argued there is a necessity to update the labour law tradition to reflect contemporary work. The well-known concept of subordination is an example.

The concept of subordination requires updating to take account of the information asymmetry in the deployment of information technologies. Information asymmetry means that employers have an advantage in relation to intrusions into employees' privacy. This advantage includes: the ways in which workers may be monitored; the personal data employers collect about them; and the processing of this collected data. The disparity in understanding, between employers and workers, of these technologies and their impact on work can be significant. In this way, information asymmetry intensifies the imbalance of bargaining power within the employment relationship by adding another layer by which employers are in a superior position; i.e., understanding the scope and range of intrusions into privacy, as well as the extent and implications of processing of data thereby collected.

Information asymmetry challenges the adequacy of accessibility in law.[41] Transparency has been invoked as a term of progress as regulations, at the European Union (EU) level, have progressed.[42] The form of transparency deployed has been one of simply informing. It is doubtful that workers would 'know exactly when and where they are in a protected sphere or, on the contrary, in a sphere in which they must expect interference from others'.[43] Can privacy at work not be infused with greater transparency?

Information asymmetry is an indication of the larger issue of the degree to which there is an advantage for employers. As noted, the architecture and case law both grant employers scope to monitor their workforces. Information technologies extend their capacities for survey workers' activities, not only including their onsite performance

40. Frank Hendrickx, 'Protection of Workers' Personal Data: General Principles' *ILO Working Paper* 62 (Geneva: International Labour Organization, May 2022), 8 ff.
41. ECtHR, *Sunday Times v. the United Kingdom*, App no. 6538/74, 26 April 1979, [49]: a law must be 'adequately accessible' and a norm cannot be a 'law' 'unless it is formulated with sufficient precision to enable the citizen to regulate his conduct'.
42. Consider the focus on transparency in Regulation 2019/1150 on promoting fairness and transparency for business users of online intermediation services.
43. *Von Hannover v. Germany*, App no. 59320/00, 24 June 2004 (ECtHR), [69].

but also extending beyond it to include off-duty conduct. Furthermore, the type of data collected has been increased, coupled with technologies that can process the range of this data into packages tailored to meet employer-focused performance measurements. To monitor the workforce, employers do not have many obligations. The guidance with which we are left (if we are advising parties) is that employers should disclose to workers there is monitoring that is being undertaken, and the uses to which the information collected may be applied. 'Should' is used to take into consideration situations such as those in *López Ribalda* and *Florindo* where there was a mixture of overt and covert surveillance deployed, with the latter form being undisclosed. Case law provides factors to consider beyond informing the workforce about surveillance, but these do not seem to be mandatory measures. Consequently, the deployment of information technologies in relation to the workforce itself illustrates the degree of subordination. The *laissez-faire* approach does not mandate distinctions such as those between the flow of communications and their content (as stated in *Bărbulescu*), or whether less intrusive means could have been used to achieve the same purpose (as in *Florindo*). Instead, employers are implicitly permitted to oversee their workforces as they think is best. This situation, however, leaves employers with the lingering possibility of a change in the law. It would serve the parties' interests better if there was a more stable set of parameters. Workers would have a better sense of their privacy at work. Employers would gain greater certainty with regard to workforce monitoring. This change could be undertaken through the following measures. Employers should be required to set out more precisely the bases for surveillance, with particular attention to the extent of monitoring (duration and scope of activities captured). Employers should have an ongoing obligation to inform workers about the full extent of monitoring activities that are undertaken. This would mean that employers will be obliged to update workers as they adapt their use of information technologies with regard to workforce surveillance. As noted above, there remains little discussion in practice regarding the data collected and processed in the course of surveillance. There is a less precise engagement of privacy as a generalized concept. And yet, the EU Charter makes such a distinction (between privacy as a broad right (Article 7) and data protection (Article 8)). It remains unclear whether these rights must be viewed as separate or linked.[44] With greater precision on this point, further considerations come into focus. For example, data may be collected and processed in the course of monitoring, but there is a question regarding whether this data collected falls within the primary objective of the monitoring, or if it is incidental to it. Such a distinction raises awareness of the importance of the purpose(s) for which monitoring has been undertaken.[45]

44. Hendrickx has contended that privacy is an overarching right within which data protection fits: Frank Hendrickx, 'Protection of Workers' Personal Data: General Principles' *ILO Working Paper* 62 (Geneva: International Labour Organization, May 2022).
45. *See* the discussion in *Data Protection Commissioner v. Doolin* 2022 IECA 117, for example, where the General Data Protection Regulation was used to note that the employer's purpose for surveillance cameras did not align with the disciplinary action it sought to take against Doolin.

§7.03 PRIVACY AS FREEDOM

Although the concept of subordination has been a fixture of labour law, the various ways in which subordination has been extended as a result of information technologies render the concept more comprehensive. Scholarship has been detailed in its examination of information technology's influence on the classification of employment. But, it has drawn less attention to the more pervasive extent of subordination as enabled by information technologies; a situation made possible by two key pillars. First, these technologies have given employers the capabilities of 'constant surveillance', where now, unlike when Charles Fried[46] used the term, surveillance approximates a constant state more than ever. Second, employment contracts (particularly the standard form terms regarding surveillance) grant employers the power to carry out this extensive monitoring. Together (the surveillance capabilities provided to employers by information technologies as well as the authority to act upon what is gathered in the course of this monitoring), there is perhaps no more vivid demonstration of the lack of trust vested in the workforce. There is no technological cure for this human bias. Nonetheless, the intrusion into workers' privacy must be recalibrated and carried out in a manner that speaks to the freedom of individuals regardless of employment classification. Faced with such significant change, labour law must also adapt, or perhaps more correctly be allowed to adapt.

If the liberal idea of freedom centres around the individual, there must be some level of curiosity about the remarkable limiting power of being identified as an employee. Privacy at work faces two connected hurdles. First, there is a perception that the opportunity to protect privacy has passed us by, and that to try to do something now is impossible (the concept being too open-ended). Second, even if privacy as a general matter may be addressed through various means, privacy at work is not a tenable concept because it encumbers the operation of a business. The response to both of these points is to argue for privacy as a matter of individual freedom in a liberal democracy.

The marketplace ethos assists in explicating the current situation. In describing the product market, Fukuyama writes that a marketplace works best 'if it is large, decentralized, and competitive'.[47] Privacy impedes this functioning of the marketplace. Privacy at work (and beyond) faces three overarching challenges simultaneously. First, technological power has been concentrated with certain actors (i.e., employers, providing them with remarkable control over the workforce, including surveillance of individuals as well as gathering and processing of personal data). A second challenge runs commensurately with the first: erosion of understanding of and appreciation for individual privacy. A third challenge is dependence: the pervasive dependence upon information technologies which function in a privacy-indifferent manner.

46. Charles Fried, 'Privacy' (1968) 77 *Yale Law Journal* 475.
47. Francis Fukuyama, *Liberalism and its Discontents* (London: Profile Books, 2022), 103.

Privacy is an essential part of freedom, as it speaks to a human desire to be separated from others. There are generalized points about privacy and the control individuals may have over their privacy. While people are social, there is a notion of limiting the extent of social interaction.[48] We do not interact with others at all points each day. It may be conjectured that we need privacy just as much as we need social interaction. The fact that there are certain activities that are done in private would seem to attest to the assertion. Still, there is an element of choice to privacy; that is, an individual may elect to not share aspects of her life with anyone else (just as one may elect to share the most private of experiences). This is about an entitlement to control what each person possesses: over information about oneself; about some space for the exclusion of others; and it can even be about the select disclosure of this information or the select invitation of others into these spaces. This information or these spaces, however, are not impregnable because others can intrude upon them. And yet, this intrusion does not automatically vitiate the entitlement. Instead, the infringement of that entitlement is recognized. And so, privacy is also an essential part of freedom. This point has not been as fully engaged in law, let alone in the labour setting. If the concept of privacy is about exclusion (removing the individual or information about the individual from the public gaze) then freedom must accompany this choice; notably the choice as to what is excluded.

To give effect to privacy as freedom in the work context, the reasonable expectation of privacy must be understood as a living concept. Although this proposition is not a partisan matter, the current situation does not necessarily speak to a balance that may be implied by the phrase reasonable expectation. Instead, the reasonable expectation of privacy appears to become remarkably malleable upon entering into an employment relationship, as demonstrated by cases such as *Bărbulescu*. Hendrickx has argued that the reasonable expectation of privacy should not be the sole determining factor because technologies (and we may add the regulation of these technologies) create an increased sense of openness and transparency (even though understanding algorithms may still be difficult).[49] For this reason, viewing privacy as an aspect of freedom offers an important framework. While the employment contract may permit limitations to freedoms of individuals, implicit is the idea that there must be some balance in these limitations. The argument put forward here is that information technologies have facilitated an imbalance in favour of employers to an extent that should be addressed with urgency; an urgency prompted by displacing the idea that the present situation becomes a precedent which will be difficult to displace.

48. Madam Justice L'Heureux-Dubé of the Supreme Court of Canada wrote of this in *R v. O'Connor*, [1995] 4 S.C.R. 411, [113] (*per* L'Heureux-Dubé). Two decades later, Daniel Solove contended that reputation and freedom are interlinked: *The Future of Reputation* (New Haven: Yale University Press, 2007).

49. Hendrickx has raised the possibility of such reasonable expectations being questioned as technologies create a greater sense of openness and transparency, particularly through monitoring technologies: Frank Hendrickx, 'From Digits to Robots: The Privacy-Autonomy Nexus in New Labor Law Machinery' (2019) 40 *Comparative Labor Law & Policy Journal* 365, 380.

§7.04 CONCLUSION

At present, it would be hard to provide either employees or employers with clear advice regarding the right to privacy at work.[50] This situation suggests part of the problem: the absence of clarity regarding privacy at work. Labour law has maintained its orthodoxy in subordination. What it has not done, however, is recognize the incremental growth in the bread of subordination facilitated by information technologies. This chapter has laid out an argument for why there is urgency in better establishing a right to privacy at work which is meaningful, accessible to both employers and employees, and living. Privacy as a living concept points to privacy's adaptation to the changing circumstances, though it does not permit a departure from the essence of the right. Privacy as freedom has been put forward as a means of not only enabling a more defined right to privacy at work but it is also suggested as a way of facilitating the deployment of the right as a living concept.

50. Consider Perulli and Sychenko's appraisal of the applicant in Case C-692/19 *B v. Yodel Delivery Network Limited* as placing 'an unjustifiable burden on the employer and renders the realisation of their right to control employee's activities almost impossible and should not be applicable to cases when the employee did not have a legitimate expectation of privacy': Perulli and Sychenko, *supra* n. 20, 295.

CHAPTER 8

The Protection of Workers' Personal Data Between General Data Protection Law and Labour Law

Rüdiger Krause

§8.01 INTRODUCTION

The monitoring of workers is not a new phenomenon but has existed for a long time. However, due to the digital transformation of the world of work, the instruments of surveillance of employees have drastically increased in the past decades.[1] It is no longer only the traditional monitoring of ICT use or video surveillance. Rather, Big Data entered the organization of work and the HR departments of companies. Algorithmic management and people analytics are increasingly being used to structure work processes and HR decision-making. At the same time, there has been a growing awareness that monitoring and surveillance of workers is not a 'natural' and unconstrained right of the employer, but an impairment of interests worth protecting by the right to privacy or the right to personality of the employees. Furthermore, in the course of a general legal development that began in the 1970s, it emerged that the processing of employees' personal data by the employer, and not just a general right to privacy, is the central legal point of reference.

It is obvious that the main driving forces behind this development are not some kind of individual 'curiosity' on the part of the employer, but hard economic factors: First, the employer has an interest in managing and monitoring employees in order to optimize their performance. Additionally, the employer is interested in efficient HR

1. Cf. European Parliamentary Research Service, Data Subjects, Digital Surveillance, AI and the Future of Work (2020); *Eurofound*, Employee Monitoring and Surveillance: The Challenges of Digitalisation (2020); *see also Tomczak/Behrend*, Electronic Surveillance and Privacy, in: Landers (ed.), The Cambridge Handbook of Technology and Employee Behavior (2019), pp. 708-742.

management, for example, to optimize transfers, promotions and training measures. Finally, the surveillance of workers is often a tool for maintaining employee discipline and deterring unlawful conduct, not least to ensure compliance with the numerous legal obligations to which the employer is subject.

As a result, employers are acquiring growing 'data power' in the sense that they are able to use employees' personal data for their own purposes, leading to increasing risks to employees' rights and freedoms.[2] Like other forms of power and information asymmetry in the employment relationship, this situation requires regulations to protect the legitimate interests of employees in the processing of their personal data in the work context. At the same time, it is clear that the processing of personal data is omnipresent in many fields of modern societies and is by no means a phenomenon limited to the world of work.[3]

Against this background, two regulatory models are conceivable: On the one hand, a set of sector-specific rules that take appropriate account of the specific processing situations in the various sectors, but which harbour the risk of ambiguities, legal inconsistencies or even contradictions. On the other hand, a cross-sectoral legal framework with common principles applicable to all fields, but with the disadvantage that this type of regulation is inevitably based on general clauses that are often vague, cause legal uncertainty for both the controller (employer) and the data subject (employee), and are not tailored to the specific problems of the respective sector (employment context).

From the outset, the European legislator has essentially opted for the second mode and created a general legal framework for the processing of personal data regardless of the sector in question, initially with the Data Protection Directive 95/46/EC and later with the General Data Protection Regulation (GDPR) (EU) 2016/679. Only for processing data in connection with electronic communications exists a more specific legal framework in Directive 2002/58/EC (ePrivacy Directive)[4] replacing the previous Directive 97/66/EC.

Consequently, it is the GDPR that regulates the processing of personal data in the employment context. Indeed, the GDPR contains a few provisions that explicitly deal with labour-related law issues.[5] However, it is mainly the responsibility of the Member States to use the opening clause of Article 88 GDPR to adopt more specific legal or collectively agreed provisions that ensure the protection of the rights and freedoms with regard to the processing of employees' personal data in the employment context. The European Parliament's call to include several labour-specific provisions directly in the GDPR[6] was not successful. There is also no directive on the protection of workers'

2. Comprehensive systematization of the general risks of processing personal data at micro (individual) and macro (structural) level by *Drackert*, Die Risiken der Verarbeitung personenbezogener Daten (2014), pp. 278-321.
3. *See* only *Zuboff*, The Age of Surveillance Capitalism (2019), who focuses on the overarching phenomenon of predicting and influencing human behaviour.
4. Cf. Art. 95 GDPR.
5. Article 9(1), (2)(b), (d) and (h) GDPR.
6. *See* Art. 82 of European Parliament legislative resolution of 12 March 2014, P7_TA(2014)0212.

personal data, an issue that has been discussed since the 1990s but failed due to a combination of legal, constitutional and political reasons.[7]

The protection of employees' personal data at the European level is therefore essentially based on a cross-sectoral regulation and not on genuine labour law.[8] Conversely, the existence of labour-specific provisions depends on the willingness of Member States to address this issue, without it being clear whether and to what extent actors at the national level (legislators and social partners) are allowed to deviate from the overarching European regulation.

This article addresses the problems arising from the situation outlined above, in particular the challenge of how to effectively protect employees' personal data against the background of general data protection law on the one hand and the specific requirements of labour law on the other.

§8.02 CONCEPTUAL ASPECTS

If the right to data protection is seen only as a subset of the right to privacy and if this right is defined in the classical way as the 'right to be let alone',[9] then the protection of employees' personal data does not seem to fit well into this concept. While there are some situations in which the employer must leave the employee alone, e.g., not monitoring workers in the locker room or in the toilet, there are also many situations in which the employer has a legitimate interest or even an obligation to process employees' personal data. To put it bluntly: the employer may have the 'right not to leave alone' its workers.[10]

It can be argued that the concept of privacy as seclusion ('snail shell') is incomplete and that the right to privacy also protects the professional sphere. This corresponds to the notion of private life in Article 8 ECHR, which, according to the case law of the European Court of Human Rights (ECtHR), is not limited to an 'inner circle' in which individuals can lead their personal lives as they see fit, but comprises to a certain degree the right to establish and develop relationships with other human beings, and thus includes also the professional life.[11] However, it does not seem

7. Cf. *Abraha*, A Pragmatic Compromise? The Role of Article 88 GDPR in Upholding Privacy in the Workplace, International Data Privacy Law 12 (2022), 276-296 (279-282) https://doi.org/10.1093/idpl/ipac015; *Simitis*, Reconsidering the Premises of Labour Law: Prolegomena to an EU Regulation on the Protection of Employees' Personal Data, European Law Journal 5 (1999), 45-62 (51-61) https://doi.org/10.1111/1468-0386.00065.
8. The only exception is Art. 9(2) of the Working Time Directive 2003/88/EC in regard to the free health assessment for workers which must comply with medical confidentiality.
9. *Warren/Brandeis*, The Right to Privacy, Harvard Law Review 4 (1890), 193-220 (195, 205) https://doi.org/10.2307/1321160.
10. *Hendrickx*, Protection of Workers' Personal Data: General Principles, ILO Working Paper 62 (2022), p. 8.
11. ECtHR 16.12.1992 – App. No. 13710/88, para. 29 – Niemietz; *see also* ECtHR 12.6.2014 – App. No. 56030/07, para. 110 – Fernández Martinez; ECtHR 17.10.2019 – App. Nos 1874/13 and 8567/13, para. 88 – López Ribalda; ECtHR 13.12.2022 – App. No. 26968/16, para. 92 – Almeida Vasconcelos Gramaxo.

necessary to analyse in detail the contested concept of privacy[12] as such and its relationship to data protection. Even if the right to privacy has a different scope and logic compared to the right to data protection,[13] which can be underpinned by the distinction between Article 7 and Article 8 of the Charter of Fundamental Rights of the European Union (CFREU),[14] there is no doubt that employees benefit from data protection law and that personal data related to professional activities are in any case covered by the right to data protection.[15] Therefore, the logic of data protection law is not alien to the world of work and the employment relationship.

From a certain perspective, however, there is a friction between data protection law on the one hand and traditional labour law thinking on the other. And indeed, at least in private employment relationships, the employer has a fundamental entrepreneurial freedom, which basically includes the freedom to collect and use all information necessary for economic success.[16] This freedom is only limited (apart from statutory law, contracts and collective agreements) by the fundamental rights of employees, which must not be violated ('harm-based approach'). Data protection law, however, goes much further and prohibits not only the violation of fundamental rights and freedoms but also any type of processing of personal data, unless it is expressly legitimized by consent or by law, which in turn means that this branch of law establishes a preliminary protection of personal interests before a specific violation occurs ('rights-based approach').[17] However, since the rights-based approach has been at the centre of data protection law from the very beginning,[18] it is only logical to apply

12. Cf. *Mulligan/Koopman/Doty*, Privacy is an Essentially Contested Concept: A Multi-Dimensional Analytic for Mapping Privacy, Philosophical Transactions, Royal Society, A 374 (2016) http://dx.doi.org/10.1098/rsta.2016.0118.
13. Cf. *Bygrave*, The Place of Privacy in Data Protection Law, University of New South Wales Law Journal 24 (2001), 277-283; *Geminn/Roßnagel*, 'Privatheit' und 'Privatsphäre' aus der Perspektive des Rechts - ein Überblick, JuristenZeitung (JZ) 70 (2015), 703-708 (707); *Lynskey*, Deconstructing Data Protection: The 'Added-Value' of a Right to Data Protection in the European Legal Order, International and Comparative Law Quarterly 63 (2014), 569-597 https://doi.org/10.1017/s0020589314000244; *Tzanou*, Data Protection as a Fundamental Right Next to Privacy? 'Reconstructing' a Not So New Right, International Data Privacy Law 3 (2013), 88-99 https://doi.org/10.1093/idpl/ipt004; *see also* CJEU 20.5.2003 - Joined cases C-465/00, C-138/01 and C-139/01, ECLI:EU:C:2003:294, para. 74 - Österreichischer Rundfunk: 'the mere recording by an employer of data by name relating to the remuneration paid to his employees cannot as such constitute an interference with private life'.
14. Cf. *Kokott/Sobotta*, The Distinction Between Privacy and Data Protection the Jurisprudence of the CJEU and the ECtHR, International Data Privacy Law 3 (2013), 222-228 https://doi.org/10.1093/idpl/ipt017.
15. CJEU 9.11.2010 - Joined cases C-92/09 and C-93/09, EU:C:2010:662, para. 59 - Schecke.
16. Cf. *Grimm*, Der Datenschutz vor einer Neuorientierung, JZ 68 (2013), 585-592 (588); *Masing*, Herausforderungen des Datenschutzes, Neue Juristische Wochenschrift (NJW) 65 (2012), 2305-2311 (2307); *Roßnagel*, Kein 'Verbotsprinzip' und kein 'Verbot mit Erlaubnisvorbehalt' im Datenschutzrecht, NJW 72 (2019), 1-5 (3); *Veil*, Die Datenschutz-Grundverordung: des Kaisers neue Kleider, Neue Zeitschrift für Verwaltungsrecht (NVwZ) 37 (2018), 686-696 (689).
17. For a comparison of the two approaches, *see Sproll*, Rechtliche Grenzen der Erhebung und Speicherung von Arbeitnehmerdaten, Zeitschrift für Wirtschaftsrecht (ZIP) 5 (1984), 23-31 (23-24).
18. At German level *see* section 3 Federal Data Protection Act (BDSG) of 1977; at European level *see* Art. 7 Directive 95/46/EC of 1995.

this approach to the employment relationship in order to avoid not only violations of personal rights but also risks to those rights. In this respect, the situation is not very different from health and safety legislation, which prohibits not only harm to the life and health of employees but also unreasonable risks that could easily lead to injury.

However, the basic concept of general data protection law leads to a specific problem when it comes to the employment context. Although one academic study identifies no less than seven different approaches to data protection law in current legal doctrine,[19] there is a broad consensus that at least the GDPR is largely based on the concept of preserving the data subject's individual control over its personal data, i.e., pursuing informational self-determination or informational private autonomy.[20] According to this approach, it is primarily the data subject itself who should have the right to dispose of its personal data. This view is reflected, for example, in the Commission's 2010 Communication on an overall approach to the protection of personal data in the European Union (EU), which states that improving control over one's personal data is one of the main objectives of this approach.[21] Accordingly, one of the main objectives of the Commission's 2012 proposal for a GDPR is to give individuals control over their own data.[22] In this sense, Advocate General *Szpunar* stated in his Opinion in the case *Orange România*: 'The guiding principle underlying EU data protection law is the self-determined decision of an individual who is able to exercise control over the use and processing of his data.'[23]

Many parts of the GDPR emphasize the central role of this model. According to Recital 7, sentence 2 GDPR, natural persons should have control over their own personal data. In addition, Article 6(1)(a) GDPR states that the – free and informed – consent of the data subject is sufficient justification for the processing of personal data.[24] As stated in Article 9(2)(a) GDPR, this also applies to the processing of special categories of personal data, i.e., sensitive data such as data concerning health or sexual orientation. In addition, explicit consent justifies or facilitates the lawfulness of automated decision-making in accordance with Article 22(2)(c) and (4) GDPR. These provisions express that the consent of the data subject is of paramount importance in the data protection concept of the GDPR. Because of the focus on the consent (and other individual rights) of the data subject, the GDPR introduces a system of 'privacy self-governance'[25] or 'data sovereignty'.[26] In such a system, data takes on the character

19. *Bieker*, The Right to Data Protection (2022), pp. 143-172.
20. *See*, for example, *Bunnenberg*, Privatautonomie und Datenschutz, JZ 75 (2020), 1088-1097 (1088, 1092-1093); *Hacker*, Datenprivatrecht (2020), pp. 161-162.
21. COM(2010) 609 final, 7.
22. COM(2012) 11 final, 2. *See also* the Commission's Communication of 2012, COM(2012) 9 final, 4-6.
23. AG *Szpunar* 4 March 2020 – C-61/19, EU:C:2020:158, para. 37 – *Orange România*.
24. *See also* Recital 42 GDPR.
25. Phrase by *Solove*, Introduction: Privacy Self-Management and the Consent Dilemma, Harvard Law Review 126 (2013), 1880-1903 (1880).
26. *See Möslein/Beise*, Datensouveränität als Privatautonomie, in: Augsberg/Gehring (eds.), Datensouveränität (2022), pp. 103-119.

of market objects and thus becomes a commodity. According to this 'commodification approach', the level of data protection is ultimately left to market mechanisms.[27]

There is a lively debate as to whether this model, which focuses on the consent of the data subject, is suitable for general data protection law and should be replaced by a model based more on specific permissions and prohibitions. This debate is not only about power asymmetry and the consequences of behavioural economics for the consent approach but also about avoiding negative externalities for other data subjects or even on a macro level for the democratic process.[28] In other words, the discussion also revolves around the question of the public interest in privacy.[29] Particularly in regard to the GDPR, Advocate General *Campos Sánchez-Bordona* challenged in his Opinion in the case *Österreichische Post* the view that safeguarding the control of the data subject on its personal data is the predominant objective of the Regulation.[30] In this context, he expressly refers to Recital 24 of Directive (EU) 2019/770 on certain aspects concerning contracts for the supply of digital content and digital services, which states that the protection of personal data is a fundamental right and therefore personal data cannot be considered a commodity.[31] A blueprint is, by way of example, Article 26(3) of the Digital Services Act which prohibits providers of online platforms from presenting advertisements to recipients of the service based on profiling as defined in Article 4, point (4) GDPR using special categories of personal data referred to in Article 9(1) GDPR.

Irrespective of this general discussion, it is obvious that the employee's consent cannot be considered an ideal expression of the private autonomy of the data subject. Consent cannot therefore serve as a central point of reference for the protection of employees' personal data.[32] Due to the employee's or applicant's dependence on the employer, consent given is regularly not free.[33] It is therefore not appropriate to place the free and informed consent of the employee at the centre of employee data protection law and to concentrate all efforts on the question in which situations these requirements are fulfilled. Rather, employee data protection law demands clear limits for the processing of employees' personal data, which must not be waived. Otherwise,

27. Cf. *Buchner*, Informationelle Selbstbestimmung im Privatrecht (2006), pp. 132-133, 176, 182-183; *Bunnenberg*, Privates Datenschutzrecht (2020), p. 85; *Denga*, Digitale Souveränität durch Datenprivatrecht?, Gewerblicher Rechtsschutz und Urheberrecht (GRUR) 124 (2022), 1113-1120 (1114).
28. *Bunnenberg*, Privates Datenschutzrecht (2020), pp. 86-126; *Engeler*, Der Konflikt zwischen Datenmarkt und Datenschutz, NJW 75 (2022), 3398-3405 (3402-3405); *Guggenberger*, Irrweg informationelle Privatautonomie (2023), pp. 132-174; *Rost*, Zur Soziologie des Datenschutzes, Datenschutz und Datensicherheit (DuD) 37 (2013), 85-91; *see also Cohen*, What Privacy is For, Harvard Law Review 126 (2013), 1904-1933.
29. *Klement*, Öffentliches Interesse an Privatheit, JZ 72 (2017), 161-170 (169-170).
30. AG *Campos Sánchez-Bordona* 6 October 2022 – C-300/21, EU:C:2022:756, paras 73 et seq. – Österreichische Post.
31. OJ 2019 L 136, 1.
32. Cf. European Parliamentary Research Service, Data Subjects, Digital Surveillance, AI and the Future of Work (2020), p. 52.
33. Cf. Art. 29 Protection Working Party (now EDPB), Opinion 2/2017 on data processing at work, WP 249, p. 23: 'Employees are almost never in a position to freely give, refuse or revoke consent'.

a bizarre situation could arise where advertising based on sensitive personal data is prohibited, while measures taken by the employer towards the employee using such data are permitted if the employee has consented and the consent is deemed to have been given voluntarily – at least exceptionally.

§8.03 DEFINITIONS AND SCOPE

Legal definitions regularly have a fundamental significance for the application of the law in concrete cases. This, of course, also applies to the application of data protection law. Therefore the question arises as to whether the central definitions of the GDPR are suitable for the protection of workers' personal data.

[A] Personal Data

First, the definition of personal data is one of the key concepts for the protection of individuals.[34] Insofar Article 4, point 1 GDPR defines personal data as any information relating to an identified or identifiable natural person. This is quasi identical to the definitions in the Council of Europe Personal Data Protection Convention 108 of 1981 (revision in 2018)[35] and the OECD Recommendation on the protection of privacy of 1980 (revision in 2013)[36] and corresponds with the definitions in other general international data protection standards.[37] So it comes with no surprise that the specific employment-related international standards, i.e., the Council of Europe`s Recommendation R(89)2 of 1989[38] and the modernized Recommendation CM/Rec(2015)5 of 2015[39] as well as the International Labour Organization (ILO) code of practice of 1997[40] provide more or less the same definition. This coherence confirms that there is common ground between general data protection law and employee data protection law in regard to personal data as an object of protection. It is therefore logical that the *Deutscher Gewerkschaftsbund* (DGB's)[41] 2022 draft for an Employee Data Protection Act explicitly refers to the definitions in Article 4 GDPR clarifying that only data related to identified or identifiable workers is workers' data.[42]

34. Cf. COM(2010) 609 final, 5.
35. Council of Europe Convention for the Protection of Individuals with regard to Automatic Processing of Personal Data (Convention 108 and Convention 108+) (1981 and 2018), para. 2(a) and Art. 2(a).
36. OECD Recommendation of the Council concerning Guidelines Governing the Protection of Privacy and Transborder Flows of Personal Data, 1980 and 2013, Annex para. 1(b).
37. Cf. Global Privacy Assembly, Policy Strategy Working Group 1: Global frameworks and standards (2020), p. 13.
38. Recommendation R(89)2 of the Committee of Ministers to Member States on the Protection of Personal Data used for Employment Purposes (1989), para. 1.3.
39. Recommendation CM/Rec(2015)5 of the Committee of Ministers to Member States on the processing of personal data in the context of employment (2015), para. 2.
40. ILO code of practice 'Protection of workers' personal data', para. 3.1.
41. The DGB is the umbrella organization of German trade unions.
42. *DGB*, Entwurf eines Beschäftigtendatenschutzgesetzes (BeschDSG) (2022), section 5(1) and (4).

[B] Responsibility

Second, the question of who is responsible is of utmost importance. In this regard, Article 4, point 7 GDPR defines, following Article 2(d) Directive 95/46/EC, the controller as every natural or legal person, public authority, agency or other body which, alone or jointly with others, determines the purposes and the processing of personal data. The Article 29 Data Protection Working Party stressed in its Opinion on the concept of controller of 2010, that in contrast to Council of Europe Convention 108, the concept is no longer used in a static manner ('controller of the file'),[43] but relates to activities reflecting the life cycle of information from its collection to its destruction and is thus more dynamic.[44] Although the Council of Europe Recommendation R(89)2 does not explicitly address this issue it seems that this recommendation follows a more static approach as well ('data on employees which are held by employers')[45] while Recommendation CM/Rec(2015)5 uses the term employer instead of controller with the consequence to define who qualifies as employer.[46] Interestingly, the ILO code of practice deals with the specific question that employers using employment agencies and provides that the employer should request the agency to process personal data consistently with the provisions of the code.[47] With the GDPR as a cross-sectoral regulation, the need for such additional rules no longer exists.

[C] Material Scope

Another problem is the material scope of application for an effective employee data protection law. It is true that most employees' personal data is processed automatically and very few data only manually, not even with the use of a filing system. However, there are some important exceptions, e.g., oral job interviews or bag and locker checks. According to Article 2(1) GDPR, the latter cases are not covered by the GDPR. However, excluding these forms of processing of workers' personal data does not fit with the objectives of labour law, as the employer exercises social power, that should also be regulated. In line with the ILO code of practice,[48] it is therefore desirable that a law on the protection of employee data is not only limited to the automated or file-based processing of employees' personal data but also includes the manual processing of such data.[49] Interestingly, the Council of Europe Recommendation R(89)2 only opposes attempts to avoid the principles of the recommendation by

43. Council of Europe Convention 108, para. 2(d). Adjusted in Council of Europe Convention 108 +, Art. 2(d).
44. Article 29 Data Protection Working Party, Opinion 1/2010 on the concepts of 'controller' and 'processor', WP 169, p. 3.
45. Recommendation R(89)2, para. 1.1.
46. Recommendation CM/Rec(2015)5, para. 2 The same legal technique can be found in the DGB's draft, but with a much more comprehensive definition who is employer, section 5(2).
47. ILO code of practice, para. 13.1.
48. ILO code of practice, para. 4.1(b).
49. Cf. *Simitis*, Reconsidering the Premises of Labour Law: Prolegomena to an EU Regulation on the Protection of Employees' Personal Data, European Law Journal 5 (1999), 45-62 (53-54).

manual processing[50] while Recommendation CM/Rec(2015)5 follows the narrower scope of the GDPR from the outset.

§8.04 PRINCIPLES OF DATA PROTECTION LAW

Article 5(1) GDPR provides six general principles for the processing of personal data as such (lawfulness, fairness and transparency; purpose limitation; data minimization; accuracy; storage limitation; integrity and confidentiality). These principles can also be found in other international data protection standards.[51] The most important principles are the subject of the following considerations, with a focus on labour law aspects.

[A] Legitimacy

The principle of legitimacy or lawfulness is key for data protection law. This principle refers to the fundamental concept that any processing of personal data (within the scope of data protection law) requires a legally accepted basis. In other words, a private individual does not have the unrestricted right to collect and store as much personal data as possible about other private individuals, even if the personal data is collected without directly invading the private sphere of the data subject. However, the processing of personal data by private individuals is of course not strictly prohibited but is first and foremost an exercise of (entrepreneurial) freedom and therefore permitted if there is sufficient justification. Or, as Recital 4 of the GDPR puts it, the right to the protection of personal data is not an absolute right.

In the employment context, the main legal basis provided by the GDPR is the necessity of processing for the performance of a contract to which the employee is a party or in order to take steps at the request of an applicant for a position prior to entering into a contract (Article 6(1)(a) GDPR) or for the purposes of the legitimate interests pursued by the controller or by a third party (Article 6(1)(f) GDPR). The problem with these legal bases is their vagueness, which leaves room for different interpretations. In principle, this legal uncertainty is unfavourable for both the employer and the employee. However, the vagueness of the GDPR and the lack of sector-specific provisions appear to be more disadvantageous for the employee, as this legal vagueness gives the employer room for manoeuvre. Even though hardly any employer will openly say that they do not care about the limits of data protection law, they will regularly claim that the processing of employees' personal data (e.g., a surveillance measure or the disclosure of data to third parties) is justified by the fulfilment of the employment contract or other legitimate interests, even if this legal claim is ultimately unfounded. At least the individual employee is unlikely to challenge the employer's view, as it is often unclear who is right and who is wrong. To a certain

50. Recommendation R(89)2, para. 1.1.

51. Cf. Global Privacy Assembly, Policy Strategy Working Group 1: Global frameworks and standards (2020), pp. 7-8. For a rearrangement of these general principles with a particular focus on the employment context, *see Hendrickx*, Protection of Workers' Personal Data: General Principles, ILO Working Paper 62 (2022), pp. 19-43.

extent, this can be seen as a problem for the enforcement of existing data protection law. However, to some extent, this is also a problem arising from the structure of the GDPR, which, in line with its nature as a cross-sectoral data protection framework, is based on general and abstract provisions.

German law has attempted to solve this problem with an employment-related general clause in the Federal Data Protection Act (*Bundesdatenschutzgesetz* (BDSG), section 26(1), sentence 1 BDSG).[52] However, the CJEU ruled that a comparable provision in the Hessian Data Protection Act is incompatible with the requirements of Article 88 GDPR because a general clause in national law that merely reiterates the condition for the general lawfulness of processing personal data already set out in Article 6(1)(b) GDPR is not specific enough with regard to the opening clause of the GDPR.[53] This ruling inevitably leads to the inapplicability of section 26(1), sentence 1 BDSG. As a result, since all efforts to come to a specific Employee Data Protection Act failed so far,[54] German courts must at least leave aside the general clause of section 26(1), sentence 1 BDSG and instead apply the more abstract provisions of the GDPR.

In that respect, French law is one step ahead, where the national data protection authority ('National Commission for Information Technology and Liberties' 'Commission nationale de l'informatique et des libertés (CNIL)') has listed eleven legitimate purposes for the processing of personal data in the employment context.[55] Together with a description of examples of the listed purposes, this legislative technique leads to significantly more legal certainty, although it seems unclear whether the list is exhaustive and whether an exhaustive list is permissible under the opening clause of Article 88 GDPR in light of Article 6(1)(f) GDPR, which basically establishes a legal ground for processing personal data if it is necessary for the purposes of the legitimate interests pursued by the controller or a third party.[56]

[B] Non-discrimination

The issue of non-discrimination deserves particular attention. In labour law, the principle of non-discrimination is of central importance and is dealt with, for example, in the Racial Equality Directive 2000/43/EC and the Equal Treatment Directive

52. 'Personal data of employees may be processed for employment-related purposes where necessary for hiring decisions or, after hiring, for carrying out or terminating the employment contract or to exercise or satisfy rights and obligations of employees' representation laid down by law or by collective agreements or other agreements between the employer and staff representatives'.
53. CJEU 30.3.2023 – C-34/21, EU:C:2023:270, paras 59 et seq., 79 et seq. – Hauptpersonalrat der Lehrerinnen und Lehrer beim Hessischen Kultusministerium.
54. Following the 2022 report by a group of experts on employee data protection (available at: https://www.denkfabrik-bmas.de/fileadmin/Downloads/Publikationen/Report_of_the_independent_interdisciplinary_Employee_Data_Protection_Advisory_Committee.pdf), the Federal Ministry of Labour and Social Affairs (*Bundesministerium für Arbeit und Soziales*) and the Federal Ministry of the Interior and Community (*Bundesministerium des Innern und für Heimat*) have agreed on a draft Employee Data Act (*Beschäftigtendatengesetz*), which was leaked in October 2024, but whose further fate is currently uncertain given the premature end of the governing coalition in November 2024.
55. Délibération No. 2019-160 of 21 November 2019, JO No. 92 of 15 April 2020.
56. Cf. CJEU 19.10.2016 – case C-582/14, EU:C:2016:779, paras 61 et seq. – *Breyer*.

2000/78/EC as well as in ILO Convention No. 111 on Discrimination in Employment and Occupation. The GDPR mentions discrimination, but only in a few recitals (Recitals 71, 75 and 85) and not directly in a provision. By comparison, the EU legislation on artificial intelligence ((AI) Act) addresses the issue of non-discrimination more than twenty times mainly in its recitals,[57] which shows that the problem of discrimination is generally linked to the use of algorithms and data analysis rather than to the protection of personal data as such. However, it is no coincidence that the ILO code of practice recalls the general principle of non-discrimination when it comes to the processing of personal data in the employment context, stating that such processing should not have the effect of unlawfully discriminating in employment or occupation.[58]

The question of whether discrimination is unlawful can only be answered in the context in which the discrimination takes place. So, if an employee is discriminated against, it is ultimately labour law and not data protection law that decides on the lawfulness of the discrimination. The question of whether personal data on political opinions or religious beliefs of a job applicant may be processed can hardly be answered solely on the basis of Article 9(2)(b) GDPR but requires an assessment under labour law as to whether a particular political opinion or religious belief is necessary for a particular job, for example, at a newspaper or a school of a religious community.

[C] Proportionality

Another key principle is proportionality, which can be found in the principle of data minimization in Article 5(1)(c) GDPR and in the formula 'processing is necessary', which is used five times in Article 6(1) GDPR. From a more general perspective, the proportionality test can be divided into three aspects: (i) the processing must be suitable to achieve the legitimate purpose; (ii) the processing must be necessary to achieve the objective in the sense that there is no less intrusive measure to achieve the same purpose; and (iii) the processing must be proportionate when weighed against the fundamental rights and freedoms of the data subject. The third requirement in particular, which is also expressed in Article 6(1)(f) GDPR, is especially problematic in cases of employee monitoring. A fair balance between the rights and interests of the employer on the one hand and the employee on the other is in most cases decisive for the outcome of a case and must ultimately be decided by the courts. For example, there are many judgments of the German Federal Labour Court (*Bundesarbeitsgericht* (BAG)) on the question of whether a certain type of monitoring of an employee is justified in terms of appropriateness.

In these decisions, the Federal Labour Court, not unlike the ECtHR,[59] carefully examines the specific aspects of the case, for example, the duration and intensity of the

57. Cf. COM(2021) 206 final and P9_TA(2024)0138.
58. ILO code of practice, para. 5.10.
59. Cf. ECtHR 5.9.2017 – App. No. 61496/08, para. 121 – Barbulescu; ECtHR 17.10.2019 – App. Nos 1874/13 and 8567/13, para. 116 – López Ribalda; ECtHR 13.12.2022 – App. No. 26968/16, para. 109 – Almeida Vasconcelos Gramaxo.

surveillance.[60] This approach leads to fairness in individual cases. However, it creates legal uncertainty because the outcome of the court's consideration of the rights and interests at stake is often difficult to predict. Furthermore, the final judgment is sometimes only issued years after the specific case and thus cannot directly influence the behaviour of the employer as the controller of workers' personal data.

Of course, it is not possible for the legislator to precisely determine the outcome of the proportionality test, in particular the aspect of appropriateness, for each future case in order to provide the employer with clear guidance as to which processing of employees' personal data is permissible and which is not. Furthermore, according to the CJEU in a case not involving employment, it is not compatible with Article 6(1)(f) GDPR for Member States to definitively prescribe the outcome of the balancing of the rights and interests in question.[61] However, it is possible to reduce the legal uncertainty arising from the structure of general data protection law for the employment context by two measures: First, by introducing more specific rules under Article 88 GDPR in terms of concrete rules for typical situations of processing of employees' personal data, such as the recruitment process, monitoring the use of ICT in the workplace, video surveillance, tracking of employees, etc.[62] Instead of relying solely on the general 'processing of personal data' approach and regarding employees as mere 'data subjects', this legal technique would mean recognizing workers as dependent persons and directly regulating employers' practices that are particularly intrusive to employees' privacy.[63] And second, by introducing the main parameters for the proportionality test to increase legal certainty in all other cases not covered by specific rules.

[D] Purpose Limitation

Another principle concerns purpose limitation in the sense that processing for another purpose must be compatible with the purpose for which the personal data was originally collected. This principle of general data protection law as such also fits well in the employment context. However, here too, the abstract criteria of Article 6(4) GDPR lead to a certain degree of legal uncertainty and give the employer considerable room for manoeuvre. Therefore, a clarification, as found in the ILO Code, that personal data collected in connection with technical or organizational measures to ensure the security and proper operation of automated information systems may not be used to

60. E.g., BAG 22.9.2016 – 2 AZR 848/15, Neue Zeitschrift für Arbeitsrecht (NZA) 34 (2017), 112, paras 28 et seq.; BAG 20.10.2016 – 2 AZR 395/15, NZA 34 (2017), 443, paras 22 et seq.; BAG 27.7.2017 – 2 AZR 681/16, NZA 34 (2017), 1327, paras 30 et seq.; BAG 23.8.2018 – 2 AZR 133/18, NZA 35 (2018), 1329, paras 24 et seq.; BAG 28.3.2019 – 8 AZR 421/17, NZA 36 (2019), 1212, paras 36 et seq., 50.
61. CJEU 7.12.2023 – case C-634/21, EU:C:2023:957 para. 70 – *SCHUFA Holding*; *see*, to that effect, also CJEU 19.10.2016 – case C-582/14, EU:C:2016:779, para. 62 – *Breyer*.
62. For particular forms of processing of workers' personal data, *see* Recommendation CM/Rec(2015)5, paras 14 et seq., and the Explanatory Memorandum, CM(2015)32 add, paras 113 et seq.
63. Cf. *Otto*, The Right to Privacy in Employment, European Labour Law Journal 6 (2015), 343-363 (362).

monitor the behaviour of workers,[64] makes sense in order to underline the importance of the purpose limitation principle. The same applies to the management of vehicles, etc., which initially serves to optimize work processes and should not be used to constantly monitor drivers.

[E] Transparency

Finally, transparency is a key feature of fair processing of personal data. Insofar, Articles 12 to 15 GDPR provide a set of transparency requirements which basically also fit in the employment context. However, there are two problems: First, it is unclear whether a covert surveillance is exceptionally allowed if it is the only option for the employer to detect thefts or other gross violations of the employment contract. The Federal Labour Court traditionally accepts such kind of surveillance as ultima ratio in its pre-GDPR case law[65] which is in line with the ILO code of practice.[66] However, it is unclear whether this case law can be maintained under the GDPR.[67] In this respect, clear guidance would make sense which might include that any intransparency for the affected employee must be substituted through transparency for the works council as a representative of the employees or the data protection authority in order to prevent the employer from deciding only on his own to survey its workers in a secret manner.

The second problem concerns the data subject's right to access under Article 15 GDPR. In principle, the CJEU follows a strict interpretation and ruled in a case that did not concern employment that 'all' personal data are the subject of the data subject's right to access and obtain a copy from the controller in accordance with Article 15(1) and (3) GDPR.[68] In the employment context, where a contractual relationship can sometimes last for many years and employees' personal data is stored not only in the HR department but also, with the increasing use of ICT, on dozens or even hundreds of electronic devices throughout the employer's organization, this approach could mean that the employer is obliged to provide information about all electronic correspondence in which a particular employee's name appears and to provide a copy of probably thousands of emails.[69] In fact, there have been cases in Germany where former

64. ILO code of practice, para. 5.4.
65. Cf. BAG 27.3.2003 – 2 AZR 51/02, NZA 20 (2003), 1193 (1195); BAG 21.6.2012 – 2 AZR 153/11, NZA 29 (2012), 1025, para. 39; BAG 22.9.2016 – 2 AZR 848/15, NZA 34 (2017), 112, paras 28 et seq.; BAG 20.10.2016 – 2 AZR 395/15, NZA 34 (2017), 443, paras 22 et seq.; BAG 29.6.2017 – 2 AZR 597/16, NZA 34 (2017), 1179, paras 30 et seq. It should be noted that some judgments do not make a clear distinction between the lawfulness of covert surveillance as such and the lawful use of the results of covert surveillance as evidence in a legal dispute regardless of its lawfulness.
66. ILO code of practice, para. 6.14(2).
67. In the affirmative *Byers*, Die Zuläsigkeit heimlicher Mitarbeiterkontrollen nach dem neuen Datenschutzrecht, NZA 34 (2017), 1086-1091 (1089-1091).
68. CJEU 4.5.2023 – case C-487/21, EU:C:2023:369, paras 20 et seq. – *Österreichische Datenschutzbehörde*.
69. Another problem not discussed here concerns the scope of the right to information if an employee is also a member of the works council and uses the same e-mail address both for business purposes and for works council activities, for this *see* LAG Köln 20 January 2023 – 9 TaBV 32/22, juris.

employees have lodged a complaint with a supervisory authority or sued the employer directly, demanding to receive all email traffic from previous years.[70] Against this background, the question can be raised whether it makes sense to restrict the right to information in such cases in order to reduce the administrative burden for the employer, especially for small and medium-sized enterprises, in accordance with Recital 13, sentence 4 GDPR. A solution to this problem could be found in Article 12(5)(b) GDPR,[71] which grants the controller the right to refuse to process a data subject's request if the request is excessive.[72] However, it is unclear whether a disproportionate effort proves that such a request is excessive.[73] The case law of the German courts offers little guidance in this respect. Two local administrative courts ruled that the request for 348 pages (of a written legal exam)[74] and even the request for 3,000 documents[75] is not excessive, while a local civil court ruled that the request for several thousand emails, which would require several weeks of work to prepare (sifting and blackening other names), is excessive.[76] The European Data Protection Board (EDPB) rejects a proportionality test in regard to data subjects' requests under Article 15 GDPR.[77] Ultimately, only the CJEU can provide a definitive answer to this problem.[78]

§8.05 SPILLOVER EFFECT

One consequence of the cross-sectoral nature of the GDPR and its applicability in the employment context is the phenomenon that the case law of the CJEU on the interpretation of the GDPR is not limited to the specific area from which the respective case originates. Rather, there is a spillover effect in the sense that such judgments are also relevant to employment cases, regardless of whether such an impact was foreseen and taken into account by the CJEU. Two examples of this effect have already been cited (incompatibility of national law with the GDPR, which definitively prescribes the

70. *Brink/Joos*, Reichweite und Grenzen des Auskunftsanspruchs und des Rechts auf Kopie, Zeitschrift für Datenschutz ZD 9 (2019), 483-488 (487).
71. By contrast, Recital 63, sentence 5 GDPR, which provides that the controller should be able to require the data subject to specify the information to which the request relates if the controller processes a large quantity of information concerning the data subject, will often not be helpful in this context.
72. Cf. CJEU 12.1.2023 – case C-154/21, EU:C:2023:3, paras 49 et seq. – *Österreichische Post AG*.
73. In the negative *Rudkowski*, Der datenschutzrechtliche Auskunftsanspruch im Arbeitsrecht, NZA 41 (2024), 1-8 (4).
74. VG Gelsenkirchen 27 April 2020 – 20 K 6392/18, ZD 10 (2020), 544, para. 89.
75. VG Stuttgart 30 November 2023 – 11 K 3946/21, juris, paras 98 et seq.
76. LG Heidelberg 21 February 2020 – 4 O 6/19, ZD 10 (2020), 313, para. 25.
77. EDPB, Guidelines 01/2022 on data subjects rights – Rights of access, Version 2.0 (adopted on 28 March 2023), paras 166, 188.
78. An additional problem concerns the probable conflict between, on the one hand, the exercise of the right of the data subject to obtain information relating to the identity of the employees of a controller who carried out operations under its authority and in accordance with its instructions and, on the other hand, the rights and freedoms of those employees, cf. CJEU 22.6.2023 – case C-579/21, EU:C:2023:501, paras 76 et seq. – *Pankki S*.

outcome of the balancing of the rights and interests in question; the data subject's right to information). Three further examples may also illustrate the possible effects of the CJEU's rulings in non-employment cases on the world of work.

[A] Automated Individual Decision-Making

First, in the case of the automated establishment by a credit information agency of a probability score based on personal data relating to a person and concerning his or her ability to meet future payment commitments, the CJEU interpreted Article 22(1) GDPR in a way that not only the final act of a human being granting a bank loan can be classified as a 'decision' within the meaning of Article 22(1) GDPR but also the establishment of the probability value which must not be considered a preparatory act.[79] Although this case has nothing to do with employment, it is of utmost importance for situations in which HR measures like recruitment, transfers or further training are driven by algorithms even if the formal decision on the measure is made by an HR manager.[80] In particular, the fact that the case involved three actors is not an obstacle to transferring it to an employment context with only two actors, in which it is regularly the employer itself who generates the output of the algorithmic system and then decides on the basis of the output.

[B] Technical and Organizational Measures

Second, the controller's obligation to implement technical and organizational measures in accordance with Articles 24 and 32 GDPR can be mentioned here. As the CJEU has ruled in two non-employment cases that the unauthorized disclosure of personal data or the unauthorized access to such data by a 'third party' is not in itself sufficient to establish that the technical and organizational measures taken by the controller were not 'appropriate' within the meaning of Articles 24 and 32 GDPR,[81] the same question cannot be answered differently once an employment case arises.

[C] Compensation

The third example concerns the right to compensation under Article 82 GDPR which is instructive in several ways. In a first step, the CJEU decided on the one hand in a number of non-employment cases that this Article must be interpreted as meaning that a mere infringement of the provisions of the GDPR is not sufficient to confer a right to

79. CJEU 7.12.2023 – case C-634/21, EU:C:2023:957, paras 44 et seq., 60 et seq. – *SCHUFA Holding*.
80. On the consequences for labour law, *see Heine*, Das Verbot der entscheidungsgleichen Datenverarbeitung, NZA 41 (2024), 33-37 (34-37); *Heine*, Die automatisierte Vorbereitung von Arbeitgeberentscheidungen, NZA 41 (2024), 1384-1389.
81. Cf. CJEU 14.12.2023 – case C-340/21, EU:C:2023:986, paras 23 et seq. – *Natsionalna agentsia za prihodite*; CJEU 25.1.2024 – case C-687/21, EU:C:2024:72, paras 38 et seq. – *MediaMarktSaturn*.

compensation.[82] On the other hand, Article 82 GDPR precludes a national rule which makes compensation for non-material damage, within the meaning of that provision, subject to the condition that the damage suffered by the data subject has reached a certain degree of seriousness.[83] In a second step, the CJEU transferred its case law to an employment case and further developed its interpretation of Article 82 GDPR in the sense that the right to compensation has no preventive or punitive character and therefore the amount may not exceed the full compensation for the damage.[84] In a third step, the CJEU picked up that case law and transferred it back into a non-employment context[85] while adding that it is not sufficient for the controller, in order to be exempted from liability under Article 82(3) GDPR, to claim that the damage was caused by the failure of a person acting under his or her authority, within the meaning of Article 29 GDPR.[86] The whole development appears like a ping-pong game in which only the internal logic of the GDPR is decisive regardless of whether the case is a non-employment or an employment case.

§8.06 GOVERNANCE

The GDPR not only contains individual rights of the data subject but also a number of provisions on the governance aiming to ensure compliance with the substantive rules on the protection of personal data, which have an impact on labour law as well.

[A] Supervisory Authorities

First of all, it is evident that the tasks of the supervisory authorities laid down in Article 57 GDPR apply also to workers' personal data. Thus, for instance, the supervisory authorities have to monitor and enforce the application of the GDPR in the employment context and handle complaints lodged by employees. In that respect, the problem is not the principle as such but the available resources because the supervisory authorities have to care for all kinds of processing personal data and cannot – unlike the labour inspection – focus only on the world of work. Nevertheless, the annual reports of the German supervisory authorities at the State level (*Bundesländer*) often contain information on employment issues. Moreover, the conference of the German data protection authorities as well as the Article 29 Protection Working Party have published

82. CJEU 4.5.2023 – case C-300/21, EU:C:2023:370, paras 31 et seq. – *Österreichische Post*; CJEU 14.12.2023 – case C-340/21, EU:C:2023:986, paras 23 et seq. – *Natsionalna agentsia za prihodite*; CJEU 14.12.2023 – case C-456/22, EU:C:2023:988, paras 21 et seq. – *Gemeinde Ummendorf*.
83. CJEU 4.5.2023 – case C-300/21, EU:C:2023:370, paras 45 et seq. – *Österreichische Post*; CJEU 14.12.2023 – case C-456/22, EU:C:2023:988, paras 16 et seq. – *Gemeinde Ummendorf*.
84. CJEU 21.12.2023 – case C-667/21, EU:C:2023:1022, paras 85 et seq. – *Krankenversicherung Nordrhein*.
85. CJEU 25.1.2024 – case C-687/21, EU:C:2024:72, paras 48 et seq. – *MediaMarktSaturn*.
86. CJEU 11.4.2024 – case C-741/21, EU:C:2024:288, paras 45 et seq. – *juris GmbH*.

several guidelines specifically for the processing of workers' personal data[87] in the past decades even though they are not genuine labour law institutions.

[B] Data Protection Officer

Some labour-specific questions arise in relation to the data protection officer. The first problem concerns the permitted level of social protection for such a person provided by Member States law. In this respect, the CJEU ruled, that the GDPR does not preclude national legislation which provides that a controller or a processor may terminate the employment contract of a data protection officer, who is a member of his or her staff in accordance with Article 37(6) GDPR, only with just cause, even if the contractual termination is not related to the performance of that officer's tasks.[88] The same applies to the dismissal of a data protection officer who is a member of staff.[89] However, this legislation must not undermine the achievement of the objectives of the GDPR.[90] In other words, from the Court's point of view, a conflict between data protection law on the one side and labour law on the other may arise, in which case data protection law takes precedence.

The second problem is the compatibility of being both, a data protection officer and chairperson of a works council at the same time. On this question, the CJEU ruled in a broad way that the data protection officer may be entrusted by the controller or processor with other tasks and duties. However, this must not result in a conflict of interests which is the case if the data protection officer determines the objectives and methods of processing personal data.[91] In its subsequent judgment, the Federal Labour Court has drawn the conclusion that the duties of a data protection officer and a chairperson of a works council are incompatible because the works council decides within its tasks and competencies conferred by the Works Constitution Act (*Betriebsverfassungsgesetz* (BetrVG)) on the purposes and means of the processing of workers' personal data. Since the chairperson is an agent of the works council and represents its interests he or she cannot simultaneously act neutrally in the same issue and monitor compliance with the GDPR. Consequently, the controller has a just cause to dismiss the chairperson of the works council from his as data protection officer.[92] In summary, the conflict between data protection law on the one hand and labour law on the other is resolved by 'unbundling' both areas of law. The Federal Labour Court, however, left

87. *See* only Art. 29 Protection Working Party, Opinion 8/2001 on the processing of personal data in the employment context, WP 48; Working document on the surveillance of electronic communications in the workplace, WP 55, Opinion 2/2017 on data processing at work, WP 249.
88. CJEU 22.6.2022 – case C-534/20, EU:C:2022:495, paras 19 et seq. – *Leistritz.*
89. CJEU 9.2.2023 – case C-453/21, EU:C:2023:79, paras 20 et seq. – *X-FAB Dresden*; CJEU 9.2.2023 – case C-560/21, EU:C:2023:81, paras 15 et seq. – *KISA.*
90. CJEU 22.6.2022 – case C-534/20, EU:C:2022:495, paras 35 et seq. – *Leistritz*; CJEU 9.2.2023, case C-453/21, EU:C:2023:79, paras 32 et seq. – *X-FAB Dresden*; CJEU 9.2.2023 – case C-560/21, EU:C:2023:81, paras 27 et seq. – *KISA.*
91. CJEU 9.2.2023 – case C-453/21, EU:C:2023:79, paras 39 et seq. – *X-FAB Dresden.*
92. BAG 6.6.2023 – 9 AZR 383/19, NZA 40 (2023), 1329, paras 24 et seq.

open whether all this also applies if someone is only an ordinary member of a works council.[93]

[C] Position of Works Councils

Since the GDPR came into force, there has been an intense debate in Germany as to whether the works council – in contrast to previous case law[94] – qualifies as an independent 'controller' within the meaning of Article 4, point (7) GDPR and whether the data protection officer may monitor not only the employer but also the works council.[95] In 2021, the German legislator added a new provision (section 79a BetrVG) to the Works Constitution Act that deals specifically with data protection. This new provision states, first, that the works council must comply with data protection law when processing personal data and, second, that the employer is responsible for the processing of personal data within the meaning of data protection law insofar as the works council processes personal data in order to fulfil its tasks.[96] With regard to the second question, the new provision lacks clear guidance. The legislator has stated in its explanatory memorandum that the data protection officer must also monitor the works council as part of the controller.[97] However, this view is not reflected in the wording of the new provision. The provision merely contains the obligation of the data protection officer to maintain confidentiality vis-à-vis the employer with regard to information that allows conclusions to be drawn about the opinion-forming process of the works council.

There is therefore an ongoing debate as to whether the data protection officer is authorized to monitor the processing of employees' personal data by the works council[98] or whether this view is incompatible with other provisions of European law, in particular Article 27 CFREU.[99] An important argument is the procedure for appointing and dismissing data protection officers. As there is no specific co-determination right of the works council under German law (in contrast to the legal situation for company doctors and occupational safety specialists, who can only be appointed or dismissed with the consent of the works council),[100] the data protection officer is only appointed by the employer and is, therefore, more or less in the employer's camp, even if he or she is formally independent. It would therefore be problematic if such a person

93. BAG 6.6.2023 – 9 AZR 383/19, NZA 40 (2023), 1329, para. 26.
94. BAG 11.11.1997 – 1 ABR 21/91, NZA 15 (1998), 385, 386 et seq.
95. *See* only *Flink*, Beschäftigtendatenschutz als Aufgabe des Betriebsrats (2021), pp. 207-224, 289-291.
96. First approach to an interpretation of section 79a BetrVG in BAG 9.5.2023 – 1 ABR 14/22, NZA 40 (2023), 1404, para. 57.
97. Bundestagsdrucksache 19/28899, 22.
98. In this sense *Brink/Joos*, Datenschutzrechtliche Folgen für den Betriebsrat nach dem Betriebsrätemodernisierungsgesetz, NZA 38 (2021), 1440-1444 (1442).
99. In this sense *Körner*, Die Auswirkungen der Datenschutz-Grundverordnung (DSGVO) in der betrieblichen Praxis (2019), pp. 65-66.
100. Cf. section 9(3), sentence 1 of the Act on Occupational Physicians, Safety Engineers and Other Occupational Safety Specialists (*Gesetz über Betriebsärzte, Sicherheitsingenieure und andere Fachkräfte für Arbeitssicherheit*).

were to monitor the data processing-related behaviour of the works council. Overall, it is regrettable that the GDPR overlooks the collision between data protection law on the one hand and labour law on the other and does not explicitly solve the problem.

§8.07 COLLECTIVE RIGHTS

It is widely recognized that the effectiveness of the protection of workers against risks arising from their personal data rests to a considerable extent on collective rights.[101] Article 88(1) of the GDPR mentions collective agreements as instruments or more specific rules to ensure the protection of the rights and freedoms when it comes to the processing of employee's personal data in the employment context. However, the GDPR itself does not establish any participation rights, but of course, does not preclude such rights so long as they do not undermine the objectives of the GDPR.

From the perspective of German law, the following aspects are important. It should be noted in advance that, according to the system of industrial relations in Germany and the firm-centred character of workers' data processing, it is primarily the works councils and not the trade unions that are at the forefront of employee data protection. Trade unions campaign for a robust Employee Data Protection Act but regularly do not make this topic the subject of traditional collective bargaining.

[A] Duty to Safeguard Employers' Compliance with Data Protection Law

The works council, in turn, has the general task of ensuring that the employer complies with data protection law, i.e., the GDPR and the BDSG, insofar as this law aims to protect employees (section 80(1), No. 1 BetrVG). This task also extends to temporary workers, but of course not to the employer's customers. Whether self-employed persons are covered is unclear and, as far as can be seen, has not yet been clarified by case law. However, the task as such is not associated with rights that go beyond mere information. For example, even if the works council detects a breach of data protection law, it cannot in principle sue the employer, but can only take informal remedial action. There are only a few exceptions: The works council has a right to demand that the employer refrain from gross violations of the employee's personal rights and a right to demand that the employer comply with works agreements on issues relating to employees' personal data.[102] In addition, under general principles of works constitution law, the works council has the right to act as a whistleblower and to inform the supervisory authority if an internal complaint is unsuccessful, although the works council as such is not mentioned in the Whistleblowing Directive (EU) 2019/1937 or the new German Whistleblower Protection Act (*Hinweisgeberschutzgesetz*).

---

101. ILO code of practice, p. 24; *Todolí-Signes*, Algorithms, Artificial Intelligence and Automated Decisions Concerning Workers and the Risks of Discrimination: The Necessary Collective Governance of Data Protection, Transfer 25 (2019), 465-481 (475-477).
102. Cf. *Flink*, Beschäftigtendatenschutz als Aufgabe des Betriebsrats (2021), pp. 120-126.

[B] Co-determination Right

Much more important is the co-determination right of the works council according to section 87(1), No. 6 BetrVG when it comes to the introduction and use of technical devices designed to monitor the behaviour or performance of the employees.[103] The Federal Labour Court ruled back in the 1970s that this provision does not require an intention of the employer to monitor the workers. Rather, it is sufficient that the technical device has the objective capacity to monitor them. If the employer and the works council cannot achieve an agreement, the employer can appeal to a conciliation board (*Einigungsstelle*) with equal representation of both sides and a neutral chairperson (section 87(2) BetrVG). Due to the increasing digitalization of the world of work, this co-determination right is a powerful instrument to protect the personal data of employees in the hands of works councils which are willing and able to use it. If the employer acts unilaterally, the labour court can bar him or her from putting the technical devices into operation at the request of the works council.[104] Thus, in Germany the legal position of works councils to influence the level of workers' personal data protection is considerably stronger than mere rights to information and consultation as provided for in the ILO code of practice[105] and the Council of Europe Recommendations[106] even if this procedural model of collective rights is still better than a purely individual approach.[107]

[C] Role of Works Agreements

The option for Member States to provide for more specific rules on employee data protection not only by law but also by collective agreements has led to preliminary ruling proceedings before the CJEU. The Federal Labour Court referred in essence two questions, first, whether works agreements are only bound by Article 88(2) GDPR and not by Articles 5, 6 and 9 GDPR, and second, whether works agreements are subject only to a limited legal review by the labour courts, i.e., in a less strict manner in comparison to Member States legislation.[108] The Federal Labour Court made it clear that it would answer both questions in the negative. There is currently neither an

103. For details, *see Däubler*, Gläserne Belegschaften, 9. Ed. (2021), paras 689 et seq., *Krause*, Sozialverträgliche Arbeitnehmerüberwachung: Technikbasierte Beschäftigtenkontrolle als Gegenstand betrieblicher Mitbestimmung im digitalen Zeitalter, in: *Gräfl et al.* (eds), 100 Jahre Betriebsverfassungsrecht (2020), pp. 353-368.
104. BAG 13.12.2016 – 1 ABR 7/15, NZA 34 (2017), 657, para. 35.
105. ILO code of practice, para. 12.
106. Recommendation R(89)2, para. 3; Recommendation CM/Rec(2015)5, para. 21(c). It is fair to say that both Recommendations provide that an agreement should be obtained, where the consultation procedure reveals the possibility of infringement of employees' right to respect for privacy and human dignity.
107. *See Ford*, Two Conceptions of Worker Privacy, Industrial Law Journal 31 (2002), 135-155 (153-155).
108. BAG 22.9.2022 – 8 AZR 209/21 (A), NZA 40 (2023), 363; *see also* BAG 25.4.2024 – 8 AZR 209/21 (B), NZA-RR 29 (2024), 389. At the CJEU under case C-65/23.

opinion of an Advocate General nor a judgment of the CJEU in this matter. Nevertheless, there is no doubt that the decision will not only clarify the two questions but will also represent a further building block in the general debate on the relationship between data protection law on the one hand and labour law on the other.

§8.08 CONCLUSIONS

The protection of employees' personal data is located at the interface between general data protection law and labour law. The relationship between the two areas of law is complex. As a rule, data protection law and labour law move in the same direction, so there is usually no friction between them when it comes to employee data protection law. However, the most pressing problem is the abstract nature of the GDPR, which leads to legal uncertainty and makes it difficult in day-to-day practice to clearly decide which processing of employees' personal data is lawful. Therefore, the most urgent demand is the creation of provisions that concretize the abstract rules and principles of the GDPR, i.e., in Germany the creation of a stand-alone legislation on the protection of workers' personal data (Employee Data Protection Act).[109]

In some situations, however, it cannot be denied that there are conflicts between data protection law and labour law. When conflicts arise, they are usually resolved by giving priority to data protection law, as the collision is usually the result of a clash between European law (data protection law) on the one hand and Member State law (labour law) on the other. In exceptional cases (conflict of interests), the friction is resolved by 'unbundling'. When interpreting the GDPR, however, sufficient consideration should be given to the national particularities of worker participation. In any case, it can be stated that workers' personal data will always have a special position in data protection law.[110]

---

109. In the same sense, the Report of the independent interdisciplinary council on employee data protection of January 2022, https://www.denkfabrik-bmas.de/fileadmin/Downloads/Publikationen/Report_of_the_independent_interdisciplinary_Employee_Data_Protection_Advisory_Committee.pdf; German Conference of the Federal and State Data Protection Supervisory Authorities (*Datenschutzkonferenz* (DSK)), Resolution of 11 May 2023, https://www.datenschutz-berlin.de/fileadmin/user_upload/pdf/publikationen/DSK/2023/2023-05_DSK-Entschliessung_Beschaeftigtendatenschutz.pdf.
110. In that sense already in 1971 *Steinmüller et al.*, Grundfragen des Datenschutzes, Bundestagsdrucksache VI/3826, 155.

CHAPTER 9

Wearable Technology to Monitor Workers' Health and Safety: Benefits, Risks, and Legal Considerations

Stefania Marassi & John Bolte

§9.01 INTRODUCTION

Heat exposure presents a significant occupational hazard for outdoor workers, potentially leading to heat strokes and even death due to exposure to extreme temperatures. Imagine being informed of a cutting-edge solution (and it does exist!): lightweight, miniaturized electronic devices known as wearables that are capable of real-time and continuous monitoring of each worker's physiological response to heat stress and can then warn those experiencing elevated levels of heat strain. To do so, these devices measure workers' physiological parameters which are indices of heat strain – body temperature and heart rate – and analyse the information retrieved, some of them using Artificial Intelligence (AI)-driven techniques.[1] The introduction of this type of device in the workplace prompts a crucial question: does the benefit of safeguarding workers' physical health through the collection and analysis of vital parameters outweigh potential risks to the respect of other fundamental rights, such as the right to data

1. Heat stress levels are usually monitored using devices like wet-bulb globe thermometers, which measure environmental parameters such as ambient temperature and air humidity. However, these devices do not account for individual differences in heat strain, i.e., the physiological and psychophysical effects of heat stress on an individual's body. Heat strain can be influenced by factors such as age, chronic diseases, gender, medications, etc. On the topic, *see* Sean R. Notley, Andreas D. Flouris & Glen P. Kenny, 'On the Use of Wearable Physiological Monitors to Assess Heat Strain During Occupational Heat Stress' (2018) 43 Appl. Physio. Nutr. Metab. 869 https://doi.org/10.1139/apnm-2018-0173. Vishal Patel et al., 'Trends in Workplace Wearable Technologies and Connected-Worker Solutions for Next-Generation Occupational Safety, Health, and Productivity' (2022) 4(1) Adv. Intell. Syst. 2100099, 8-9 https://doi.org/10.1002/aisy.202100099.

protection and the right to (mental) health in the workplace, which might be jeopardized by constant monitoring?

Research, commercialization, and adoption of wearables are rapidly expanding. This fast-emerging technology has already countless applications across various industry sectors, including healthcare, fitness, professional sports, and fashion, to name a few.[2] The world of work is also embracing this trend with numerous examples showcasing the integration of such technology in the work floor: smart hats that monitor workers' fatigue by measuring brain waves with sensors integrated into headbands, sensor-enabled insoles that track metrics related to the wearer's movement and location to alert safety managers if a lone worker falls, and scan glove scanners used to optimize workflows and spur workers' productivity.[3]

In an occupational setting, these devices offer novel opportunities to improve business efficiency by monitoring workers' productivity and performance (e.g., ring barcode scanners). Additionally, they could contribute to enhancing occupational health and safety (OHS) by providing on-the-spot training and assistance to workers in carrying out their tasks (e.g., virtual reality glasses and wearable robots known as exoskeletons), monitoring various environmental and/or physiological parameters to alert them of imminent risks for their safety and health (e.g., smart hats), and promoting healthy lifestyle habits, such as walking, as part of initiatives like corporate wellness programs (e.g., fitness trackers).[4]

Yet, their deployment in the workplace is of concern for the respect of workers' fundamental rights, including the right to privacy and data protection and the right to health and safety at work. Equipped with different types of sensors, these devices can capture a wide array of (personal and sensitive) data about the wearer and the surrounding environment, including heart rate variability, breathing rate, sweat rate, location, ambient temperature, and the presence of gases. Employing diverse techniques, including AI-driven algorithms like machine learning, they can analyse the gathered information and provide insights into, or even predictions about, the wearer's health status, behaviour, and workplace safety. The information obtained by the employer may extend beyond the purpose for which these devices were originally introduced and could potentially be misused to make discriminatory decisions against workers. For instance, in the scenario presented above, this could involve dismissing workers who are considered less productive due to lower heat resistance.

---

2. *See, e.g.*, for the healthcare sector, Shouvik Mukherjee, 'State of the Art in Smart Portable, Wearable, Ingestible and Implantable Devices for Health Status Monitoring and Disease Management' (2022) 22(11) Sensors 4228 https://doi.org/10.3390/s22114228; for the fashion industry, Giovanni Ziccardi, 'Wearable Technologies and Smart Clothes in the Fashion Business: Some Issues concerning Cybersecurity and Data Protection' (2020) 9(2) Laws 12 https://doi.org/10.3390/laws9020012; for fitness and professional sports, Skyler R. Berman, 'Bargaining over Biometrics: How Player Unions Should Protect Athletes in the Age of Wearable Technology' (2020) 85 Brook L Rev 543 https://doi.org/10.2139/ssrn.4881551.
3. For other examples, *see* Patel et al., *supra* n. 1, 4-20.
4. *See, e.g.*, European Agency for Safety and Health at Work (EU-OSHA), 'Smart Digital Monitoring Systems for Occupational Safety and Health: Workplace Resources for Design, Implementation and Use' (Report, 2022), 18 ff.

Similarly, the use of wearable technology may introduce new OHS risk factors such as constant oversight, loss of workers' autonomy, and work intensification, all of which could have significant consequences for workers' mental health and overall well-being. This is particularly evident when these devices are employed as algorithmic management tools to monitor workers' performance and productivity,[5] as also highlighted by the recent decision of the French Data Protection Authority (Commission nationale de l'informatique et des libertés (CNIL)). The CNIL indeed fined *Amazon France Logistique* EUR 32 million for its excessive surveillance practices in two distribution centres, which were deemed to violate several provisions of the General Data Protection Regulation (GDPR). These practices involved, among others, requiring workers to use scanners that collected real-time data concerning the speed of task execution, idle time, and latency time.[6] Having said that, similar considerations can be made about wearables and other (digital) technologies that are intended to enhance workers' health and safety.[7]

In light of the above, this chapter sets out to conduct an exploratory study of the use of wearables that are *specifically* designed for OHS monitoring, and the legal implications it entails.[8] Despite the rapid advancements in this technology, this topic has garnered limited attention.[9] This contribution, therefore, intends to address this

5. On the topic, *see, e.g.*, Aude Cefaliello & Miriam Kullmann, 'Offering False Security: How the Draft Artificial Intelligence Act Undermines Fundamental Workers Rights' (2022), 13(4) European Labour Law Journal 542, 559 https://doi.org/10.1177/20319525221114474; EU-OSHA, 'Artificial Intelligence for Worker Management: An Overview' (Report, 2022), 20 ff. and 71; Alex J. Wood, 'Algorithmic Management: Consequences for Work Organisation and Working Condition' (European Commission, 2021), 9-11; Phoebe V. Moore, 'Data Subjects, Digital Surveillance, AI and the Future of Work' (European Parliamentary Research Service, 2020), 24-25.
6. Commission nationale de l'informatique et des libertés (CNIL), Délibération de la formation restreinte n°SAN-2023-021 du 27 décembre 2023 concernant la société AMAZON FRANCE LOGISTIQUE. For a commentary on the decision *see* Stefania Marassi & John Bolte, 'Leveraging Data Protection Law for Protecting Workers' Fundamental Right to Health and Safety in the Workplace: the Amazon Case' (2024), 10(2) International Labor Rights Case Law 263-268, https://doi.org/10.1163/24056901-10020021 and Michele Molè, 'Minimised Work Surveillance Exists under the GDPR: Amazon France and the DPA Sanction', Global Workplace Law & Policy, 4 March 2024, https://global-workplace-law-and-policy.kluwerlawonline.com/2024/03/04/minimised-work-surveillance-exists-under-the-gdpr-amazon-france-and-the-dpa-sanction/.
7. *See, e.g.*, Aída Ponce Del Castillo & Michele Molè, 'Worker Monitoring vs Worker Surveillance: The Need for a Legal Differentiation', in Aida Ponce Del Castillo (ed.), Artificial Intelligence, Labour and Society (ETUI, 2024), 164-165; EU-OSHA, 'Smart Digital Monitoring Systems for Occupational Safety and Health', *supra* n. 4, 34-39; EU-OSHA, 'Artificial Intelligence for Worker Management: Implications for Occupational Safety and Health' (Report, 2022), 8 ff.
8. The use of wearable devices for efficiency monitoring (e.g., Amazon handheld scanners) is outside the scope of this contribution. However, a brief reference to these devices will be included in section §9.02 to provide context to the types of devices that are specifically developed to be used for OHS monitoring.
9. For an exception *see, e.g.*, EU-OSHA 'Smart Digital Monitoring Systems for Occupational Safety and Health', *supra* n. 4. Legal literature has also started examining the use of wearables as self-tracking devices in the context of corporate wellness programs and the data protection implications: *see, e.g.*, Philippa Collins & Stefania Marassi, 'Is That Lawful? Data Privacy and Fitness Trackers in the Workplace' (2021) 37(1) International Journal of Comparative Labour Law and Industrial Relations 65 https://doi.org/10.54648/ijcl2021003; Céline Brassart Olsen, 'To Track or Not to Track? Employees' Data Privacy in the Age of Corporate Wellness, Mobile Health, and GDPR' (2020) 10(3) Int'l Data Privacy L. 236-252 https://doi.org/10.1093/idpl/ipaa004; Bart

gap in the academic and European Union (EU) policy debate, which has primarily revolved around the data protection and OHS legal challenges posed by digital technologies when employed as algorithmic management tools to, for instance, monitor workers' performance and productivity.[10]

In doing so, first, it provides a comprehensive overview of different types of wearables currently being researched or already available in the market as well as their applications in the field of OHS and the way they collect and analyse data. Given the limited legal literature on the subject, this part draws on literature from different fields of study such as electrical engineering, OHS, and information technology.[11]

Second, it identifies and examines the main legal challenges stemming from the deployment of wearables for OHS monitoring from two legal angles and the corresponding European regulatory frameworks: on the one hand, the EU Framework Directive 89/391/EEC, as these devices could be viewed as tools for safeguarding workers' health and safety in the workplace, thus aligning with the employer's duty of care obligations under this regulatory instrument, while also introducing new OHS risk factors; on the other hand, the GDPR as the use of such devices may lead to infringements of workers' data protection rights. In this respect, this contribution focuses on the principle of lawfulness and the principle of purpose limitation, which will be used to illustrate how the deployment of wearable technology for OHS monitoring may raise questions regarding compliance with data protection law.

§9.02 WEARABLE TECHNOLOGY

[A] Definition and Classification

Wearables are smart, portable, electronic devices that are body-worn (on, near, or in the human body) or attached to/embedded in garments or other clothing accessories

---

Custers & Helena Ursic, 'Worker Privacy in a Digitalized World under European Law' (2018) 39(2) Comp. Lab. L. & Pol'y J. 323; Kirstie Ball, 'Electronic Monitoring and Surveillance in the Workplace' (Publications Office of the European Union, Luxembourg, 2021), 25; Moore, 'Data Subjects, Digital Surveillance, AI and the Future of Work', *supra* n. 5, 21-23.

10. *See, e.g.*, Aude Cefaliello, Phoebe V. Moore & Robert Donoghue, 'Making Algorithmic Management Safe and Healthy for Workers: Addressing Psychosocial Risks in New Legal Provisions' (2023) 14(2) European Labour Law Journal 192-210 https://doi.org/10.1177/20319525231167476; Valerio de Stefano & Mathias Wouters, 'AI and Digital Tools in the Workplace Management and Evaluation: An Assessment of the EU's Legal Framework' (European Parliamentary Research Service, Study, 2022); Eurofound, 'Employee Monitoring and Surveillance: The Challenges of Digitalization' (Publications Office of the European Union, Luxembourg 2020); Antonio Aloisi & Elena Gramano, 'Artificial Intelligence is Watching You at Work: Digital Surveillance, Employee Monitoring and Regulatory Issues in the EU Context' (2019) 41(1) Comp. Lab. L. & Pol'y J. 95; Custers & Ursic, *supra* n. 9.

11. *See, e.g.*, John Howard et al., 'Advanced Sensor Technologies and the Future of Work' (2022) 65 Am J Ind Med. 3 https://doi.org/10.1002/ajim.23300; Ekaterina Svertoka et al., 'Wearables for Industrial Work Safety: A Survey' (2021) 21(11) Sensors 3844; Jayden Khakurel, 'Tapping into the Wearable Device Revolution in the Work Environment: A Systematic Review' (2018) 31(3) Information Technology & People 791 https://doi.org/10.1108/itp-03-2017-0076; Patel et al., *supra* n. 1.

(e.g., footwear).[12] They integrate different types of sensors to detect and measure (indoor) environmental parameters, for instance, chemical, and physical agents such as hazardous substances and ultraviolet (UV) radiation, and/or the wearer's physiological parameters (e.g., heart rate, breathing rate, brain activity, perspiration, blood pressure, skin temperature, etc.), biomechanical parameters (movement and activity with inertial measurement units) as well as position (e.g., with GPS).[13]

Different classifications of wearables have been made in literature, for instance, based on their applications, functions, and placement.[14] This contribution uses the position of the device to distinguish between two main categories: (a) 'body-worn' wearables, including 'on and near body' and 'in body' devices, and (b) wearables affixed to or embedded in clothing or clothing-related accessories (smart wearable textile).

[1] Body-Worn Wearables: 'On and Near Body'

Not only there is noticeable research on devices that are worn by a worker on the body or as an (external) accessory to it, but several devices have also already been commercialized and have made their way into the workplace. Three main clusters can be distinguished depending on the body segment on which the wearable is placed: (a) head/ear-mounted devices; (b) wrist-worn and handheld devices; and (c) upper/lower/full-body devices. This distinction, however, is not always clear-cut as for some workplace applications wearables form a 'sensor system',[15] where different sensors are placed on different parts of the body at the same time.

Concerning the first cluster, smart eyewear, which includes augmented and virtual reality (AR and VR)[16] smart glasses, smart contact lenses,[17] headsets, head-mounted displays, and smart helmets, is an example of wearable technology that businesses in sectors such as logistics, aviation, aerospace, and transportation have

---

12. To the authors' knowledge, legal literature has not addressed the definition of wearable. However, the term wearable has been defined in scholarly writings of other disciplines (e.g., data science, electrical engineering): *See, e.g.*, Khakurel, *supra* n. 11, 792.
13. This classification/distinction is drawn from Svertoka et al., *supra* n. 11, 5.
14. *See, e.g.*, Elena Stefana et al., 'Wearable Devices for Ergonomics: A Systematic Literature Review' (2021) 21 Sensors 777, 2 https://doi.org/10.3390/s21030777; Aleksandr Ometov, 'A Survey on Wearable Technology: History, State-of-the-Art and Current Challenges' (2021) 193 Computer Networks 108074, 6 ff. https://doi.org/10.1016/j.comnet.2021.108074; Naghmeh Niknejad, 'A Comprehensive Overview of Smart Wearables: The State of the Art Literature, Recent Advances, and Future Challenges' (2020) 90 Engineering Applications of Artificial Intelligence 103529, 2 https://doi.org/10.1016/j.engappai.2020.103529; Sungmee Park & Sundaresan Jayaraman, 'Wearables: Fundamentals, Advancements, and a Roadmap for the Future', in Edward Sazonov (ed.), *Wearable Sensors: Fundamentals, Implementation and Applications* (Academic Press: Cambridge, MA, USA, 2020) 10-11.
15. Stefana et al., *supra* n. 14, 13.
16. For an in-depth analysis of AR and VR, *see* Jeffrey M. Hirsch, 'Future of Work' (2020) 3 University of Illinois Law Review 889, 901-906.
17. Suranga Seneviratne et al., 'A Survey of Wearable Devices and Challenges' (2017) 19(4) IEEE Communications Surveys & Tutorials 2573, 2584 (e.g., Google Glass and Google Contact Lenses) https://doi.org/10.1109/comst.2017.2731979.

already started to use.[18] Devices like AR and VR smart glasses and head-mounted displays can be used to enhance safety and productivity. For example, in warehouses, they can provide information on how to handle packages based on their content taking into account toxicity, fragility, inflammability, etc. As they allow workers to remain hands-free while performing their tasks, they can also be useful in reducing mistakes, speeding up work production processes, and, more in general, monitoring occupational productivity for quantity, speed of action, and quality performance purposes. Moreover, they can provide on-site virtual training and deliver instructions on how to perform complicated tasks[19] or handle hazardous situations in the workplace.[20]

Research is also been carried out on the use of personal exposure monitoring devices, aka exposimeters, or badges that are mounted or clipped on the worker's (fore)head. In this regard, personal dosimeters can quantify the accumulated dose of, *inter alia*, personal ultraviolet (UV) exposure, especially for outdoor workers like farmers, seafarers, and construction workers.[21] Furthermore, potential applications of earwear in the workplace (e.g., earables like in-ear electroencephalography (EEG) devices and ear-moulded plugs that can estimate core body temperature) are being investigated too as these devices could provide useful insights on, for instance, the level of (office) workers' attention and occupational heat strain.[22]

As to the second cluster, wrist-worn devices (e.g., smart watches, wrist bands, activity trackers) and handheld devices (e.g., gloves and ring barcode scanners) have not only drawn the attention of scholars of different disciplines (e.g., sociology, electrical engineering) but have also started finding experimental and real context applications in the workplace.[23] By way of example, handheld devices are already widespread in the retail, manufacturing, logistics, and e-commerce (warehouses) sectors where businesses deploy them to optimize production processes and workflows.[24]

The potential of using such wrist-worn devices for OHS applications is also evident. In this respect, for instance, research is being conducted on the use of wrist-worn devices for environmental sensing: UV exposimeters and dosimeters embedded in wristbands are illustrative examples of wearables that can measure individual exposure to, respectively, light or physical hazards like vibration and noise.[25] At the same time, companies have started deploying fitness trackers in the

18. Future Today Institute (FTI), 'Tech Trends', 173, 177, 298; Patel et al., *supra* n. 1, 11-12.
19. *See, e.g.*, EU-OSHA, 'Smart Digital Monitoring Systems for Occupational Safety and Health', *supra* n. 4, 26-27; Richard A. Bales & Katherine V.W. Stone, 'The Invisible Web at Work: Artificial Intelligence and Electronic Surveillance in the Workplace' (2020) 41(1) Berkeley J Emp & Lab L 1, 8-9; Phoebe V. Moore, 'The Mirror for (Artificial) Intelligence: In Whose Reflection?' (2019) 41 Comp. Lab. L. & Pol'y J. 47, 63-64 https://doi.org/10.2139/ssrn.3423704; Patel et al., *supra* n. 1, 11-12.
20. Hirsch, *supra* n. 16, 904.
21. *See, e.g.*, Alois W. Schmalwieser, 'Review on Occupational Personal Solar UV Exposure Measurement' (2021) 12 Atmosphere 142 https://doi.org/10.3390/atmos12020142.
22. FTI, *supra* n. 18, 297; Notley et al., *supra* n. 1, 876.
23. For a list of commercially available products *see* Seneviratne et al., *supra* n. 17, 2574 ff.
24. Patel et al., *supra* n. 1, 9.
25. Svertoka et al., *supra* n. 11, 9; Patel et al., *supra* n. 1, 5.

workplace as part of corporate wellness programs. Legal literature and news reports point to a widespread practice in American companies, which attempt to promote healthy lifestyle habits by monitoring different physiological parameters of their workforce.[26]

Regarding the third and last cluster, upper/lower/full body wearables include a wide range of devices that can be worn on the trunk, and upper and lower extremities (limbs).[27] These have a wide range of OHS applications, for example, monitoring vital parameters, detecting awkward postures, assisting workers in heavy lifting tasks, and measuring personal exposure to dangerous substances in the workplace. OHS studies and industry reports point to several examples of research being conducted on this category of wearables and several real-life applications: chest straps that monitor workers' vital signs to tackle stress at work;[28] IMU sensors placed in different body segments (e.g., back and shoulders of construction workers) that capture and analyse real-time movement and muscle activity to detect ergonomic hazards;[29] upper, lower, or full-body exoskeletons (e.g., in the form of safety vests, exosuits) that serve as lift aids in heavy handling tasks in the manufacturing industry;[30] and miniaturized as well as heavier and bulkier personal exposure monitors that can measure in real-time and continuously workers' personal exposure to hazardous substances such as coal dust and particulate matter (also called airborne particles).[31]

[2] Body-Worn Wearables: 'In Body' Devices

'In-body' devices can be applied to the surface of the skin, either adhered to it or tattooed (electronic epidermal wearables), placed through/underneath the skin (electronic transdermal wearables), or inserted in the human body (implantable/

26. *See, e.g.*, Moore, 'Data Subjects, Digital Surveillance, AI and the Future of Work', *supra* n. 5, 21-23.
27. Hands are excluded in the upper extremities sub-category as they are included in the wrist-mounted and hand-held devices. Moreover, the category 'upper/lower/full body wearables' also includes wearables that can be clipped on – or attached with velcro to – clothes, e.g., tags that track and detect personnel in real-time (e.g., Zebra dart tag, or AeroScout T2 Wi-Fi Active RFID tag: information available athttps://vandrico.com/wearables/device/aeroscout-t2-wi-fi-active-rfid-tag.html, accessed on 1 February 2024), or devices that measure personal exposure (e.g., Sunsprite personal light tracker, which measures the wearers' light exposure: information available at https://vandrico.com/wearables/device/sunsprite-personal-light-tracker.html, accessed on 1 February 2024).
28. *See, e.g.*, Katie Scott, 'BNP Paribas Uses Wearable Technology to Help Staff Tackle Physical and Mental Stress', Employee Benefits (23 May 2019, 6 am), https://employeebenefits.co.uk/bnp-paribas-wearable-technology-stress/.
29. *See, e.g.*, DorsaVi, ViSafe, *Creating Safer Workplaces Through Wearable Sensor Technology* (2017), available at https://www.dorsavi.com/wp-content/uploads/2020/12/dorsaVi-myViSafe-Brochure-US-A806.A.pdf (accessed on 1 March 2024).
30. On exoskeletons, *see, e.g.*, EU-OSHA, 'The Impact of Using Exoskeletons on Occupational Safety and Health' (Discussion paper, 2019); Ifeoma Ajunwa, 'Algorithms at Work: Productivity Monitoring Applications and Wearable Technology' (2018) 63 St Louis U LJ 21, 40.
31. On personal exposure monitors *see, e.g.*, American Industrial Hygiene Association (AIHA), 'The Future of Sensors: Protecting Worker Health Through Sensor Technologies' (2016) 62.

ingestible).[32] These devices, some of which require a medical procedure to be inserted into the human body (e.g., microchips), are capable of measuring and monitoring a wide array of physiological and bio-mechanical (movement, posture) parameters depending on the purpose for which they are being used.

The use of in-body devices is spreading out in the healthcare industry.[33] In the world of work, the pace at which this tech advancement is unfolding is not as fast as in the medical sector. Yet, there are studies from different fields on the (potential) use of electronic epidermal wearables (e.g., skin patches) and ingestible pills for OHS monitoring.[34] Some products have started to be commercially available for use in the workplace too.[35] In particular, OHS scholars have started investigating and reporting the benefits that temperature-sensing capsules (ingestible pills) and skin patches may have for protecting the health and safety of workers who are exposed to extreme temperatures (e.g., firefighters).[36] Recently, EU-OSHA has also indicated that electronic epidermal wearables (e.g., skin patches) could become a promising sensing technology in the health and safety field.[37]

Additionally, a few businesses have begun experimenting with microchipping their employees already starting from 2004, when the news reported that the Mexican Government implanted 160 of its officials for access control in a department with sensitive data.[38] Since then, a few American and European tech-savvy companies and start-ups have made headlines by giving the possibility to employees to have passive radio frequency identification (RFID) microchips implanted underneath their skin between the thumb and the forefinger to log on to their computer, swipe into the company's premises (or restricted areas) without a badge, pay in vending machines, and print.[39] It is in this context that this tech development has drawn the attention of

32. This contribution follows the literature strand that includes in-body sensor devices in the category of wearables: *see, e.g.*, Ometov et al., *supra* n. 14, 7-8 and Svertoka et al., *supra* n. 11, 5.
33. *See, e.g.*, Yali Zheng et al., 'Wearing Sensors Inside and Outside of the Human Body for Early Detection of Diseases', in Edward Sazonov (ed.), *Wearable Sensors: Fundamentals, Implementation and Applications* (Academic Press: Cambridge, MA, USA, 2020) 94-99.
34. *See, e.g.*, Sara Amendola et al., 'UHF Epidermal Sensors: Technology and Applications', in Edward Sazonov (ed.), *Wearable Sensors: Fundamentals, Implementation and Applications* (Academic Press: Cambridge, MA, USA, 2020) 151-152.
35. *See, e.g.*, Patel et al., *supra* n. 1, 9; Christopher Legner, 'Sweat Sensing in the Smart Wearables Era: Towards Integrative, Multifunctional and Body-Compliant Perspiration Analysis' (2019) 296 Sensors and Actuators 200, 212-213 https://doi.org/10.1016/j.sna.2019.07.020.
36. *See, e.g.*, Howard et al., 'Advanced Sensor Technologies', *supra* n. 11, 6-7; Juri Taborri et al., 'Preventing and Monitoring Work-Related Diseases in Firefighters: A Literature Review on Sensor-Based Systems and Future Perspectives in Robotic Devices' (2021) 18(18) Int J Environ Res Public Health. 9723, 6-7 https://doi.org/10.3390/ijerph18189723.
37. EU-OSHA, 'Smart Digital Monitoring Systems for Occupational Safety and Health', *supra* n. 4, 13, 19-20.
38. Dario A. Rodriguez, 'Chipping in at Work: Privacy Concerns Related to the Use of Body Microchip (RFID) Implants in the Employer-Employee Context' (2019) 104 IOWA L. REV. 1581, 1599; European Parliament, 'The Use of Chip Implants for Workers' (Study for the EMPL Committee, 2017).
39. For examples, *see* European Parliament, 'The Use of Chip Implants for Workers', *supra* n. 38, 16-18.

legal scholars, policymakers, and legislators.[40] OHS applications could be envisaged for these implantable too, for instance, to protect workers' health and safety by limiting access to dangerous areas of a company.[41]

[3] Smart Wearable Textile

Smart textile, also known as e-textile or smart garment, is a rapidly evolving sensing technology[42] that includes conductive fabrics or sensors embedded directly into clothing (e.g., shirts, pants) or other accessories (e.g., insoles, belts, shoes, socks, boots) through different types of fabric manufacturing techniques such as knitting, weaving, embroidery, printing, coating.[43] Thanks to their ability to sense the user and the environment, smart textiles can monitor physiological (e.g., heart rate, temperature, sweat, and especially its biomarkers), bio-mechanical (e.g., motion, pressure, bending, twisting), and environmental parameters (e.g., dangerous gases such as ammonia). Some e-textiles also have sensory and haptic applications and are therefore also able to dynamically respond and adjust to changes that occur in the surroundings (e.g., environmental conditions like the presence of a dangerous chemical gas) and in the wearer (moisture in sweat).[44] For example, smart thermoregulating t-shirts can autonomously activate cooling functions when the wearer is warm and sweet.[45] Smart compression, heating, or electrical stimuli are additional examples.[46]

E-textile holds promising applications in various fields and industries, from sports and fitness to healthcare, fashion, space, and defence.[47] This has sparked a wave of interest from European institutions, researchers, and manufacturers. The research and use of smart textiles in the workplace for OHS monitoring is still in its infancy.[48] However, the progress made in the above fields may pave the way to smart garment

---

40. *See, e.g.*, Seili Suder & Merle Erikson, 'Microchipping Employees: Unlawful Monitoring Practice or a New Trend in the Workplace?', in Martin Ebers & Marta Cantero Gamito (eds), *Algorithmic Governance and Governance of Algorithms:* Data Science, Machine Learning, and Law 1 (Springer 2021); Custers & Ursic, *supra* n. 9, 326-327; European Parliament, 'The Use of Chip Implants for Workers', *supra* n. 38; Rodriguez, *supra* n. 38, 1604 ff.
41. Suder & Erikson, 'Microchipping Employees', *supra* n. 40, 81-82.
42. The market for e-textiles will be worth over USD 1.3 billion by 2031, information available at: https://www.idtechex.com/en/research-report/e-textiles-and-smart-clothing-2021-2031-technologies-markets-and-players/828 (accessed on 10 March 2024).
43. For a definition of smart textile, *see* Matteo Stoppa, 'Wearable Electronics and Smart Textiles: A Critical Review' (2014) 14 Sensors 11957, 11958 https://doi.org/10.3390/s140711957; Howard et al., 'Advanced Sensor Technologies', *supra* n. 11, 6.
44. Seneviratne et al., *supra* n. 17, 2580-2581.
45. For an example, *see* Heiq Smart Temp, available at https://www.heiq.com/products/textile-technologies/heiq-smart-temp-thermoregulation/ (accessed on 10 March 2024).
46. Howard et al., 'Advanced Sensor Technologies', *supra* n. 11, 6.
47. For examples of smart wearable textiles in different sectors, *see* Mukherjee, *supra* n. 2, 12; FTI, *supra* n. 18, 228; Anna Knack et al., 'Digital Age: Wearable devices: Implications of Game-Changing Technologies in Services in Europe' (Eurofound Working Paper, 2019) 18.
48. Research has been already conducted on the design and development of smart clothing and smart footwear for some occupations, for instance, first emergency responders (e.g., firefighters), construction workers, and fishermen. On first emergency responders *see* PROETEX February 2006-January 2010, http://www.proetex.org/, and Tanja Radu et al., 'Wearable Sensing Application: Carbon Dioxide Monitoring for Emergency Personnel using Wearable

applications in different industrial and non-industrial working environments. Some manufacturers have started marketing products that find – or could find – applications in different occupations.[49] Also, some scholars have started highlighting that the sensing capacity of this technology could open up opportunities to monitor and protect workers' health and safety.[50] By way of example, chemical/gas sensors embedded in a garment or footwear could detect toxic chemical gases that can have serious health consequences for workers in different industries (e.g., firefighters, cleaning personnel), for example, carbon dioxide (CO_2) and ammonia (NH_3).[51] Along similar lines, location and movement sensors incorporated in safety shoes and insoles could provide information about the position of lone workers who are in need because, for instance, they have fallen.

[B] Wearable Data Processing

Wearables gather real-time and continuously a wide range of raw data, which are then usually transferred/streamed (e.g., wirelessly or using Bluetooth technology) to a paired device (e.g., a smartphone) or the cloud for further analysis.[52] Machine learning algorithms can be used to process the dataset and the information analysed is then translated into an understandable and actionable format for the worker or whoever needs, or would like to, have access to it, e.g., a site manager, or an OHS professional. In this regard, wearables (or the paired application on the smartphone) can trigger (visual, auditory, haptic) alert signals and provide real-time feedback and coaching on how a worker has to perform a work-related task.[53] Additionally, summary reports about workers' exposure to an occupational risk factor (e.g., graphical representations of the percentages of high or low-risk postures – squatting or stooping – among the workforce) can be automatically produced at the end of the day or a work session and viewed in (cloud-based) dashboards on computer desktops.[54]

Sensors' (2009) 3(10) Int J Electron and Commun Eng. 1794, 1797; on construction workers, *see* Stefana et al., *supra* n. 14, 9 ff.; on fishermen, *see* Seneviratne et al., *supra* n. 17, 8.

49. An example is XSole PTI insoles, https://traxxs.net/en/#solutions (accessed on 10 March 2024).
50. *See, e.g.*, Howard et al., 'Advanced Sensor Technologies', *supra* n. 11, 7, and Isacco Gualandi et al., 'Textile Chemical Sensors Based on Conductive Polymers for the Analysis of Sweat' (2021) 13 Polymers 894, 1 https://doi.org/10.3390/polym13060894.
51. Howard et al., 'Advanced Sensor Technologies', *supra* n. 11, 6; Seungse Cho et al., 'Smart Electronic Textiles for Wearable Sensing and Display' (2022) 12(14) Biosensors 222, 7-8 https://doi.org/10.3390/bios12040222.
52. Svertoka et al., *supra* n. 11, 9; Senevirtate et al., *supra* n. 17, 2597; Khakurel, *supra* n. 11, 792.
53. For examples, *see* Timothy Fort et al., 'The Angel on Your Shoulder: Prompting Employees to Do the Right Thing Through the Use of Wearables' (2016) 14 Nw. J. Tech. & Intell. Prop. 139, 148-150; Sol Lim & Clive D'Souza, 'A Narrative Review on Contemporary and Emerging Uses of Inertial Sensing in Occupational Ergonomics' (2020) 76 International Journal of Industrial Ergonomics 102937, 11 https://doi.org/10.1016/j.ergon.2020.102937; Stefana et al., *supra* n. 14, 10-12, 15.
54. For an example of a cloud-based dashboard in an off-the-shelf wearables see the belt-mounted wearable Reflex that is used for biomechanical analysis of workers' movement, information available at https://www.wearkinetic.com/injury-reduction/ (accessed on 10 March 2024).

By way of example, the wearable device DorsaVi ViSafe is an off-the-shelf wearable that can be used to detect and monitor workers' movement. To do so, it integrates mini-sensors that are positioned on the workers' lower back and shoulders and that gather data related to the workers' motion and muscle activity. The device uses Bluetooth technology to transmit real-time motion data to a compatible application in a smartphone or tablet. Data are synchronized to the cloud and can be seen on a computer dashboard. DorsaVi ViSafe provides real-time visual alert signals as well as instant and continuous feedback to workers on a paired application on the smartphone. Workers can view a colour-coded graph displaying how much time in percentages they have spent in one of the three-movement risk zones (low, moderate, high movement risk one) as well as a colour-coded heat map showing how risky the movements they are doing are for parts of the body where the wearable sensors are placed. When their movement risk is classified as 'high', workers can view a video that displays how to carry out the task with correct movements.[55]

[C] OHS Applications

Wearable technology presents novel opportunities to protect workers' health and safety. Specifically, these devices can be used to protect workers' (and visitors') safety by preventing and mitigating (imminent) risks (e.g., falls, human-machine collisions, road traffic accidents) whose occurrence could result in work-related accidents and, particularly, fatal or nonfatal injuries. To do so, they measure and monitor a wide array of worker and environment-related parameters depending on the purpose and can alert workers of (imminent) dangers to their physical safety. Three examples can illustrate how wearables could contribute to protecting workers' physical safety in the workplace.

First, in high-risk occupations such as construction, various types of (biomechanical) sensors (e.g., stretch, strain, and inertial sensors) can be embedded in workers' clothing or directly affixed to the skin to detect falls and near falls by analysing the wearer's movement and human body strain (e.g., bending).[56] Second, smart caps can be used to measure and detect workers' fatigue as well as send alert signals when the worker is too fatigued and this could result in occupational accidents. This is done by collecting and analysing workers' physiological parameters that are proxies of fatigue, such as brain waves, heart rate variability, and breathing patterns. This is particularly relevant in industry sectors where fatigue is a workplace hazard as workers work long hours, often in poor and stressful working conditions, taking

55. Information available at DorsaVi, myViSafe, App User Manual, available at https://help.dorsavi.com/wp-content/uploads/sites/9/2022/03/GD4577-DS-myViSafe-App-User-Manual-INT-A5 37.F10.pdf (accessed on 2 November 2024).
56. Harish Chander, 'Wearable Stretch Sensors for Human Movement Monitoring and Fall Detection in Ergonomics' (2020) 17 Int. J. Environ. Res. Public Health 3554, 2 https://doi.org/10.3390/ijerph17103554.

insufficient rest (e.g., transportation, construction, manufacturing, and mining).[57] Third, wearables that can track workers, visitors, and assets' location using real-time location systems (e.g., GPS) can be used to impede access to restricted and/or hazardous areas (e.g., nuclear plants), alert workers of the proximity of sources of danger such as operating equipment (e.g., forklifts and pallet jacks),[58] locate the exact position of lone and remote workers (e.g., in the mining sectors)[59] and detect areas in the company where there is a high concentration of hazardous agents (e.g., chemical in oil and gas industry), the so-called hotspot detection.

Furthermore, wearables can play an increasingly important role in protecting workers against the development of occupational diseases, i.e., 'any disease contracted as a result of an exposure to risk factors arising from work activity'.[60] To do so, they can measure and monitor a wide range of the wearer's physiological parameters and, as a result, produce a (quick) assessment of a worker's health status and risk as well as provide him/her with direct feedback on how to change the way the tasks are executed.[61] Also, they can serve as early warning systems.

By way of example, there is noticeable research on the use of wearables to assess biomechanical risks that could lead to musculoskeletal disorders (MSDs). This is traditionally done with observations of the worker while he/she performs the tasks.[62] Using different types of sensors (e.g., stretch and inertial sensors), wearables can now monitor real-time the wearer's movement as well as provide a direct, *ex ante* assessment of the ergonomic risks, and on-the-spot feedback and training to the worker (e.g., through vibrations)[63] on how to modify the way the tasks are carried out.[64]

Also, wearables can be used to assess workers' personal UV exposure in addition to traditional tools and methods such as UV protective clothes, surveys, questionnaires, and sun habit diaries. In this respect, research studies are being conducted on the use of polysulphone film (PSF) badges (e.g., VioSpor) worn, for example, on the workers' back, and electronic UV monitoring dosimeters (e.g., Scienterra) mounted on hats and headbands. These devices can quantify the personal solar UV exposure of outdoor workers in sectors like agriculture (e.g., farmers, winegrowers, seafarers, workers working in greenhouses), construction, and transportation (e.g., flight pilots).[65]

57. N.R. Adão Martins et al., 'Fatigue Monitoring Through Wearables: A State-of-the-Art Review' (2021) 12 Front. Physiol. 790292, 2 https://doi.org/10.3389/fphys.2021.790292.
58. Patel et al., *supra* n. 1, 7-8.
59. Rodriguez, *supra* n. 38, 1594.
60. Protocol of 2002 to the Occupational Safety and Health Convention of International Labour Organization (ILO) (Art. 1(b)).
61. For an example, *see* Patel et al., *supra* n. 1, 7.
62. Ranavolo Alberto et al., 'Wearable Monitoring Devices for Biomechanical Risk Assessment at Work: Current Status and Future Challenges – A Systematic Review' (2018) 15 Int. J. Environ. Res. Public Health 2001, 2 https://doi.org/10.3390/ijerph15092001.
63. For an example, *see* Patel et al., *supra* n. 1, 18.
64. Alberto et al., *supra* n. 62, 2; Stefana et al., *supra* n. 14, 13-15.
65. Schmalwieser, *supra* n. 21.

§9.03 WEARABLES' OHS MONITORING: BENEFITS, RISKS AND LEGAL IMPLICATIONS FROM AN OHS AND DATA PROTECTION PERSPECTIVE

The integration of wearables in the workplace for OHS monitoring can be seen as a double-edged sword. On the one hand, it offers employers new opportunities to mitigate occupational risks, thus aligning with the duty of care obligation to guarantee a healthy and safe working environment as laid down in European and national legislations (e.g., Framework Directive 89/391/EEC). Yet, on the other hand, it has the potential to introduce new OHS risk factors and bring about concerns regarding the respect of workers' data protection rights due to the extensive collection, combination, and analysis of (personal) data, particularly when utilizing AI-driven analysis techniques. These are two sides of the same coin that are challenging to reconcile. The following two sub-sections will delve into these two perspectives.

[A] Wearables' OHS Monitoring as a *Means* to Protect Workers' Health and Safety

Literature and policymakers have started acknowledging that wearable technology holds significant benefits for workers:[66] these devices could be used as a *means* to guarantee a healthy and safe working environment, thereby complementing existing instruments and methods (e.g., observations, breathing zone sampling), some of which are beginning to be viewed as inaccurate, too subjective and slow.[67] In particular, traditional methods and instruments to identify, assess, and monitor OHS hazards and risks are usually based on quantitative, but *ex post*, analysis of samples (e.g., of air contaminant) in laboratories, or on subjective techniques such as observations on how workers perform their tasks (e.g., in ergonomics).

In comparison, wearables present new opportunities: they conduct real-time, continuous, and remote measurements and monitoring, enabling employers to adopt direct, on-the-spot, OHS intervention strategies, be it, for instance, alerting workers that they are exposed to noise exposure levels that exceed a certain threshold or coaching them on the correct posture, ergonomically-wise, to manually handle heavy loads or keep prolonged positions. Having said that, however, it is unclear whether, and to what extent, employers could introduce wearable technology within the current EU regulatory framework.

---

66. For instance, *see* OECD, 'Using AI in the Workplace: Opportunities, Risks and Policy Responses' (OECD Artificial Intelligence Papers, March 2024, No. 11), 6; OECD, 'Using Artificial Intelligence in the Workplace: What Are the Main Ethical Risks?' (Report, 2022), 35; EU-OSHA, 'Artificial Intelligence for Worker Management: Implications', *supra* n. 7, 14 ff.; EU-OSHA, 'Smart Digital Monitoring Systems for Occupational Safety and Health', *supra* n. 4, 18 ff.; Rafael Zorzenon et al., 'What is the Potential Impact of Industry 4.0 on Health and Safety at Work?' (2022) 153 Safety Science 105802; Stefano & Wouters, *supra* n. 10, 6 ttps://doi.org/10.1016/j.ssci.2022.105802.
67. *See, e.g.*, John Howard, 'Artificial Intelligence: Implications for the Future of Work' (2019) 62 Am J Ind Med. 917, 920 https://doi.org/10.1002/ajim.23037.

The EU OHS acquis is based on the principle of prevention.[68] In this respect, employers need to continuously take steps and measures to prevent and reduce occupational risks:[69] as part of a company's OHS management, employers need to assess the occupational risk factors (e.g., extreme temperatures, noise, vibrations, UV radiations) that can affect workers' health and safety,[70] and based on this evaluation, they then need to adopt preventing measures (e.g., encasing a noisy machine).

Article 5(1) Framework Directive 89/391/EEC embodies this principle, setting forth, broadly, the employers' general duty of care towards workers, namely 'a duty to ensure the safety and health of workers in every aspect related to the work'.[71] As for what employers need to do to fulfil this duty, Article 6(1) reads that '[w]ithin the context of his responsibilities, the employer shall take *the measures necessary* for the safety and health protection of workers (...)'. Necessary measures are, according to AG Mengozzi, those measures that are '*appropriate and sufficient* for that purpose [protecting workers' health and safety]'.[72]

The content of the measures needs to be derived from the general principles of prevention laid down in Article 6(2) Framework Directive 89/391/EEC,[73] including the principle of the hierarchy of control measures to prevent and reduce occupational risks. According to this principle, employers' primary goal is to eliminate occupational hazards. This could take place by, for instance, physically removing them (e.g., not using a noisy machine), thereby reducing the risk to zero, or replacing a dangerous substance or process with a non-dangerous or less dangerous one. When elimination or substitution is not possible, employers need to manage and minimize the residual risk by introducing control and protective measures. In order of priority, these include engineering control measures (e.g., general ventilation, installing barriers to prevent access to dangerous areas), administrative (organizational) control measures (e.g., limiting the time workers spend in a noisy working environment), collective (e.g., ventilation systems) and personal protective measures (e.g., masks, helmets, safety shoes).

Could (or should) then wearables be considered necessary measures that employers need to put in place to protect workers' health and safety, also in line with the principle of hierarchy of control measures? This is a question that legal literature has yet to explore in depth and that needs to be subject to further research.[74] A few initial

68. *See* Art. 1(1), Council Directive of 19 June 1989 on the introduction of measures to encourage improvements in the safety and health of workers at work (89/391/EEC), 29 June 1989, No. L184/1.
69. The notion of prevention in the Directive includes 'all the steps or measures taken or planned at all stages of work in the undertaking to prevent or reduce occupational risks' (Art. 3(d) Framework Directive 89/391/EEC).
70. Articles 6(1) and 9(3) Framework Directive 89/391/EEC.
71. On the broad formulation, *see* Case C-127/05, *Commission v. United Kingdom* [2005] ECLI: EU:C:2007:338, Opinion of AG Mengozzi, ECLI:EU:C:2007:30, para. 118.
72. *Ibid.*, para. 103 [italics by the authors].
73. Opinion of AG Mengozzi in *Commission v. United Kingdom, supra* n. 71, paras 101 and 107; *see also* Edoardo Ales, 'Occupational Health and Safety: a European and Comparative Legal Perspective', in André den Exter (ed.), *European Health Law* (Maklu Press Antwerp, 2017) 50.
74. However, EU-OSHA has begun to explore this subject and suggests that wearables could play a significant role in the risk assessment process mandated on employers under the current EU OHS

considerations can be made: while it is difficult to view wearables as measures that eliminate or substitute a source of occupational risks or as engineering and administrative measures, these devices could serve to monitor the effectiveness of the measures implemented by the employer.[75] For instance, suppose that local exhaust ventilation systems (engineering control measures) are put in place to reduce the risk of exposure to chemical agents. Wearables could be used to measure real-time the level of workers' exposure, potentially combining it with workers' location data. The information retrieved could trigger a twofold OHS intervention by the employer: first, workers could be promptly alerted when the level of exposure reaches a defined threshold and invited to wear personal protective equipment (PPE) (e.g., a respiratory mask); second, the information regarding the inadequacy of the control measure could lead to the selection of a more appropriate response to the occupation hazard in question.

[B] Wearables' OHS Monitoring as a *Source* of OHS Risks and Potential Breaches of Workers' Data Protection Rights

The use of wearables for OHS monitoring introduces novel risks and challenges from both an OHS and data protection standpoint. Specifically, similar to other digital technologies (e.g., cobots, AI-powered recruitment software, etc.),[76] wearables may present OHS risk factors that can endanger workers' physical safety and health as well as mental health.

Given their nature – they are electrical devices, equipped with batteries and sensors – the use of such devices can pose potential risks to workers' physical safety in the event of malfunction.[77] This could occur, among others, in case of battery failure, when the device overheats and catches fire, or when it is not (fully) waterproof.[78] Additionally, workers' physical health may be compromised too when the wearable

regulatory framework. *See* EU-OSHA, 'Smart Digital Monitoring Systems', *supra* n. 4, 25. For a criticism on this approach, *see* Ponce del Castillo & Molè, *supra* n. 7, 163-165.

75. EU-OSHA, 'Artificial Intelligence for Worker Management: Implications', *supra* n. 7, 14.
76. On the topic, *see, e.g.*, Cefaliello, Moore & Donoghue, *supra* n. 10; Maciej Jarota, 'Artificial Intelligence in the Work Process. A Reflection on the Proposed European Union Regulations on Artificial Intelligence from an Occupational Health and Safety Perspective' (2023) 49 Computer Law & Security Review 105825, 2-3 https://doi.org/10.1016/j.clsr.2023.105825; Adrián Todolí-Signes, 'Making Algorithms Safe for Workers: Occupational Risks Associated with Work Managed by Artificial Intelligence' (2021) 27(4) Transfer: European Review of Labour and Research 1, 4 ff. https://doi.org/10.1177/10242589211035040; European Parliament, Health and safety in the workplace of the future (Briefing requested by EMPL committee 2019); Phoebe V. Moore, 'The Threat of Physical and Psychosocial Violence and Harassment in Digitalized Work' (International Labour Office, Geneva, 2018) 2-15; EU-OSHA, 'Artificial Intelligence for Worker Management: Implications', *supra* n. 7, 8 ff.; EU-OSHA, 'Foresight on New and Emerging Occupational Safety and Health Risks Associated Digitalisation by 2025' (European Risk Observatory, Report, 2018), 46-64.
77. *See, e.g.*, EU-OSHA, 'Foresight on New and Emerging Occupational Safety and Health Risks', *supra* n. 76, 54 on smart PPE.
78. EU-OSHA, 'Smart Digital Monitoring Systems for Occupational Safety and Health', *supra* n. 4, 35; Howard et al., 'Advanced Sensor Technologies', *supra* n. 11, 4-5; EU-OSHA, 'Foresight on New and Emerging Occupational Safety and Health Risks', *supra* n. 76, 48.

intended to mitigate a specific OHS risk does introduce new ones. For instance, studies carried out by EU-OSHA indicate that exoskeletons can help prevent MSDs. At the same time, however, their use can lead to the occurrence of other MSD risk factors as they may exert pressure on other parts of workers' bodies. Also, they could cause skin irritation, increased cardiovascular load, and injuries in case of malfunctioning, *inter alia*.[79]

Furthermore, the use of wearables introduces OHS risk factors that could have significant consequences for workers' mental health. Studies on the topic have primarily focused on risk factors that are prevalent in digital (AI-powered) technologies that are used for algorithmic management purposes. In this respect, literature and European policy documents have identified several psychosocial risk factors capable of inducing stress, anxiety, and depression among workers. Examples encompass work intensification, potential breaches of privacy rights, fear of discriminatory uses by the employer, constant and continuous oversight, and erosion of workers' autonomy.[80] By way of example, devices such as smart gloves and hand-held scanners deployed in warehouses and logistic centres monitor workers' productivity by tracking the amount of work and the pace at which workers are required to perform their tasks. This may lead to workers feeling pressed to perform as fast as they can, thus increasing the pace of work and heightening workplace stress.[81] The same can be said for smart eye devices (like VR/AR head-mounted devices) that are used as on-the-spot training instruments.[82]

Having said that, recent studies conducted by EU-OSHA have started to underline that new smart OHS monitoring systems, including wearable technology, do present alike risk factors. By way of example, while being an advantage compared to conventional OHS instruments, real-time measurements imply a constant and extensive collection and (AI-powered)analysis of (personal) data that may lead to a potential violation of workers' data protection rights, a factor that could contribute to anxiety and stress.[83] Specifically, from a data protection perspective, the use of these devices raises several questions. As mentioned in the introduction of this contribution, the

79. EU-OSHA, 'Smart Digital Monitoring Systems for Occupational Safety and Health', *supra* n. 4, 34; EU-OSHA, 'Foresight on New and Emerging Occupational Safety and Health Risks', *supra* n. 76, 48; Jarota, *supra* n. 76, 2.
80. Cefaliello & Kullmann, 'Offering False Security', *supra* n. 5, 559; Todolí-Signes, *supra* n. 76, 4-9; Stefano & Wouters, *supra* n. 10, 43-44; EU-OSHA, 'Foresight on New and Emerging Occupational Safety and Health Risks', *supra* n. 76, 55; EU-OSHA, 'Artificial Intelligence for Worker Management: An Overview', *supra* n. 5, 13-15.
81. European Parliament, 'Addressing AI Risks in the Workplace: Workers and Algorithms (Briefing, 2024), 3; Moore, 'The Threat of Physical and Psychosocial Violence and Harassment', *supra* n. 76, 11.
82. Phoebe V. Moore, 'OSH and the Future of Work: Benefits and Risks of Artificial Intelligence Tools in the Workplace', in Vincent G. Duffy (ed.), *Digital Human Modeling and Applications in Health, Safety, Ergonomics and Risk Management. Human Body and Motion* (Springer International Publishing 2019) 301-302.
83. EU-OSHA, 'Foresight on New and Emerging Occupational Safety and Health Risks', *supra* n. 76, 57; EU-OSHA, 'Smart Digital Monitoring Systems for Occupational Safety and Health', *supra* n. 4, 36-38. *See also*, Ponce del Castillo & Molè *supra* n. 7, 162-164.

GDPR principles of lawfulness and purpose limitation are used to illustrate these concerns.

First, assuming that wearables process workers' personal (sensitive) data, it is unclear what legal basis under the GDPR an employer could invoke to use wearable technology to monitor its workforce's health and safety at work.[84] Regarding consent, for example, data protection and labour law scholars as well as data protection authorities have consistently stated that, with a few limited exceptions, it is not the desirable legal ground to use in an employment context given the inherent power imbalance between employers and employees.[85] When it comes to wearable technology, this has been asserted also about the use of implantables (microchips) and fitness trackers in the workplace.[86]

However, could consent be used (in combination with another legal basis) as a permissible legal ground to process workers' data for 'benign' reasons, namely when there are benefits for the workers such as safeguarding them from the occurrence of accidents and diseases in the workplace?[87] This is a particularly relevant question as wearables, among other OHS monitoring technologies (e.g., drones, cobots), have the potential to enhance and personalize the level of protection. In this regard, one can think about wearables that are used for proximity detection, namely, they track workers' location to warn them of the immediate proximity to dangers such as moving machinery, or those that monitor health-related metrics (e.g., skin/core body temperature and heart rate variability) to alert outdoor workers of the potential risk of heat strokes.

Second, it is unclear under the GDPR how employers could deploy wearables for monitoring OHS, while at the same time complying with the principle of purpose limitation. This principle seeks to limit the data controller's use of the gathered and processed personal data and make sure that data are not processed and used beyond what a data subject could reasonably expect.[88] Thus, what remains within a data subject's reasonable expectation when wearables are utilized for the specific purpose of protecting his/her health and safety?

84. Regulation (EU) 2016/679 of the European Parliament and of the Council of 27 April 2016 on the protection of natural persons with regard to the processing of personal data and on the free movement of such data, and repealing Directive 95/46/EC (GDPR) (Text with EEA relevance) (OJ L 119 4.05.2016, p. 1, Arts 6 and 9).
85. Custers & Ursic, *supra* n. 9; Art. 29 Data Protection Working Party (WP 29), 'Opinion 2/2017 on Data Processing at Work', Adopted on 8 June 2017, 17/EN, WP 249, 6-7, 23; European Data Protection Board (EDPD), 'Guidelines 05/2020 on Consent under Regulation 2016', Adopted on 4 May 2020, 9.
86. Custers & Ursic, *supra* n. 9. Autoriteit Persoonsgegevens (Dutch Data Protection Authority), AP: Verwerking gezondheidsgegevens wearables door werkgevers mag niet (8 March 2016), https://autoriteitpersoonsgegevens.nl/nl/nieuws/apverwerking-gezondheidsgegevens-wearables-door-werkgevers-mag-niet (accessed on 10 March 2024); WP 29, 'Opinion on Data Processing at Work', *supra* n. 85, 17-18.
87. On the topic of consent and micro-chipping employees, *see, e.g.*, Suder & Erikson, 'Microchipping Employees', *supra* n. 40, 76 ff.
88. WP 29, 'Opinion 03/2013 on Purpose Limitation', Adopted on 2 April 2013, 00569/13/EN, WP 203, 11; Olsen, *supra* n. 9, 240.

Businesses might use these devices to safeguard employees from a specific OHS risk and, as a result, adopt intervention strategies consistent with the original purpose such as implementing new working protocols to reduce the OHS risk and using early warning signs. Yet, at the same time, they might obtain information about workers' performance, behaviour, a health conditions that go beyond the original purpose of the data processing. This may also lead to employers 'abusing' the extra information gathered and making management decisions (e.g., dismissal, promotions) to the detriment of less productive or healthy employees.[89] For example, wearables that detect and measure UV exposure could provide information about how many breaks workers take in indoor environments, so indirectly giving an insight into workers' behaviour and potential productivity. Likewise, monitoring sleep parameters using an actigraphy worn on the wrist may be relevant in the transport industry to evaluate the recovery of long-haul drivers and avoid (fatal) injuries due to accidents. Nevertheless, these devices may also give information concerning sleep disorders (e.g., sleep apnea) that are unknown to the individuals.

§9.04 CONCLUSIONS

This contribution aimed to explore the use of wearable technology in the workplace for OHS monitoring, mapping out the type of devices currently being researched and off-the-shelf solutions as well as identifying their applications and functioning. Also, it intended to identify the main legal implications of deploying such technology in the workplace from two distinct perspectives: OHS and data protection.

Undoubtedly, wearables designed for OHS monitoring are making their way into the world of work. The examples are numerous: devices worn 'on the body' like earables, placed 'in the body' like smart patches or integrated into working garments like boots and insoles. Their sensing capacity enables the measurement of a wide variety of metrics related to the worker and/or the environment, thereby enabling employers to monitor real-time and continuously their workforce's safety and health status.

It is contended that wearables have the potential to improve the protection of workers' health and safety, particularly as tools that could complement existing traditional OHS monitoring methods and instruments. Their deployment in the workplace may therefore be in line with the employers' obligation to secure a safe and healthy working environment under the existing EU regulatory framework. In this regard, wearables could function as an added layer of OHS preventive measures; for example, they could serve as early warning signals prompting workers to take decisions that could save their lives such as breaks when heat strain is reaching a defined threshold.

Nonetheless, due to the large amount of data processed, the potential repercussions for workers' data protection rights cannot be overlooked. In this respect, this

89. John Henniger, 'Wearable Technology and Employer Wellness Programs: Gaps and Solutions' (2018) 12 OHIO St. Bus. L.J. 197, 201.

contribution has identified that under the GDPR, the extent to which employers have a legal basis to introduce such devices in the workplace is unclear and requires further guidance. Also, even considering the potential benefits of this technology, it remains unclear how to draw a line between the OHS-related purpose used by employers for introducing such devices in the workplace, and the (potential) misuse that could be made of the information retrieved. Along similar lines, the use of wearables could lead to new OHS risk factors, which employers are mandated to identify and assess in the risk assessment process under the current EU-OHS regulatory framework.

A complex and challenging legal dilemma hence comes to the forefront. Employers must ensure a safe and healthy working environment and employees have a fundamental right to health and safety at work. To what extent do we then allow technologies that can – or have the potential to – ensure more effective and individualized protection of workers' health and safety if this benefit may come to the detriment of data protection rights and the emergence of other OHS risk factors? In other words, could we argue that OHS monitoring justifies a 'relaxation' of workers' data protection rights?

Unlike scenarios in which wearables are used for electronic performance monitoring, the core issue here lies in the balance between, on the one side, employers' responsibility and liability to guarantee a safe and healthy working environment and workers' fundamental right to health and safety at work, and, on the other side, workers' fundamental rights of data protection and health and safety at work, the latter put at risk by new OHS risk factors brought about by the use of wearable technology. The EU-OHS regulatory framework and the GDPR provide different lenses through which to examine this subject. Their response to whether, and if so to what extent, wearables' OHS monitoring is/should be allowed, may differ too. Further research is therefore needed to shed light on how to carry out the delicate balancing exercise between workers' rights and interests and employers' responsibilities and managerial prerogatives.

CHAPTER 10

Subsidiarity and Technology: The Case of Remote and Platform Workers

Julia López López

§10.01 THE PRINCIPLE OF SUBSIDIARITY AS A DISTRIBUTIVE AND COOPERATIVE PRINCIPLE

The principle of subsidiarity has a determining role – one that is not only regulatory but also political – in the distribution of competences in the different areas of the organization of labour relations both at the international level and in national social law. At the international level, the subsidiarity-based defence of the individual against state interference, to the extent that proves to be compatible with broadly established objectives, has been a classic interpretation that has been strongly defended by some authors.[1] In a crucially important institutional matter, at the international level, the role of the international human rights courts plays a very important role in the debates on the principle of subsidiarity in the defence of cooperative models between the different actors.[2]

However, at the level of the European Union (EU), the subsidiarity principle stands as one of the keys to the organization of relations between the Union and the Member States.[3] From the perspective of the EU, the bases regarding this point are found in Article 5, paragraph 3 of the Treaty on EU and Protocol 2 on the principle of subsidiarity and proportionality, which deals with competences that are not exclusive to the EU and in circumstances in which the member countries cannot achieve the

1. Carozza, P., https://scholarship.law.nd.edu/law_faculty_scholarship/564.
2. *See* Iglesias, M., Subsidiarity and International Human Rights Courts: Deference to States or Cooperative Division of Labor?, Derecho PUCP, Revista de la Facultad de Derecho 79, 2017, 191-222.
3. Sciarra, S., Solemn Hearing 2023 Recourse to and Discourse on the European Convention: An Asset for Democracies, Strasbourg, 27 January 2023, European Court of Human Rights.

Community objectives; in these cases, the EU intervenes proportionally to guarantee these objectives.[4] One of the most complex aspects of the application of the subsidiarity principle is the monitoring of compliance with the objectives by the different actors and levels of management.[5] Within these international and EU debates on the principles of organization of the system of sources and distribution of management powers, which affect in a way the handling of labour relations, it is interesting to focus on how the subsidiarity principle has shaped the impact that technology has had as an element of the definition of employment relations and labour rights, taking as a reference of remote work and platform work. Technology has gone from being simply an instrument of work to being more broadly an indicator of inclusion or not within a certain status of the employment relationship. As a consequence, technology and the way its new capabilities are handled serve to define the conditions and labour rights through which the system of sources and principles in the organization of employment relationships can be traced. The multilevel structure of the system of sources for the organization of employment relationships[6] and the combination of hard and soft law is one of the main characteristics of the current regulation of labour law.[7] In this line, the Parliament Resolution of 24 June 2021 – on the adequacy of European regulations and subsidiarity and proportionality – affirms that digital innovation is advancing rapidly and that it is necessary to take into account for the future that the rules reflect digital innovation, without prejudice to the principles of application of the principles of subsidiarity and proportionality.

§10.02 LABOUR STATUS AND TECHNOLOGY: REMOTE WORK AND FRAMEWORK AGREEMENT

Remote work is the first form of employment that should be analysed when studying how technology defines labour status and how regulatory actors distribute competencies based on subsidiarity and proportionality. The pandemic produced an increase in remote labour relations that has been stabilizing, with a pattern that differs by sector and company, as reported in the data.[8] The increase in the number of forms of remote work, in its different versions, has prompted the need for a legal and regulatory treatment that builds on different patterns of reference regarding the arrangement of the system of sources. In this sense, the ordering role of the subsidiarity principle that implements mechanisms of participation of the different multilevel actors presents in

4. *See* Craig, P. (2004), Competence: Clarity, Conferral, Containment and Consideration. *ElRev*, 29, 323.
5. *See* Tilyndite, L., Subsidiarity: Mechanisms for Monitoring Compliance European Parliamentary Research Service, July 2028. Bogg, A. (2016). Subsidiarity or Freedom of Association? A Perspective from Labor Law. *American Journal of Jurisprudence*, 61(1), 143-174 https://doi.org/10.1093/ajj/auw007.
6. *See* Prassl, J., The Interaction of EU Law and National Law: Between Myth and Reality, in Bogg, A., Costello, C. & Davies, ACLO Research Handbook on EU Labour Law (2016), Elgar, pp. 42-64.
7. *See* Falkner, G., et al., Complying with Europe. EU Harmonization and Soft Law in the Members States, CUP, 2005.
8. Eurofound, 'Telework in the EU: Regulatory Frameworks and Recent Updates', 2022.

the case of remote work a complex reality of sources encompassing both conventional and other legal sources that are also governed by the principle of proportionality.

A relevant starting point at the EU level involves how the telework management rules are structured through a framework agreement. In 2002, the European Trade Union Confederation (ETUC), the Union of Industrial and Employers' Confederations of Europe (UNICE)/the European Association of Craft, Small and Medium-Sized Enterprises (UEAPME) and the European Centre of Enterprises with Public Participation (CEEP) signed a framework agreement on telework 'in order to provide greater security for employed teleworkers in the EU'. The aim of the agreement was to develop a general framework at the European level for the working conditions of teleworkers and to reconcile the common needs of employers and employees for flexibility and security. The basis of the European telework agreement is to recognize the same overall protection as for workers working on company premises.

The Agreement defines remote work on two axes, technology and the location factor. The remote worker uses technology and performs his work outside the company's premises. The Agreement structures the organization of remote work on the principle of the voluntariness of remote status and the right to equality and non-discrimination for the workers involved. The Framework Agreement on remote work develops, in addition to the principles of regulation at the EU level, a set of rights and working conditions for these workers.

Among other fundamental rights is the respect for the private life of the worker that must be guaranteed by the reasonableness and proportionality of the firms' means of surveillance of the worker. The employer has the responsibility to facilitate, instal and maintain the necessary equipment for teleworking. With a basis in the principle of subsidiarity, the agreement provides for the employer's responsibility, under national law and collective agreements, for the costs arising from the loss or damage of equipment and data used by the teleworker. With regard to health law and its management, in the Agreement the employer is responsible for ensuring health and safety at work. The Agreement refers to the Community level of subsidiarity with reference to Directive 89/391/EEC and the specific directives as well as to national laws and relevant collective agreements. The agreement stipulates that the employer, workers' representatives and the competent authorities will have access to the telework site, within the limits set out in the laws and collective agreements of the member countries. The occupational health of teleworkers is thus guaranteed at the Community level by the Directives and by the Framework Agreement with specific reference to the role of standards and collective agreements at the level of the member countries. It is very interesting to see how the Agreement integrates the Community Directives within the system of sources of management of this form of employment and how collective bargaining is developing different models at the national level with very different characteristics but with a common element, namely the emphasis on consensus as a principle of management of labour relations.[9]

9. *See* on the different models of collective bargaining, Liukknune, U. (ed.), Collective Bargaining in Labour Law Regimes, A Global Perspective, Springer, 2020.

The irradiation of the contents of the Framework Agreement on telework has served to develop, with different models at the level of the member countries, the regulation of remote work. If we take as a reference the *Spanish* case, as in the Framework Agreement, the technological and locational elements vertebrate the regulation that is defined in Articles 1 and 2 of the norm as 'that work at a distance that is carried out by means of the exclusive or prevalent use of computer, telematic and telecommunication means and systems, understanding by prevalent that it is at least 30% of the working time'. There are therefore three elements that make up this employment relationship, the locational, the technological and the quantitative.

Of the principles and rights included in the Framework Agreement, the Spanish model of regulation (as is also the case in other member countries) incorporates the right to equal treatment and non-discrimination for remote workers in its Articles 4 and 5. Thus it is established that 'companies are obliged to avoid any discrimination, direct or indirect, particularly on grounds of sex, age, seniority or professional group or disability, of remote workers'. As a key instrument in the elimination of discrimination, companies are obliged, in their equality policies, to take into account remote workers in the diagnosis, implementation, application, follow-up and evaluation of equality measures and plans. Spanish legislation specifically includes the obligation of companies to apply measures against sexual harassment, harassment based on sex, harassment for discriminatory reasons and harassment in the workplace. As part of the equality and non-discrimination policies, Spanish legislation on the development of telework recognizes the right to equality and non-discrimination in the reconciliation of work and personal life.

The Spanish norm of development of remote work establishes a series of guarantees for the worker that are established through a very formalized contract, with content established in the norm or in accords and collective bargaining agreements. It is a question of guaranteeing the rights of workers through a minimum obligatory content – including among other matters an inventory of the means, equipment and tools that the development of remote work demands – the enumeration of expenses as well as form of quantification of the compensation that obligatorily the company must pay and the moment and form for said payment. The role of collective bargaining agreements is very relevant in this matter. The modification of the conditions established in the remote work accord, including the percentage of attendance, must be the object of an agreement between the company and the employee, formalized in writing prior to its application. This modification is to be made known to the legal representation of the workers.

The right to equality and non-discrimination, which, as we have seen, was one of the keys to the negotiated organization of conditions for telework established in the EU, was complemented by the principle of voluntariness, which, like the aforementioned right, has been developed by the member countries. Thus, in the *Spanish* case, Article 5 of the law establishes that remote work will be voluntary for the worker and for the employer, with the formulation established in the agreement for the implementation of remote work. The realization of remote work can be agreed from the moment of conclusion of the contract or subsequently and the principle of voluntariness or agreement also governs the reversibility of this form of work. In this sense, remote working is reversible for both the company and the workers, and the implementation and reversibility processes, as established in the regulations of the *Spanish* case, are based on negotiation.

The regulation develops, within its treatment of labour rights and working conditions, important contents such as, among others, the right to have a time record and digital disconnection as a limitation on the use of technological means of business and work communication during rest periods within the maximum duration of the working day. This stipulation is linked to the workers' rights to health and rest.

The right to occupational health is enshrined within the fundamental rights of remote workers, connected on the one hand, with the agreed working time conditions and on the other hand with the worker's right to privacy and intimacy. Data protection is reinforced by Spain's Organic Law 3/2018, of 5 December, on Personal Data Protection and the guarantee of digital rights, in accordance with the principles of suitability, necessity and proportionality of the means used. According to the terms of this law, the company shall be obliged in the use of its powers of control and surveillance of remote workers to respect the consideration of their dignity and take into account, where appropriate, their personal circumstances, such as the concurrence of a disability.

The Spanish legal standard includes and develops the principle of consensus or negotiation, which was already established as a procedure in the European Framework Agreement, to establish or make use of the employment relationship of remote workers for personal reasons of the teams.

The company must take into account the social uses of such means and the particularities of remote work while also guaranteeing the implementation of digital disconnection. The latter right, as a company policy, must be specified following a prior hearing of the workers' representatives in order to achieve a reasonable use of the technological means and to eliminate computer fatigue.

The principle of subsidiarity which is at the core of the organization of remote work presents some very original and specific characteristics because it is the Framework Agreement of the year 2000 which has served as a reference for the models of development of this form of work which experienced its explosion somewhat later, in the context of the pandemic. The subsidiarity principle is also present, as a basis for their hybrid element, in mixed forms of employment that are legally defined, for example, in the *Spanish* case when the remote component is less than 30% of working time. Equality and non-discrimination, as well as voluntariness, are components of the EU organization of this type of work that radiates to the organization of remote work at the level of the member countries with different contents and manifestations of this principle. The key is that from the communitarian level, remote work has an origin of regulation in a Framework Agreement that has acted as a ground of regulation in the member countries that adopt its basic principles of voluntariness and non-discrimination. The principles of subsidiarity and proportionality frame this process of conversion of conventional norms in the EU to legal development norms and agreements within the member countries. It is interesting to see how the configuration by collective bargaining is inserted in the general framework of study and analysis of the competences of the different actors in the organization of the locational and technological element in employment relations from subsidiarity, proportionality and consensus.

The regulation of remote and platform work has been taken up in different countries of the EU with different models. Belgium, Croatia, Greece, Malta, Portugal and Spain have modified their legislation to implement the Platform Working Directive with a specific interest in the control of Artificial Intelligence as will be seen in the *Spanish* case below.[10]

§10.03 SUBSIDIARITY AND PLATFORM WORKERS: THE IMPLEMENTATION OF THE PRINCIPLES OF REGULATION OF THIS FORM OF WORK THROUGH THE DIRECTIVE

A second case to be taken into account in examining the forms of employment that combine remote workplaces and technology is platform jobs. The regulation of this form of employment presents, as in the case of remote workers, a complex multilevel network that makes it necessary to frame the debates from a standpoint that incorporates the principles of subsidiarity and proportionality. More than 28 million people in the EU work in platform jobs and the forecast is that this figure will rise to 43 million by 2025.[11]

On 8 February 2024, the Proposal for a Directive of the European Parliament and of the Council on improving the working conditions of workers in digital platforms was approved. As with telecommuting, the specificity of this type of work and the precarious situation of these workers has justified an EU regulation implemented through the application of the principle of subsidiarity, in this case through a Directive.

The points of reference of this Community intervention at the level of regulation of this form of work – as stated in the explanatory memorandum of the EU regulation – is to comply with the sustainability objectives set out in Article 3 of the Treaty on EU[12] and to fight against 'social exclusion and discrimination as well as to promote social justice and protection and equality between women and men', to promote solidarity between generations and to generate 'economic, social and territorial cohesion and solidarity between Member States'.

The definition of principles and minimal floor rights for platform workers is set out in the Charter of Fundamental Rights of the EU, which must be applied when EU

10. https://www.eurofound.europa.eu/en/resources/article/2024/regulatory-responses-algorithmic-management-eu.
11. https://www.consilium.europa.eu/es/policies/platform-work-eu/.
12. Article 3.3 of the Treaty 'The Union shall establish an internal market. It shall work for the sustainable development of Europe based on balanced economic growth and price stability, a highly competitive social market economy, aiming at full employment and social progress, and a high level of protection and improvement of the quality of the environment.'

rules are implemented at the level of the member countries. The Charter of Fundamental Rights has played a role in the system regulating sources of employment relationships, including those of platform workers. The contents of rights and principles that are to be developed through the principle of subsidiarity are found, among other places, in Article 8 of the Charter which states that everyone has the right to the protection of personal data, in Article 12 of the Charter on the right to freedom of peaceful assembly and freedom of association at all levels, in Article 16 on the freedom of enterprise and in Article 21 of the Charter on the right to equality and non-discrimination. Article 27 of the Charter protects the right of workers to information and consultation in the enterprise. Under Article 31 of the Charter of Fundamental Rights of the EU, every worker has the right to just and fair working conditions which respect his or her health, safety and dignity.

The EU level therefore guarantees, through the Charter of Fundamental Rights and the Community Directives, a series of labour rights for remote workers and regarding platform workers, through the principle of subsidiarity and proportionality, minimum rights that must be applied by the member countries in order to achieve the Community's objectives.

Along with the hard law standards at the EU level, it is significant to note the multiple mentions in the European Pillar of social rights, (principle 5) on the right of workers - regardless of their type of contract or duration, to fair and equitable treatment in terms of working conditions with access to social protection and training in accordance with the law and collective bargaining agreements; on rights to information on their working conditions (principle 7) as well as the right of workers to be informed of the reasons for dismissal and to be given a reasonable period of notice before dismissal and the right of workers (principle 10) to a high standard of working conditions (principle 7) and the right of workers to be informed of the reasons for dismissal and to be given a reasonable period of notice before dismissal (principle 10) and to a high level of occupational health and safety protection and to the protection of their personal data in the context of employment.

Moving down to the level of secondary legislation, EU law has regulated platform work through the new Directive trying to respond to the fact that 'when platforms operate in several Member States or across borders national authorities do not have easy access to data on digital platforms, such as the number of persons performing platform work, their employment status or their working conditions'.

The Community regulation enshrines several principles: first, the principle of participation and information for workers in the implementation of the use of automated monitoring and decision-making systems affecting their recruitment and their working conditions. Second, it prohibits the use of automated monitoring systems for the processing of some personal data of those who work for digital platforms, such as biometric data or data on the emotional or psychological state of these people. Third and finally, the decisions to be made in an automated way must be evaluated by individuals. Among other points, the Directive on transparent and predictable working conditions[13] provides for measures aimed at protecting the working conditions of persons in atypical employment relationships, recognizing the right to receive information, probationary periods, minimum predictability of work and measures for on-call contracts.

The Directive on platform workers introduces the right to information and consultation on artificial intelligence, breaking the asymmetries that occur on this issue between workers and companies.[14]

This Directive presents several important interactions with a series of more specific Directives including the following: The mention of Directive (EU) 2023/970 of the European Parliament and of the Council of 10 May 2023 reinforcing the application of the principle of equal pay for equal work or work of equal value for men and women through pay transparency measures and enforcement mechanisms;[15] Directive 2003/88/EC of the European Parliament and of the Council on working time;[16] Directive 2008/104/EC on temporary agency work[17] as well as those relating to occupational health, temporary duration of contracts, part-time work and secondment. These interactions have been of decisive importance, carrying many specific implications. In the field of social protection, the regulations on the coordination of national social security systems apply to both employees and self-employed persons working through platforms in cross-border situations. All these norms create a constellation of references to define labour rights for platform workers.

However, it is important to complete the regulatory frame at the international level, the Convention No. 135 (1971) of the International Labour Organization (ILO) concerning Workers' Representatives, currently ratified by twenty-four Member States, states that workers' representatives may be trade union or non-union, workers' representatives may be persons recognized as such under national law or practice, either trade union representatives, i.e., representatives appointed or elected by the trade unions or their members, or elected representatives, i.e., representatives freely chosen by the workers of the undertaking, in accordance with the provisions of national laws or regulations or collective agreements; or elected representatives, i.e., representatives freely chosen by the workers of the undertaking in accordance with the provisions of national laws or regulations or collective agreements, and whose functions do not extend to activities that are recognized in the country as the exclusive prerogative of trade unions. This Convention specifies that, where there are both union representatives and elected representatives in the same enterprise, such representation shall not be used to undermine the positions of the unions concerned or their representatives, and that cooperation between the elected representatives and the unions concerned or their representatives should be encouraged.

13. Directive 2019/1152 of the European Parliament and of the Council of 20 July 2019 on transparent and predictable working conditions in the EU, OJEU L 2019-81159.
14. Adams-Prassl, J., et al. (2023), Regulating Algorithmic Management: A Blueprint. *European Labour Law Journal*, 14(2), 124-151 https://doi.org/10.1177/20319525231167299.
15. 'OJEU' No. 132 of 17 May 2023.
16. (OJ L 299 of 18.11.2003).
17. (OJ L 327 of 5.12.2008).

Member States have ratified ILO Convention No. 98 (1949) on the Right to Organize and Collective Bargaining, according to which measures which tend to encourage the formation of workers' organizations dominated by an employer or an employers' organization, or to support workers' organizations financially or otherwise, with a view to placing such organizations under the control of an employer or an employers' organization, are considered acts of interference against which ILO Member States must protect workers' organizations.

§10.04 SPANISH DEVELOPMENT REGULATIONS: PRESUMPTION OF LABOUR AND PLATFORM WORK

The regulation of the technological factor in employment relations, as has been argued in this chapter, has had an impact, among other aspects, on the status of platform workers, with the *Spanish* case being a model that includes participation as a key principle in the regulation of this form of work. However, Spanish management of this regulatory terrain enters fully into the protection of these workers through the presumption of employment that is included in the regulation.

Thus, Spain's Workers' Statute[18] has been amended to introduce a new letter d) in Article 64.4, with the following wording: 'To be informed by the company of the parameters, rules and instructions on which the algorithms or artificial intelligence systems that affect decision-making that may affect working conditions, access to and maintenance of employment, including profiling, are based.' Also, a new twenty-third provision is introduced, with the following wording on the presumption of labour in the field of digital delivery platforms, establishing that 'by application of the provisions of Article 8.1 of the Workers' Statute, it is presumed to be included within the scope of this law the activity of persons who provide paid services consisting of the delivery or distribution of any consumer product or merchandise, by employers who exercise the business powers of organization, management and control directly, indirectly or implicitly, through the algorithmic management of the service or working conditions, through a digital platform'.

The analysis of employment relationships that combine the locational element with the technological one presents a series of common characteristics on the one hand and differential ones on the other, but above all, they are today, in the current framework of digitized labour relations, an example of the hybridization of factors identifying the type of employment.

§10.05 THE HYBRIDIZATION OF EMPLOYMENT MODELS

The principle of subsidiarity and proportionality has been decisive in shaping the role of the different actors in the regulation of increasingly complex remote and platform labour relations with an aspect of interest in this application. The role of collective bargaining for remote workers on the one hand, and the presumption of labour on the

18. Royal Legislative Decree 2/2015 of 23 October.

other hand in the case of platform workers, stand as the most relevant aspects to see the interrelations of the different forms of employment within labour law. Thus, the current development of forms of employment does not allow a simple differentiation between remote work and face-to-face work but, together with the relationships that present the elements of identification required in the different models, face-to-face work has been transformed with greater or lesser intensity in the different cases into hybrid work that combines locational and technological factors. This hybridization of types of work is due in some cases to the very identity of the company or sector, in other cases to labour flexibility and in others to the mechanisms for reconciling family and work life but these convergences challenge all the regulatory systems to adapt principles and rights to the new reality.

CHAPTER 11
Work as a Code: Humanization of Labour in the Robot Age

Simon Taes

§11.01 INTRODUCTION

There is a growing trend of deploying 'smart' or 'autonomous' robots across various industries. For example, autonomous mobile robots in warehouses retrieve goods from racks and deliver them to designated locations or accompany workers by providing on-screen instructions. Smart glasses guide warehouse workers through augmented reality, ensuring efficient and accurate workflows. In manufacturing, robotic arms assemble products with high precision, while in agriculture, autonomous drones and harvesters optimize crop management and harvesting. In healthcare, robots assist in surgeries and routine tasks like medication delivery, and in retail, they manage inventory by scanning shelves and automating restocking. These examples underscore the widespread impact of robotization, which raises significant questions about the future of work and the adequacy of current labour laws.

This increasing appearance of robotization processes has various consequences for the nature of work and raises a broad range of legal questions. This is part of a broader discourse on the impact of emerging technologies in the workplace and represents a continuation of the debate on digitalization and platform work. Within this context, PRASSL already compared humans as a 'service' and algorithms as 'bosses'.[1] This contribution seeks to extend these comparisons by focusing on the meaning of work in a robotized work environment and by arguing that the human element of work cannot be fully encapsulated by a code or a sequence of tasks assigned to or performed

1. J. Adams-Prassl, 'What If Your Boss Was an Algorithm? Economic Incentives, Legal Challenges, and the Rise of Artificial Intelligence at Work', *Comp. Lab. L. & Pol'y J.* 2019, No. 1, 123-153; J. Prassl, *Humans as a Service*, Oxford, Oxford University Press, 2016, 208 p.

by a robot. Additionally, it contends that the debate on digitalization and artificial intelligence (AI) needs to be expanded to include the implications of the human-robot interaction, as specific social and legal issues related to this interaction are often overlooked in the discussions on the implementation and use of new technologies in the workplace.

This contribution aims to explore the implications of robotization for human work and to assess the extent to which labour law is equipped to address these implications. The analysis is structured into three parts. The first section of this contribution concerns the concept of robotization and its impact on the workplace. The second section delves deeper into the implications of the robotized working environment for human work, drawing on the results of research from social sciences. In this section, it is also argued that labour law needs to address these implications. The final section proposes an approach to equip labour law with safeguards to address these implications by examining legislative principles.

§11.02 ROBOTIZATION AND THE EVOLVING HUMAN-ROBOT INTERACTION

Robotization as a phenomenon is subject to a continuously changing technological evolution. It can be defined as *'the innovative automation processes in which human labor is replaced by artificial intelligent physical systems, involving both repetitive and non-repetitive manual and cognitive tasks'*.[2] New technologies push today's robotization processes beyond the automation techniques of the previous century, in which machines repeatedly carried out a process or set of specific actions.

On the contrary, robots nowadays are increasingly becoming more autonomous. This increased autonomy of robots is based on the combination and integration of various AI tools into physical objects that are equipped with sensors, moving arms, grippers, and other physical components.[3] The use of AI allows robots to understand the captured information in their environments by these sensors (cameras, microphones, lasers, etc.). The technological improvement in the field of these sensors enables robots to perceive this information better. The improvement in the fields of actuators adds flexibility and mobility for robots to move and react to the processed information in their environment. Other parts of robots aim to establish and improve the communication between machines and systems. This implies that robotization processes are nowadays designed by means of robots that are more autonomous and mobile. These 'intelligent' robots have the advantage of being more flexible and dynamic, allowing them to be used in multifunctional capacities in workplaces.

Robots that are currently caged in separated environments will increasingly be replaced by mobile robots that operate among and together with workers. In particular, the robots' perception of their surroundings, their improved communication abilities and actions in the physical world strengthen the interaction and collaboration between

2. S. Taes, *Robotisering en arbeidsrecht*, Brugge, die Keure, 2024, 39.
3. *Ibid.*, 43-45.

workers and robots. This implies that the increasing autonomy of robots will have most likely an impact on the decision-making processes and human behaviour in the workplace, as these autonomous robots become more interactive with workers and determine to some extent the organization of work and the actions workers perform in this human-robot interaction. This section explains how this interaction is changing in current robotization processes.

In the past, the human-robot interaction relied typically on a dichotomy between teleoperation (robots being remotely controlled by humans) and supervisory control (humans overseeing autonomous systems and intervening as necessary).[4] The traditional industrial robots were not designed for direct collaboration with human workers.[5] The interaction was rather indirect: the operator gave instructions (a sequence of actions) to the robot and the robot provided information to the operator about its environment, task, and status.

However, this dichotomy becomes outdated in the context of autonomous robots. This means that the interaction between workers and robots changes in relation to the level of autonomy that the robot possesses in terms of their characteristics of programming, remote control, monitoring and collaboration. The level of autonomy a robot impacts, therefore, the communication and interaction with workers. This is demonstrated by the applications of robots leading to various forms of interaction with robots that are currently introduced in workplaces. The interaction between humans and robots becomes more present with the advancements in smart technologies and improved sensors. In essence, three main types of human-robot interaction can be distinguished.

The first type of human-robot interaction concerns the limited interaction that occurs when robots and employees are present in the same work environment simultaneously. In this so-called coexistence between humans and robots, human decision-making is not replaced, and they work on separate tasks.[6] An example of this is social robots that welcome and assist customers or visitors in shops and hospitals.

The second type is the human-robot cooperation, which is characterized by humans and robots sharing the same working environment, as well as a common goal. This cooperation between humans and robots occurs in production processes, in which workers maintain control over the robots and the use of technologies is predominantly based on human activity.[7] This entails that the autonomy of these robots may increase, but they are still used as instruments. This kind of cooperation can arise when the robot mimics the employee's movements or the robot's movements are adjusted in a

4. M. Goodrich & A. Schultz, 'Human-Robot Interaction: A Survey', *Foundations and Trends in Human-Computer Interaction* 2007, 204-205.
5. S. Thrun, 'Toward a Framework for Human-Robot Interaction', *Human-Computer Interaction* 2004, 17.
6. M. De Looze & T. Bosch, 'Mensgerichte Technologie' in: S. Dhondt & E. Dessers (red.), *Robot zoekt collega*, Tielt, Lannoo, 2022, 75; TNO, *Opkomende risico's voor arbeidsveiligheid: werken in dezelfde ruimte als een cobot*, https://publications.tno.nl/publication/34627025/Kpi5oy/TNO-2018-R11463.pdf, 12-13.
7. *Ibid.*

different way by the employee's actions. A clear example of the human-robot cooperation takes place when surgeons are working together with robots to perform operations on their patients.[8]

The third type refers to the human-robot collaboration. This type contains all aspects of cooperative interaction in which physical contact between humans and robots is possible.[9] This type refers to the interaction of robots actively engaging in collaboration with workers and performing tasks alongside them. The robot can dynamically adjust movements and actions to suit the worker and task status. Collaborative robots or cobots are a typical example of this interaction. Cobots aim to work together with a worker and provide assistance to them during the performance of various tasks. In this way, physically demanding and risky tasks can be delegated to the cobot, allowing workers to focus on other tasks to achieve common goals.[10]

Hence, the increased technological capacities and autonomy of robots lead to a strengthening of the interaction and cooperation between humans in diverse ways. This means that the question is not whether workers will interact with robots in the workplace, but rather in what way this interaction between workers and robots occurs in the context of robotization. It can be expected that the increased autonomy of robots may result in increased ways of interactions between robots and workers.

§11.03 HUMAN WORK IN ROBOTIZED WORKPLACES

Robotization and the changing interaction between humans and robots have been the research object in studies from social sciences. In particular, the consequences of robotization for quality of work have been examined in research. This research reveals that it is not evident to make general statements about the exact effects of robotization on the quality of work. The outcomes demonstrate that these effects can be both positive and negative, depending on how the robotization processes are implemented within a particular organization. Robotization can redefine, therefore, the meaning of human labour, as this process leads to a new redistribution of labour between humans and machines by replacing workers' cognitive abilities and physical strength. This section focuses, in other words, on the impact of the human-robot interaction on human labour in the workplace and the shifting role of the workers in the robotized working environment.

For instance, it has been found that robots contribute to reducing physical work pressure, while they can lead to adverse effects on the mental workload due to

8. R. Van Den Hoven Van Genderen, 'Robo Sapiens and Data Protection', *Jusletter IT* 2018, https://juslet-ter-it.weblaw.ch/en/issues/2018/24-Mai-2018/robo-sapiens-and-dat_2fce043b7d.html, 8.
9. TNO, *Opkomende risico's voor arbeidsveiligheid: werken in dezelfde ruimte als een cobot*, https://publications.tno.nl/publication/34627025/Kpi5oy/TNO-2018-R11463.pdf, 13.
10. D. Romero et al., 'Towards an Operator 4.0 Typology: A Human-Centric Perspective on the Fourth Industrial Revolution Technologies', *International Conference on Computers & Industrial Engineering* 2016, 5.

increased work pressure and less decision-making autonomy for workers.[11] This increased mental workload occurs, in particular, when robots impose the work pace on workers who interact and work with them or supervise them continuously when they perform their tasks. The use of wearables or swarm bots in warehouses may illustrate these consequences. These devices can be considered tools that assign tasks to workers and instruct them, among others, to pick up an item and deliver this within a predetermined time period. To achieve this task allocation, these devices have to be able to monitor continuously the location of workers and to process a lot of data of the work organization and the work performance of workers.

In addition, some types of interaction with robots may impact the autonomy and decision-making of workers. Robots are used in some applications as an extension of the worker and do not make any decisions on their own. In other cases, however, workers depend on the information provided by robots or the decisions they make autonomously without any human intervention. These applications limit the decision-making and autonomy of workers because they do not allow decisions that derive from the foreseen work organization in an environment in which all aspects of these robotization processes are connected with each other.[12] This means that, contrary to earlier robotization processes, workers have less control over the robots' movements and actions. However, this changes when robots attain a certain degree of autonomy during their interactions with humans. This changing role of robots in their interaction with humans affects not only robots but also humans themselves. The increasing interaction between humans and robots results in robots taking over some level of human control. Hence, the increased robots' autonomy may lead to decreased workers' autonomy when performing their tasks.[13] Not only does the degree of autonomy of a robot determine how it interacts with a human but also the way it is implemented in the workplace.

Furthermore, research in social sciences illustrates that collaboration with robots can impact the utilization of employees' skills and the meaningfulness of the tasks within their jobs as some tasks are delegated to robots. This means that the part of the tasks performed by workers can be both very simplified or complicated in the interaction with robots. As a result, workers can become under- or overskilled in relation to the required tasks to perform their jobs when robots collaborate with

11. A. Andreeva & G. Yolova, 'On Humanizing Work in the Digital Age' in: M. Rahman, R. Goel, A.P. Gomes & A. Uzzaman (eds), *Redefining Global Economic Thinking for the Welfare of Society*, Pennsylvania, IGI Global, 2022, 184; E. Peruffo, R. Rodriguez Contreras, I. Mandl & M. Bisello, *Game-Changing Technologies: Transforming Production and Employment in Europe*, Luxemburg, Publications Office of the European Union, 2020, 36; M. Douwes, M.A. Huysmans, K.O. Kraan & M.P. De Looze, 'Robotisering en de gevolgen voor arbeidsbelasting en het arbeidsdeskundig vak', *AKC Onderzoekscahier* 2017, No. 21, 21.
12. Y. Vereycken, M. Ramioul & M. Hermans, 'Old Wine in New Bottles? Revisiting Employee Participation in Industry 4.0', *New technology, work, and employment* 2021, 54-57.
13. R. Maslowski, J.D. Vlasblom, J. Rözer & A. Smit, *Robotisering en de kwaliteit van werk: Een kennissynthese,* Den Haag, Sociaal en Cultureel Planbureau, 2021, 65 and 68.

them.[14] A final aspect impacted by the human-robot interaction is the social interactions in the workplace. If workers collaborate with robots, this may result in fewer interactions with their colleagues or supervisors.[15]

To conclude, this section provided a synthesis of the research in social sciences on the potential consequences of robotization and the human-robot interaction in the workplace for human work. This shows that the human-robot interaction has an impact on many aspects of human work and, therefore, alters the meaning of work in the robotized work environment.

§11.04 LABOUR LAW AS A QUEST TO HUMANIZE THE ROBOTIZED WORKPLACE

The transformation of human work through robotization raises legal issues that require some measures of safeguards within labour law. This is demonstrated by the broader debate in legal scholarship on the modernization of labour law, which refers to some legal implications associated with robotization. For instance, FAIOLI considered AI and intelligent machines a third element in the employment relationship, alongside the worker and employer.[16] According to GRAMANO, the mechanization of work processes through new technologies is shifting the traditional legal parameters for defining work relationships.[17] HENDRICKX argued that legal research needs to focus on the implications of robots for the roles of workers and employers in the employment relationship.[18] In this regard, WEISS referred to collaborative robots in the context of Industry 4.0 and to AI systems used in managing employee recruitment, task allocation, controlling work performance, and imposing sanctions for shortcomings.[19]

---

14. International Federation of Robotics, *Robots and the Workplace of the Future*, https://ifr.org/downloads/papers/IFR_Robots_and_the_Workplace_of_the_Future_Positioning_Paper.pdf, 16; European Centre for the Development Of Vocational Training, *Insights into Skill Shortages and Skill Mismatch*, www.cedefop.europa.eu/files/3075_en.pdf, 13; S.K. Parker, 'Beyond Motivation: Job and Work Design for Development, Health, Ambidexterity, and More', *Annual Review of Psychology* 2014, 663 and 670; Sociaal-Economische Raad [Social-Economic Council], *Verkenning en werkagenda digitalisering; Mens en technologie: samen aan het werk*, www.kennisbanksocialeinnovatie.nl/nl/kennis/kennisbank/ser-notitie--verkenning-en-werkagenda-digita-lisering--mens-en-technologie--samen-aan-het-werk/1363/share/email/1363, 71.
15. M. De Looze & T. Bosch, 'Mensgerichte Technologie' in: S. Dhondt & E. Dessers (red.), *Robot zoekt collega*, Tielt, Lannoo, 2022, 68; C. Hinojosa & X. Potau, 'Advanced Industrial Robotics: Taking Human-Robot Collaboration to the Next Level', *Eurofound working paper* 2017, https://euagenda.eu/upload/publications/untitled-150335-ea.pdf, 24.
16. M. Faioli, 'Artificial Intelligence: The Third Element of the Labour Relations' in: A. Perul-Li & T. Treu (eds), *The Future of Work Labour Law and Labour Market Regulation in the Digital Era*, Alphen aan den Rijn, Kluwer, 2021, 177-190.
17. E. Gramano, 'Work Performance and Organisational Flexibility: At the Core of the Employment Contract' in: T. Addabbo et al. (eds), *Performance Appraisal in Modern Employment Relations*, Cham, Palgrave Macmillan, 88.
18. F. Hendrickx, 'From Digits to Robots: The Privacy-Autonomy Nexus in New Labor Law Machinery', *Comparative Labor Law & Policy Journal* 2019, Vol. 40, No. 3, 367.
19. M. Weiss, 'Digitalisation and Basic Principles of Labour Law' in: T. Gyulavári and E. Menegatti, *Decent Work in the Digital Age European and Comparative Perspectives*, Oxford, Hart Publishing, 2022, 21.

Moreover, it has been highlighted before that the integration of AI in workplaces appears to further reinforce technological surveillance by granting access to workers' data and analysing these data with limited human programming.[20] This active analysis of workers' data through technology goes beyond passive surveillance, as it allows one to assess productivity and work performance. This has been noticed already in the context of digital labour platforms that use algorithms to select platform workers who are not subject to performance ratings or supervision by a manager. In this way, technology is increasingly capable of taking over tasks previously performed by a manager.[21] It is not only about the exercise of supervision but also about the automated decision-making concerning employees in terms of their evaluation and analysis of work performance. This automated decision-making by employers occurs increasingly in all aspects of the employment relationship, from recruiting job candidates to managing and dismissing workers.[22] An example of this is data-driven phenomenon of people analytics, which involves processing information about employees to make automated decisions about hiring, promotion, and termination. This enables an increasing number of aspects of the employer's authority executed through technological means. This would result in shifting the responsibility of the employer to algorithms as sophisticated assessment and decision-making systems that cannot always be explained due to the complex combination of data collection and machine learning analyses.

This evolving use of technologies from monitoring to managing workers may imply that the legal concerns related to robotization also shift. The traditional legal concerns about the emergence of robots and machines in the workplaces relate to job displacement due to automation, because these devices can perform a wide array of routine physical labour and transform the nature of work and jobs. As discussed in the previous section, this transformation of work by robotization processes has positive and negative implications for both workers' physical and mental health as the interaction with robots becomes increasingly necessary to perform tasks in the workplace.

As robots become more capable of performing tasks independently by the integration with AI tools, robotization processes nowadays introduce additional legal issues similar to digitalization processes. As mentioned above, robots are increasingly able to monitor workers' activities in the workplace through the collection of a vast amount of data in their surroundings via their sensors.[23] Cameras, microphones and GPS tracking systems, for instance, may enable them to acquire more and faster information about workers. Devices, such as wearables, provide managers with more

20. OVIC, *Closer to Machine: Technical, Social and Legal Aspects of AI*, Melbourne, Office of the Victorian Information Commissioner, 2019, 36.
21. J. Adams-Prassl, 'What If Your Boss Was an Algorithm? Economic Incentives, Legal Challenges, and the Rise of Artificial Intelligence at Work', *Comp. Lab. L. & Pol'y J.* 2019, 123.
22. K. Kellogg, M. Valentine & A. Christin, 'Algorithms at Work: The New Contested Terrain of Control', *Academy of Management Annals* 2020, No. 1, 373-376.
23. E. Bryndin, 'Increase of Safety Use Robots in Industry 4.0 by Developing Sensitivity and Professional Behavioral Skills', *American Journal of Mechanical and Industrial Engineering* 2020, 9.

information on workers' performance and movements that can be used during staff assessments. The use of technology in electronic monitoring impacts the employment relationship as it allows the employer access to more information to monitor and assess the workers' performance more accurately.

This dual capacity means that robots not only gather and process data but also act within the physical world, for instance, by retrieving goods, assembling products, and even interacting with humans in dynamic environments. For this reason, robots cannot be considered merely data processing tools to monitor workers and productivity but are also tools that are physically present in the workplace and perform physical tasks together with workers or not. Unlike purely digital AI tools, autonomous robots are physical entities capable of performing both manual and cognitive tasks that could be carried out by workers. This ability to access and respond to data in real-time, coupled with physical action, distinguishes robots from digital AI-systems.[24] Therefore, the legal issues related to the health and safety risks of interacting with physical machines are combined with the legal issues related to the use of machines for workers' surveillance and assessment. This implies that the legal questions related to automation and digitalization will probably appear cumulatively in the context of robotization. Hence, other measures and safeguards in labour law need to be considered to address these combined issues.

A starting point to examine these potential safeguards in labour law is the shift that can be noticed within the employment relationship towards techno-subordination in relation to robotization. Techno-subordination refers to the use of technology to exercise employers' powers to manage, instruct and evaluate workers.[25] In other words, the performance of the employment relationship depends increasingly on the capabilities of AI-tools and robots. HENDRICKX questions in this regard whether workers can work for a robot and to whom or what workers would be subordinated.[26] Various aspects of robotization impact, as mentioned in the previous section, the roles and responsibilities of workers and employers in the employment relationship when working with autonomous robots in the workplace. This means that techno-subordination can be strengthened on both sides of the employment relationship: robots as tools to exercise the employer's authority and to perform the worker's tasks.[27] The increasing autonomy of robots enables them to exercise their assigned tasks more independently, ultimately leading to a more distinct identity within the employment relationship. In this regard, autonomous robots could be considered a mediator in the employment relationship with the potential to impact it significantly by altering the social relations in the workplace. This occurs when they exercise the powers of employers and monitor workers by processing the perceived and recorded data on

24. O. Görür, B. Rosman, F. Sivrikaya & S. Albayrak, 'Social Cobots: Anticipatory Decision-Making for Collaborative Robots Incorporating Unexpected Human Behaviors', *Proceedings of the 2018 ACM/IEEE International Conference on human-robot interaction* 2018, 2.
25. F. Hendrickx, 'From Digits to Robots: The Privacy-Autonomy Nexus in New Labor Law Machinery', *Comparative Labor Law & Policy Journal* 2019, No. 3, 380.
26. F. Hendrickx, 'Regulating New Ways of Working: From the New "Wow" to the New "How"', *ELLJ* 2018, 204.
27. S. Taes, *Robotisering en arbeidsrecht*, Brugge, die Keure, 2024, 137-138.

human behaviour and movements through their sensors. This robot surveillance differs from human monitoring, as robots do not have the freedom and intentions that humans possess.[28] Their perception and movements are based on their learning capabilities and algorithms directing them to make certain actions or assessments and steering them in their decision-making processes. This raises the question of whether robots are able to exercise the authority of employers without possessing such 'human' intentions and, in particular, to make assessments about the human performance of work.

In this context, it is urged to pay attention to the humanization of work since technological devices threaten to consider workers as objects solely tasked with achieving the employer's goals. Technology is associated, in this regard, with the commodification of human labour and its dehumanizing consequences. DE STEFANO mentioned in this regard that the interaction between workers and AI and robots can lead to new forms of dehumanization when these devices are used to exercise the powers of managers and are granted similar rights and obligations as managers.[29] In this context, the interaction between humans and robots can lead to new forms of dehumanization when workers have to physically interact with robots in a shared workplace. SUPIOT also acknowledges the dehumanization of work as one of the risks that the digital revolution can bring, especially when workers are part of a communication network constantly processing an increasing volume of information about them.[30] He argues that physical control over workers is now being exerted through intellectual control in the sense that computer programs shape human work.[31]

Building further on these findings, robotization can be considered a new risk that reduces work to a mere commodity, stripped of its human dimensions and confined to codes and algorithms. Robots in the workplace may strengthen, therefore, this risk of dehumanization when they are applied as a decision-making tool to perform the employment relationship, not able to understand the human aspects of work and all circumstances in which it is performed.

Considering it one of its core principles, labour law aims to ensure that work is not considered merely a commodity. This principle expresses the idea that human work cannot be reduced to a sequence of tasks predetermined by an algorithm, the result of a series of zeroes and ones in a code or a chain of actions performed by a robot. Labour law has, therefore, a major role in protecting the human side of work in the workplace. This idea is not entirely new as this was also included in the framework on the humanization of work.[32] This framework was already developed in the seventies to

28. UNESCO, *Report of Comest on Robotics Ethics*, 2017, https://unesdoc.unesco.org/ark:/48223/pf0000253952#: ~ :text = COMEST % 20concludes % 20therefore % 20that % 2C % 20in,that % 20 States % 20reconsider % 20this % 20practice, 42-43.
29. V. De Stefano, 'Negotiating the Algorithm: Automation, Artificial Intelligence, and Labor Protection', *Comp. Lab. L. & Pol'y J.* 2019, 23.
30. A. Supiot, 'The Tasks Ahead of the ILO at Its Centenary', *International Labour Review* 2020, No. 1, 119.
31. A. Supiot, 'Labour Is Not a Commodity: The Content and Meaning of Work in the Twenty-First Century', *International Labour Review* 2021, No. 1, 4.
32. T.M. Fraser, *Human Stress, Work and Job Satisfaction*, Genève, International Labour Office, 1984, 21-22.

address the adverse effects of automation but it becomes relevant again in the context of AI and autonomous robots in the workplace. Moreover, humanization of work can be linked with the fundamental principles of labour law and be seen as a means of protecting human dignity. This means that the humane treatment of workers must be encompassed within labour law as part of the functions of this legal domain.[33] This is also included in the fundamental right to work that aims to safeguard the physical and psychological integrity of the individual during the development of the work and to guarantee that the individual is in a position to act both physically and psychically at least as long as the work continues.[34]

§11.05 RIGHT TO PRIVACY AS HUMANIZATION TOOL FOR THE ROBOTIZED WORKPLACE

The previous sections elaborated on the impact of robotization on work and in what way labour law should address the legal issues related to this technological and social phenomenon. It is argued in this regard that it is pivotal to safeguard the human aspects of work and to further develop the idea of humanization of work. For this reason, the legal measures should aim to protect workers' physical and mental integrity to allow them to work in the robotized workplace. As shown in this section, the right to privacy is able to provide a solid foundation to develop these legal measures but this requires that all aspects of the right to privacy are included and that this right is linked to the protection of the physical and mental integrity of workers.

The right to privacy usually appears in cases of the electronic monitoring of workers. It is considered highly relevant to address legally the consequences of the use of devices and technologies to surveil and assess workers' performance by processing workers' personal data. For instance, wearables may provide workers insight into their health status or warn them if they are in a hazardous situation, but these devices can also show information on their performance. Working Party 29 (WP29)[35] expressed, therefore, its concerns about this use of technology in the workplace, because this information may also be used by their employers to monitor the workers' location and intrude on their private life.[36]

The right to respect for private life, under Article 8 of the European Convention on Human Rights, also considered assessing whether such tools to monitor workers electronically are justified and proportionate to the pursued aim. As well-established in its case law in the context of video surveillance or the monitoring of electronic communication, the European Court of Human Rights (ECtHR) refers to the right to privacy as the right to establish and develop relationships with other people and the

33. P. Gilabert, 'Dignity at Work' in: H. Collins, G. Lester & V. Mantouvalou (eds), *Philosophical Foundations of Labour Law*, Oxford, Oxford University Press, 2018, 71.
34. UN Committee on Economic, Social and Cultural Rights (CESCR), General Comment No. 18: The Right to Work (art. 6 of the Covenant), 6 February 2006, E/C.12/GC/18, available at www.refworld.org/docid/4415453b4.html, No. 7.
35. Article 29 Data Protection Working Party.
36. Opinion of WP29 of 8 June 2017 on data processing at work, No. 2/2017, 20.

possibility to develop an own social identity.[37] Interestingly, the Court ruled in the *Antovic and Mirkovic* case that video recording in the workplace as such without the aim to monitor workers already amounts to an interference with their private lives, because in this space relationships with other people are established and developed. This finding could be highly relevant in the context of robotization. It implies that the mere observation of workers by the cameras of robots could be considered an interference with their private lives and requires a justification and needs to comply with the proportionality principle.

The right to privacy is, however, broader than the right to establish relationships in the workplace. According to the ECtHR, the interpretation of this concept as a 'private circle' in which an individual may determine his own life and completely isolate himself from the outside world that does not fall within this circle would be too restrictive. It thus includes the right to personal development both in terms of personality and autonomy, the physical and psychological integrity of a person and also other values such as the well-being, dignity and development of personality.

The ECtHR also applies this right in other kinds of cases that concern the workers' health and safety as this is also interpreted as the positive obligation of States to protect the physical and mental integrity of workers. The Court emphasized, in particular, that mental health is even a 'crucial' part of private life.[38] In these kinds of cases, on the protection of workers' health and safety, the Court examines, among others, whether Member States have adopted sufficient safeguards in their legislation. This is explicitly mentioned in another case, in which the Court held that the Norwegian government had failed to fulfil its obligation in Article 8 when divers had not received appropriate information to assess the health and safety risks associated with their activities, as this information is considered a part of the preventive measures to protect them from harm.[39] This right was also violated when an employer did not take any measures nor established any procedures for a victim of sexual harassment.[40] In another case concerning a worker suffering from a depression allegedly caused by high work pressure, the Court found no violation of the right to private life, because the investigation by the national authorities was sufficient and the national legislation provided for complaint procedures and, where appropriate, compensation for non-pecuniary damage.[41]

The Court held a similar assessment in the *Spadijer* case that concerned a person harassed at work by colleagues. Although the Court stated that not every act or measure that negatively affects a person's moral integrity constitutes an interference with private life, it would be when it has long-lasting consequences for a worker's well-being. Moreover, Judge YUDKIVSKA interprets in the concurring opinion the scope of the right to privacy broader and emphasized that the protection of human

37. ECtHR 28 February 2018, No. 70838/13, Antović and Mirković/Montenegro, para. 40; ECtHR 5 September 2017, No. 61496/08, Barbulescu/Romania, para. 70.
38. ECtHR 6 February 2001, No. 44599/98, Bensaid/United Kingdom, para. 47.
39. ECtHR 5 December 2013, No. 52806/09, Vilnes e.a./Norway, para. 245.
40. ECtHR 30 November 2022, No. 47358/20, C./R, paras 69-83.
41. ECtHR 10 December 2015, No. 36656/14, Dolopoulos/Greece, paras 53-57.

dignity should not be limited to physical trauma or severely traumatic experiences. It should also provide protection from other negative emotions: '*Human dignity is harmed when a person is marginalised, disregarded or degraded, and the concept of an attack on human dignity today includes not only physical trauma, not only deeply traumatic experiences in, for example, a war- or disaster-related context, but many other negative emotions. This being so, protection from bullying as an attack on human dignity (actually the very aim of bullying is dehumanisation – a destruction of human dignity) in the modern world clearly relates to a "minimally decent" life*' (own underlining).[42] This case law demonstrates a clear connection between the right to privacy and the legal measures to protect the physical and mental health and integrity of workers.

This broad interpretation of the right to privacy is also reflected in legal scholarship. HENDRICKX distinguishes several types of privacy, namely information privacy, communicative privacy, physical and psychological privacy and self-determination. Information privacy concerns the control that a person can exercise over personal information. Communicative privacy ensures that the communication between the persons concerned remains confidential. This also refers to physical and mental privacy in relation to one's own life and thoughts and physical and mental integrity and self-determination in terms of control over one's own personality.

Considering the abovementioned impact on the various elements of work, all these aspects of the right to privacy will become highly relevant in the context of robotization processes. The Austrian Data Protection Agency (OVIC) argued, for instance, that the development of technology has brought about a new concept of data protection, as informational privacy was impacted by the computerized databases and again by algorithmic tools and the use of AI in combination with drones, camera networks and digital tracing. HENDRICKX also argued that the emergence of AI, automated decision-making and robots leads to the next phase in the development of the right to privacy, in which personal autonomy may play a major role.[43] This means that the various aspects of the right to privacy may not be overlooked, as the autonomy and integrity of workers can be impacted through the use of AI, algorithmic intelligence and robots. Wearables, for instance, can provide useful information about the health and movements of people, which means these devices may bring questions about both physical and information privacy. This consideration can also be extended to the effects of robotization on workers' autonomy.[44] This social significance of robots in the workplace implies that they are not more objects or tools but are capable of affecting the development of workers' social identity as well.

Therefore, there is a need to develop legal measures that address the social and legal implications of robotization and, in particular, protect all aspects of the right to privacy. This requires that these measures not only address the use of robots to monitor

42. Concurring opinion judge YUDKIVSKA in ECtHR 9 February 2022, No. 31549/18, Spadijer/ Montenegro.
43. F. HENDRICKX, 'Privacy 4.0 at Work: Regulating Employment, Technology and Automation', *Comparative Labor Law & Policy Journal* 2019, vol. 41, 166.
44. R. CALO, 'Robotics and the Lessons of Cyberlaw', *Calif. L. Rev.* 2015, (513) 532.

workers electronically by means of their sensors but also provide broader protection to mitigate risks for the workers' integrity related to the adverse effects of the interaction and cooperation with robots in the workplace. The existing measures based on the right to privacy aim primarily to protect the informational privacy and the protection of personal data of workers. These measures will be essential to deal with some implications of robotization, but they need to be complemented by and combined with other innovative legal measures that focus on providing protection to other aspects of the right to privacy, such as the workers' integrity and autonomy. For this reason, the final section of this contribution delves deeper into a specific field of labour law that has already developed and established various measures to protect these important aspects of working lives, namely the principles related to occupational safety and health regulation. It elaborates, in addition, the meaning of these principles for the protection of workers' integrity and autonomy in robotized working environments.

Occupational safety and health as a humanization tool for the robotized workplace.

Similar to the right to privacy, the principles and legislation on the occupational safety and health of workers have been developed and adapted in light of technological and social evolutions. At first, these instruments addressed particularly hazardous working conditions (such as specific substances or situations) to protect the safety of workers. However, since 1980, legislators started to develop a new comprehensive approach for the protection of occupational safety and health.[45] The instruments did not impose precise legal obligations anymore but did rather contain general principles to guarantee health and safety in the workplace. For instance, the European Union (EU) adopted in 1985 a 'new approach' to legislative harmonization concerning the health and safety of citizens, which entailed the abandonment of the practice of incorporating detailed technical specifications and the provision of only the essential requirements in these European directives.[46] This new approach led a few years later to the adoption of the Framework directive on occupational safety and health in the workplace, which contains '*measures to encourage improvements in the safety and health of workers at work*' and the general principles '*concerning the prevention of occupational risks, the protection of safety and health, the elimination of risk and accident factors, the informing, consultation, balanced participation in accordance with national laws and/or practices and training of workers and their representatives*'.[47] This comprehensive approach to occupational safety and health is also reflected in the CJEU's interpretation of the concepts 'safety' and 'health' in this directive because the CJEU refers to the definition of 'health' in the preamble to the Constitution of the World

45. International Labour Office, ILO standards-related activities in the area of occupational safety and health: An in-depth study for discussion with a view to the elaboration of a plan of action for such activities, https://www.ilo.org/sites/default/files/wcmsp5/groups/public/%40ed_protect/%40protrav/%40safework/documents/publication/wcms_177455.pdf, 12-13.
46. Commission of the European Communities, Completing the internal market, No. COMC85 310 final, 14 June 1985, 19-20.
47. Article 1 Council Directive of 12 June 1989 on the introduction of measures to encourage improvements in the safety and health of workers at work (89/391/EEC), *OJ L* 26 June 1989, No. 183, 2. (hereinafter: 'OSH Framework Directive').

Health Organization: '*a state of complete physical, mental and social well-being that does not consist only in the absence of illness or infirmity*'.[48] This implies that the protection of occupational safety and health is broadened from various risks related to specific working conditions to a holistic view of every aspect concerning workers' physical, mental and social safety and health with regard to work. It includes a broad range of measures regarding workers' health and safety aiming to protect their integrity and autonomy as part of their work.

To pursue this goal, the legal framework of OSH needs to be able to correspond adequately to the implications of robotization. One may argue, therefore, that the holistic approach to workers' health and safety needs to be sufficiently broad in the robot age and to provide protection in light of the emerging risks of the human-robot interaction and its abovementioned impact on the quality of work. For instance, this implies that the robot age will require measures and risk assessments to protect workers' cybersecurity and perhaps even their cyber health in order to properly address the risks of robotized workplaces. This would require that the occupational safety and health obligations are clarified in the context of these technological advances and entail that risk assessments also ensure the (cyber) well-being of workers, in terms of cybersecurity of the 'connection' between devices and workers, the impact on ergonomics and the increased (mental) workload due to the constant monitoring of the workplace or the machine-based work rate imposed by algorithms.[49] Therefore, measures need to be adopted that sufficiently deal with these risks related to the human-robot interaction for workers' physical and mental safety and health become paramount in safeguarding OSH in the robotized workplace.

The OSH legal framework already provides in a rather extended way protection to workers' health and safety. The EU directive on OSH, for instance, imposes the general obligation to employers '*to ensure the safety and health of workers in every aspect related to the work*'.[50] This reflects the holistic approach to workers' health which can be relevant to safeguard the workers' integrity in every aspect of their work affected by the interaction with robots. Moreover, the OSH Directive requires that employers have to evaluate the risks related to workers' safety and health and have to take the necessary measures for protection. It refers, in particular, to the provision of information, training, means and organization and to the prevention of OSH risks.[51] Notwithstanding the importance of the other measures, this contribution delves deeper into the *ex ante* approach to avoid any risks to workers' health and safety in the robotized workplace. The OSH directive provides a specific list of general principles to prevent OSH-related risks by implementing measures, such as '*(a) avoiding risks; (b) evaluating the risks which cannot be avoided; (c) combating the risks at source; (d) adapting*

48. CJEU 12 November 1996, No. c-84/94, United Kingdom of Great Britain and Northern Ireland v. Council of the European Union, para. 15.
49. International Labour Organization, Safety and health at the heart of the future of work Building on 100 years of experience, ISBN 978-92-2-133152-0 (web pdf), Geneva, 2019, 31; EU-OSHA, Foresight on new and emerging occupational safety and health risks associated with digitalization by 2025, 6-7.
50. Article 5 OSH Directive.
51. Article 6 OSH Directive.

the work to the individual, especially as regards the design of work places, the choice of work equipment and the choice of working and production methods, with a view, in particular, to alleviating monotonous work and work at a predetermined work-rate and to reducing their effect on health (e) adapting to technical progress; (g) developing a coherent overall prevention policy which covers technology, organization of work, working conditions, social relationships and the influence of factors related to the working environment' (own underlining).[52]

These principles may provide guidance to address the adverse implications of robotization for work. In particular, the above-underlined principles can be considered the measures enhancing human control over work, as they require that the work has to be adapted to the worker and that predetermined work-rate has to be avoided. This finding may become increasingly important in robotized workplaces. They safeguard the human aspects of work and aim to avoid a machine-based work-rate. In that way, the deprivation of human autonomy can be avoided when workers are able to remain in control over their work in cooperation with robots and their work is not (only) determined by the objectives of algorithms. The importance of these kinds of measures is also reflected in the AI Act, as it contains the principle of human oversight over high-risk AI systems requiring the design and development of these systems to allow effective oversight by persons to prevent and minimize the risks to health, safety or fundamental rights associated with the intended use or reasonably foreseeable misuse of these systems.[53] These prevention principles offer, therefore, a solid basis to develop measures protecting not only workers' health and safety but also their integrity and autonomy.

This protection by the *ex ante* approach can be strengthened by combining this with the principles of data protection. It has already been mentioned that the *ratio legis* of these principles is to safeguard the informational self-determination of individuals and to regulate or restore the informational imbalance between controllers and data subjects.[54] In other words, they aim to ensure human control over personal information and offer similar legal protection in comparison to the OSH principles. They require, for instance, measures to protect the security and integrity of personal data and to assess risks in the context of the data protection impact assessments.[55] The combination of the data protection principles and the OSH principles may strengthen, among others, the protection of workers in terms of their cybersecurity (and health) in digital work environments and when workers interact with AI systems or robots in physical workplaces.

52. Article 6.1 OSH Framework Directive.
53. Article 14 Regulation of 13 June 2024 of the European Parliament and of the Council laying down harmonised rules on artificial intelligence and amending Regulations (EC) No. 300/2008, (EU) No. 167/2013, (EU) No. 168/2013, (EU) 2018/858, (EU) 2018/1139 and (EU) 2019/2144 and Directives 2014/90/EU, (EU) 2016/797 and (EU) 2020/1828 (2024/1689), *OJ L* 12 July 2024, No. 144.
54. Recital 7 GDPR; Guidelines of EDPB of 4 May 2020, on consent under Regulation 2016/679, No. 05/2020, 11; Opinion of WP29 of 9 April 2014 on the notion of legitimate interests of the data controller under Art. 7 of Directive 95/46/EC, No. 844/14/EN WP 217, 36.
55. Article 35 GDPR.

This section explained the reason to include the OSH perspective in the development of legal measures to address the challenges of robotization impacting various aspects of work. In this regard, reference is made to the importance of the obligation to assess the risks related to all aspects of work and the principles to prevent these risks safeguarding workers' integrity and control over their work. It has also been argued that the combination of the OSH and data protection principles, instead of a stand-alone perspective, would be able to protect more adequately the workers' integrity and self-determination in robotized workplaces. These existing principles could reinforce each other, as the data protection perspective already aims to provide protection to the informational privacy and the OSH perspective ensures that other aspects of the workers' privacy are not overlooked. The combination of both the OSH and data protection principles may provide, therefore, a solid foundation to develop legal measures to address the challenges related to robotization and to establish a safe, meaningful and productive human-robot interaction in the workplace.

§11.06 CONCLUSION

Robotization as a technological and social phenomenon in various kinds of workplaces and sectors is able to have profound implications for the work performed by workers. It is argued in this contribution that labour law has a major role in addressing the implications of the increasing interaction between workers and robots in order to limit its adverse consequences and strengthen its beneficial effects on the quality of work. Labour law should develop in this regard an approach based on the idea of the humanization of work because it opposes the idea that work could be merely expressed in a code that enables robots to perform tasks in the workplace. To pursue the objectives of humanization of work, legal safeguards in labour law should be developed that are derived from the right to privacy protecting workers' integrity and self-development. This contribution argues, moreover, that measures need to be implemented in the legal framework based on the combination of the principles in the current OSH and data protection legislation. These measures would enable labour law to achieve an effective humanization of work and to flourish human work in robotized workplaces.

CHAPTER 12
How Privacy Shapes the Meaning of Work: Developing Freedom and Autonomy in Labour Law

Frank Hendrickx

§12.01 INTRODUCTION

In the modern workplace, privacy has emerged as a fundamental concern and has become more and more intertwined with the role of freedom and autonomy in relation to work. As the world of work evolves under the influence of major game-changing patterns, particularly with the advent of the growing use of digital technologies[1] and, more recently, with the rise of remote work, boundaries between personal and professional spaces are increasingly blurred and critical questions arise about the role of privacy and its legal development in labour law.

This chapter explores how privacy influences the perception and reality of work, focusing on its impact on individual freedom and autonomy within the workplace. This is approached through concepts and legal developments within the labour law discourse and the perspective of the fundamental right to privacy. It attempts to explore and develop further understandings and narratives of the meaning of work in relation to the privacy notion, in light of legal developments in the employment sphere. As the concept of privacy is intriguing, due to its growing, multiple meanings and its 'open-textured' character,[2] the question arises as to how these meanings can relate to the meaning of work and how they influence contemporary discussions on the

1. F. Hendrickx & V. De Stenano (eds), *Game Changers in Labour Law: Shaping the Future of Work*, in *Bulletin of Comparative Labour Relations*, Vol. 100, Alphen aan den Rijn, Kluwer Law International, 2018.
2. M. Otto, *The Right to Privacy in Employment: A Comparative Analysis*, Bloomsbury Academic, London, 2016, 221 pp.

employment relationship in the context of which freedom and autonomy are growing relevant concepts.

The right to privacy has originally been phrased as 'the right to be left alone' by Warren and Brandeis in nineteenth-century legal thought.[3] This definition of the right to privacy can be seen as the right to have a private space and to keep private or personal information away from third parties or the wider public. It could be viewed as a right to maintain control over one's personal information, and to define the boundaries of one's own private life.

In the context of work, and due to further legal developments, the concept of privacy has extended beyond mere 'informational privacy'. As will be further elaborated below, it has evolved to encompass the ability to manage the flow of information about oneself, the exercise of informational self-control, as well as to create or claim a personal space – or personal life – even within professional settings, and to make autonomous decisions without undue external interference. Privacy in the workplace, therefore, is not merely about protecting (personal or private) information, or having a private (physical) space, but seems fundamentally connected to the preservation of individual dignity, identity, freedom and autonomy.

Freedom and autonomy are inherently linked to privacy and are two pillars that underpin the core ethical, philosophical and legal values of work. Both concepts enable overlapping spheres, preferences and values in a workplace debate. In a more philosophical understanding, autonomy and freedom are, like privacy, rich and complex notions. They receive different meanings and have appeared for a long time in the history of philosophical thought. Autonomy and freedom, although overlapping, are often defined in different ways. Autonomy may refer to personal self-development and self-determination. 'Put most simply, to be autonomous is to govern oneself, to be directed by considerations, desires, conditions, and characteristics that are not simply imposed externally upon one, but are part of what can somehow be considered one's authentic self.'[4] Freedom could be seen as being free from limitations. Berlin conceptualized freedom as encompassing, negatively, as 'the degree to which no man or body of men interferes with my activity', and positively, something that 'derives from the wish on the part of the individual to be his own master'.[5] The idea of self-governance and self-determination, including self-realization, seems to reflect in both notions of autonomy and freedom. It will be argued that privacy is a useful perspective to capture these dimensions of human and working life.

Before elaborating some reflections in relation to some key issues in contemporary labour law, a concise overview of the meaning of work debate is first provided below, as well as a brief exploration of the relationship between the notions of privacy,

3. S.D. Warren & L.D. Brandeis, 'The Right to Privacy', *Harvard Law Review* 1890, Vol. 4(5), 193-220 https://doi.org/10.2307/1321160.
4. J. Christman, 'Autonomy in Moral and Political Philosophy', *The Stanford Encyclopedia of Philosophy* (Fall 2020 Edition), Edward N. Zalta (ed.), https://plato.stanford.edu/archives/fall2020/entries/autonomy-moral/.
5. I. Berlin, *Four Essays on Liberty*, Oxford, Oxford University Press, 1969, 121, 122 and 131.

freedom and autonomy. Subsequently, departing from a significant degree of conceptual interdependency, this contribution then develops some narratives of labour law in relation to the role of freedom and autonomy in relation to the employment relationship's assumptions (and realities) of authority and subordination, as well as in relation to the idea of personal development, identity and control in the work context.

§12.02 THE MEANING OF WORK DEBATE

The relationship between privacy, freedom, and autonomy in the workplace is complex and multifaceted. The most evident view on the role of these three key concepts could be seen in relation to information privacy, monitoring and surveillance. A broad understanding is that privacy is under pressure due to technological surveillance and monitoring of workers, and through massive data collection and processing, with deeper implications arising from big data, people analytics, algorithmic management, or broader, the increasing presence of robots and artificial intelligence (AI) in the work environment. This also brings concerns of diminished autonomy and freedom, as workers may be intensively monitored or assessed and pressured to conform to certain goals or behaviours. However, the relationship between privacy, freedom and autonomy will also be concerned with degrees and expectations in relation to the fostering of trust, the empowerment of individuals, self-governance and determination, and the development of human relations. That may enhance an overall sense of autonomy and freedom at work. The privacy debate, when followed in its legal context, is precisely developing these values and meanings.

The relevance of the meaning of work is related to this debate. The meaning of work itself is increasingly shaped by the degree to which privacy is recognized and develops. In many instances, autonomy and freedom are seen as major values in giving meaning to work, but also privacy can be seen as a prerequisite for meaningful work. Privacy is capable of underpinning the intrinsic values that workers may derive from their professional lives.

This meaning of debate follows from the fact that our societies are strongly focused on work and the role of work. Work receives a central place not only in the creation of societal welfare but also in personal life. Work, according to some, is a '*necessity of life*',[6] allows one to live a life, and forms one's identity and future. There is, however, not one single meaning of work.[7] Furthermore, the search for the meaning of work is not new. It grew along with the philosophy of work and labour. With the Enlightenment, the question received a new bearing, since this era of thought provided a subjectivistic perspective, with humans as rational and productive beings, oriented towards a 'makeable' reality, a vision which continued to remain within a Romantic

6. H. Applebaum, *The Concept of Work: Ancient, Medieval, and Modern*, State University of New York Press, Albany, 1992, xii (660 pp.).
7. Cf. M. Cholbi, 'Philosophical Approaches to Work and Labor', *The Stanford Encyclopedia of Philosophy* (Summer 2023 Edition), Edward N. Zalta & Uri Nodelman (eds), https://plato.stanford.edu/archives/sum2023/entries/work-labor/.

perspective, since work then was seen as an emanation of self-realization or self-development.[8] With industrialization and the globalization of the world of work, the hard reality made work appear more instrumental, work as a mere 'means to an end', as a way to receive an income and to maintain a family. However, this appeared a too simplistic view.[9] The twenty-first century brought again fundamental changes to the world of work, with a post-Fordistic and technology-driven world of work.[10] It has led to increased attention to the meaning of work[11] with rising literature on the subject.[12] The idea that work has various meanings seems evident in a complex society. With '*Generation Z*' entering the labour market, work may imply various goals, desires and understandings, but both 'making money', as well as individual self-development and meaningful human relationships come standing central.[13] At the same time, the more socio-political and ethical meanings of work receive more attention, including influences from values such as justice, respect equality. It would seem that the world of work has a need for what is called a '*paradigm of meaning*'.[14]

Within this contemporary context of rich and modern understandings of the meaning of work, notions such as privacy, freedom and autonomy play an important role. An interesting dimension is that these concepts are developed in legal discourses on work and the workplace and thus help to appreciate, through these notions, the reciprocity between work-meanings and modern legal discourses in labour law.

§12.03 PRIVACY, FREEDOM AND AUTONOMY

Privacy is not only increasingly encapsulated in legal discourses of labour and employment law but is also more and more a vector of freedom and autonomy.[15] The very concept of privacy has more and more found its way to give meaning and context to labour law, employment law discourses and understandings of what it means to work. This is strongly connected with how privacy comes to the fore in relation to broader developments. Automation and technology are widely recognized as forces

8. N.H. Smith & J-Ph. Deranty, 'Work, Recognition and the Social Bond: Changing Paradigms', in Nicholas Smith & Jean-Philippe Deranty (eds), *New Philosophies of Labour: Work and the Social Bond*, Leiden/Boston, Brill, 2012, p. 5 (381 pp).
9. N.C. Morse & R.S. Weiss, 'The Function and Meaning of Work and the Job', *American Sociological Review* 1955, Vol. 20(2), 191-198 https://doi.org/10.2307/2088325.
10. Global Commission on the Future of Work, *Work for a brighter future*, ILO, Geneva, 2019, 75pp.
11. The literature links the changing world of work with the changing meaning of work: cf. C. Baldry et al., 'Work Attachment, Work Centrality and the Meaning of Work in Life', in *The Meaning of Work in the New Economy*, in *The Future of Work Series*, Palgrave Macmillan, London, 2007, p. 2.
12. For a social-scientific literature overview: C. Bailey et al. 'A Review of the Empirical Literature on Meaningful Work: Progress and Research Agenda', *Human Resource Development Review* 2019, Vol. 18(1), 83-113 https://doi.org/10.1177/1534484318804653.
13. C. Seemiller & M. Grace, *Generation Z: A Century in the Making*, New York, Routledge, 2019 (Figure 3.2.).
14. A. Di Fabio & D.L. Blustein, 'From Meaning of Working to Meaningful Lives: The Challenges of Expanding Decent Work' (Editorial), *Frontiers in Psychology* 2016, Vol. 7(1119), 1 (pp. 1-2) https://doi.org/10.3389/fpsyg.2016.01119.
15. F. Hendrickx, 'Privacy 4.0 at Work: Regulating Employment, Technology and Automation', *Comp. Lab. Law & Policy Journal* 2020, Vol. 41(1), 147-172.

that shape labour and employment relations, and inevitably, the meaning of work. The advent of machines and new technologies has prompted work organizations to adjust and labour laws to evolve in response to these changes, including relevant roles for privacy rights. Changing meanings of work, from traditional employment to more flexible and digital arrangements, further highlight the importance of privacy rights. As work becomes increasingly reliant on digital tools, worker privacy is subjected to new forms of surveillance and data collection. This makes it essential for privacy rights to evolve in a way that responds to the unique challenges posed by the modern work context.

The impact of technology on the development of the right to privacy, furthermore, has brought increasing emphasis on the concept of personal data protection.[16] It could be seen as a more specific development, but obviously part of the broader privacy rights evolution. In the European Union (EU), the right to privacy and the right to personal data protection are both seen as fundamental rights, which can exist in their 'own right', enshrined in two separate articles (Articles 7 and 8) of the Charter of Fundamental Rights of the EU (CFREU). The 'General Data Protection Regulation (GDPR)'[17] has become a lead document and conceptual framework to discuss privacy-related challenges in relation to personal data processing in a work context. However, the strong interdependency of privacy and data protection cannot be overlooked. The right to privacy includes the right to data protection, as is confirmed in the European Human Rights Court's case law.[18] This has also been the approach in the International Labour Organization (ILO) Working Paper on 'the protection of workers' personal data' (2022).[19] Furthermore, within the complexity of the new world of work, with changing work-life relations and fundamental rights developments, it is crucial to recognize that the evolution of privacy, including data protection rights, has occurred in parallel with these broader phenomena such as globalization, the evolution of new ways of working, changing societies and the shifting meanings of work.

Against this broader background, 'the right to be let alone' as forwarded by Warren and Brandeis,[20] can also receive new understandings, which, in turn, can lead to stronger links with the concepts of freedom and autonomy. Privacy is also seen through the lens of identity and personal development, which is connected to self-determination and self-governance, attached to freedom and autonomy.

16. Ph. Moore, 'Data Subjects, Digital Surveillance, AI and the Future of Work', *STUDY Panel for the Future of Science and Technology*, EPRS – European Parliamentary Research Service Scientific Foresight Unit (STOA) PE 656.305 – December 2020, p. 32; https://www.europarl.europa.eu/RegData/etudes/STUD/2020/656305/EPRS_STU(2020)656305_EN.pdf.
17. Regulation (EU) 2016/679 of the European Parliament and of the Council of 27 April 2016 on the protection of natural persons with regard to the processing of personal data and on the free movement of such data, and repealing Directive 95/46/EC (General Data Protection Regulation) *OJ* L 119, 4.5.2016, 1-88.
18. *See Leander v. Sweden*, ECtHR 26 March 1987, Series A No. 116, p. 22, §48.
19. F. Hendrickx, *Protection of Worker's Personal Data: General Principles*, ILO Working Paper nr. 62, 5 May 2022, 55 p., https://www.ilo.org/global/publications/working-papers/WCMS_844343/lang--en/index.htm.
20. Warren & Brandeis, *supra* n. 3.

Human relationships are constitutive of persons as human beings and necessary conditions to develop oneself as a human. Charles Fried has developed a privacy understanding that speaks to this dimension. It concerns a view of 'privacy as a context for respect, love, friendship and trust'.[21] It is a concept that is necessarily relational and connected to the very idea of privacy as personal or human integrity[22] as well as to notions of respect and self-respect.[23]

In this manner, the right to privacy can also be seen as 'the right to be let alone' in judging oneself, and thus a right to self-governance, to be free from others' judgment or interference in relation to one's identity, to personal development and human interaction. The suggested understanding of privacy as a form of self-judgment and immunity from judgment by others[24] forms a good link with self-determination, also seen in a relational context. Individuals are not isolated beings. Personal identity, meaning and respect come through the understanding of the context of society in which one is situated.

Privacy, in that sense, can still be understood in a modern manner according to the views of Warren and Brandeis, as a space for individuals that is determined for him/herself.[25] This space is not necessarily a physical space, not necessarily a 'place', but can be an invisible or moral space. It is a space of autonomy and freedom, a space in which individuals can be free from interference and make fundamental life options themselves.[26] This also implies that individuals are protected against control from others over one's personality and identity.

This approach to privacy is obviously strongly connected with the notions of freedom and autonomy. Autonomy is, therefore, an important dimension of privacy.[27] Privacy is a notion which can be used, to cover issues that can also be captured under the notions of freedom and autonomy.[28] In the scholarship of the past century, Beddar already brought 'the right to talk and listen freely, to read and write, to meet with

21. Ch. Fried, 'Privacy', *Yale Law Journal* 1968, Vol. 77(3), 477 https://doi.org/10.2307/794941.
22. *Ibid.*
23. *Ibid.*, 482.
24. J.L. Johnson, 'A Theory of the Nature and Value of Privacy', *Public Affairs Quarterly* 1992, Vol. 6(3), 286 (271-288).
25. Cf. 'the right to be let alone': Warren & Brandeis, *supra* n. 3, 193; *Conclusions of the Nordic Conference of Jurists on the Right to Privacy May*, 1967; J. Velu, 'The European Convention on Human Rights and the Right to Respect for Private Life, the Home and Communication', in Arthur Henry Robertson (ed.), *Privacy and Human Rights*, Manchester, Manchester University Press, 1973, 108: 'the right to be let alone to live one's own life with the minimum degree of interference'.
26. J.H.F. Shattuck, *Rights of Privacy*, Skokie, National Textbook Company, 1977, 122.
27. J. Hirshleifer, 'Privacy: It's Origin, Function and Future', *Journal of Legal Studies* 1980, Vol. 9(4), 649 https://doi.org/10.1086/467659.
28. J. Wagner DeCew, 'The Scope of Privacy in Law and Ethics', *L.P.* 1986, 162 https://doi.org/10.1007/bf00190759; Beddard includes '*the right to talk and listen freely, to read and write, to meet with others, to exchange ideas*' within a privacy concept. R. Beddard, *Human Rights and Europe*, Cambridge, Cambridge University Press, 1993, 114; Cf: Denning: 'the freedom of every law-abiding citizen to think what he will, to say what he will, and to go where he will on his lawful occasions without let or hindrance from any other persons', A. Denning, *Freedom under the Law*, Londen, Stevens & Sons, 1949, 5; M.A. Hogg, 'The Very Private Life of the Right to Privacy', in The David Hume Institute, *Privacy and Property*, Edinburgh, Edinburgh University Press, 1994, 2.

others, to exchange ideas' under the privacy concept.[29] Denning opposed this with the understanding that 'the freedom of every law-abiding citizen to think what he will, to say what he will, and to go where he will on his lawful occasions without let or hindrance from any other persons' belongs under a freedom concept.[30] This overlap caused some authors to deny a privacy right where a 'right to freedom' could be invoked.[31] However, while there is no full overlap between privacy, freedom and autonomy, it has become clear that many dimensions of freedom and autonomy are playing an increasingly important role in the right to privacy. Wagner DeCew has called it 'a subset of autonomy cases', or 'liberty cases in virtue of their concern over decision-making power, whereas privacy is at stake because of the nature of the decision'.[32] In this sense, personal lifestyle and personal identity, personal self-governance, can be seen through the lens of privacy, and protected through the right to privacy, even if some would rightly point out the fact that it concerns autonomy and freedom.[33]

That privacy, indeed, also covers autonomy, freedom and self-determination is an approach that is not new in legal development. Not only can it be traced back to the original 'right to be let alone'-concept but it has also found a basis in European legal development. In the earlier years of the Council of Europe's human rights protection mechanisms, the European Commission for Human Rights pointed out in its case of *Brüggeman and Scheuten* that 'the right to respect for private life is of such a scope as to secure to the individual a sphere within which he can freely pursue the development and fulfilment of his personality'.[34] It would be more common to adopt that (early European) view nowadays.

Contemporary debates about the role of autonomy and freedom in the employment relation illustrate this evolvement, as well as the case law of the European Court in relation to the right to privacy in the work environment.

29. R. Beddard, *Human Rights and Europe*, Cambridge, Cambridge University Press, 1993, 114.
30. A. Denning, *Freedom under the law*, London, Stevens & Sons, 1949, 5.
31. F. Davis, 'What Do We Mean by "Right to Privacy"?', *S.D.L.R.* 1959, 230; J.J. Thomson, 'The Right to Privacy', *Philosophy and Public Affairs* 1975, 313.
32. Wagner DeCew, *supra* n. 28, 164-165: 'Many privacy issues, such as protection from electronic surveillance, have no connection with autonomous decision-making. Also, many self-determined choices, to drive a loudspeaker through a quiet neighborhood, for example, can be made by an individual but are not in any further sense private decisions. A subset of autonomy cases, however, certain personal decisions regarding one's basic lifestyle, can plausibly be said to involve privacy interests as well. They should be viewed as liberty cases in virtue of their concern over decision-making power, whereas privacy is at stake because of the nature of the decision.'
33. Cf. J.A. Swanson, *The Public and the Private in Aristotle's Political Philosophy*, Ithaca, Cornell University Press, 1994, 3 and 7; '*the notion that certain human involvements are defective, lose all or much of their* value or special quality, when the agent concerned is not free to act on his own preferences or in his own way' (W.L. Weinstein, *The Private and the Free: A Conceptual Inquiry*, Vol. XIII, Nomos, 1971, 37); 'There is a fundamental belief in the uniqueness of the individual, in his basic dignity and worth as a creature of God and a human being, and in the need to maintain social processes that safeguard his sacred individuality' (A.F. Westin, *Privacy and Freedom*, New York, Atheneum, 1967, 33).
34. *Brüggeman and Scheuten v. Germany*, E.C.R.M. 12 July 1977, Nr. 6959/75, *D.R.*, Vol. 10, §55; *X v. Germany*, E.C.R.M. 30 September 1975, Nr. 5935/12, *D.R.*, Vol. 3, 46; *F v. Switzerland*, E.C.R.M. 10 March 1988, Nr. 11680/85, *D.R.*, Vol. 55, 178.

§12.04 UNDOING SUBORDINATION WITH THE RIGHT TO BE LET ALONE

While the right to privacy seen as 'the right to be let alone' is challenging for labour law, this is certainly the case for finding it linked with freedom and autonomy. While the right to privacy has now much broader facets, the original 'definition' is intriguing once given new contemporary meanings.

A classic starting point would be that privacy in the employment context needs to be qualified by the employment relationship would imply, as 'a general rule', a subordinate relationship. As we wrote before, 'contemporary labour law is still predominantly based on the view that the work relationship supposes "authority" on the part of the employer or the "subordination" of the employee. The idea is that working under the authority of the other party is part of the agreement between the parties to the employment relationship. When making an employment agreement, one party agrees to perform work for remuneration under the authority of the other party. Authority becomes a constitutive element of the contract. As a consequence thereof, it is generally assumed in labour law that this implies different legal powers and rights for the employer: the right of the employer to lead and direct the workplace, to organise the work, to give orders and instructions, to exercise control'.[35]

This approach is far from outdated. On the contrary, it is still central in current thought and the practice of employment relationships, even if the scope of labour law is under debate. However, new evolutions take place. One dimension is the growth of 'autonomous workers' and 'dependent self-employed' persons.[36] Another dimension is technology, where – even for autonomous workers – control levels seem to be increasing. Furthermore, at least partly in relation to this, legal scholarship is increasingly concerned with 'employer power' and the legitimization in labour law of the authority of one party (the employer, or the principal) over the other (the worker).[37] The link between subordination on the one hand, and freedom and autonomy on the other hand, seems easily made. In more contemporary debate, labour law's general assumption is confronted with the finding that 'the employment relationship subjects an employee to the exercise of market and social power at the hands of his/her employer',[38] knowing that power imbalances and the concept of subordination can be highly problematic.[39] Davidov has pointed at the democratic deficit problem, as workers who follow orders while being governed by hierarchy, give up autonomy and

35. Quote taken from: F. Hendrickx, 'Regulating New Ways of Working: From the New "Wow" to the New "How"', *ELLJ*, Vol. 9(2), 200 https://doi.org/10.1177/2031952518781449.
36. Cf. A. Perulli, 'Subordinate, Autonomous and Economically Dependent Work: A Comparative Analysis of Selected European Countries' in Giuseppe Casale (ed.), *The Employment Relationship. A Comparative Overview*, ILO and Hart Publishing, 2011, 137-167.
37. A. Aloisi, 'Regulating Algorithmic Management at Work in the European Union: Data Protection, Non-discrimination and Collective Rights', *IJCLLIR* 2024, Vol. 40(1), 44 https://doi.org/10.54648/ijcl2024001.
38. D. Cabrelli & R. Zahn, 'Theories of Domination and Labour Law: An Alternative Conception for Intervention?', *IJCLLIR* 2017, Vol. 33(3), 345 https://doi.org/10.54648/ijcl2017015.
39. V. De Stefano & N. Countouris, *Lifting the Private-Law Veil: Employer Authority and the Contractual-Coating of Worker Subordination*, Osgoode Legal Studies Research Paper No.

freedom 'without being able to participate in this government'.[40] The language of 'subordination' in a labour law discourse becomes more interesting, but also under pressure, in light of a privacy discourse.

The past has shown that the introduction of the right to privacy in the workplace had to be legitimized (including debates in relation to the 'horizontal application' of human rights). Nowadays, the debate may shift to the idea that it is authority and subordination which must be legitimatized. The right to privacy challenges the traditional departure point of labour law, envisaging a subordinated worker. The right to privacy is the right to be let alone, while authority and subordination would imply an employer's right 'not to leave the worker alone'. Obviously, a worker is only subordinated to the employer with a view to the exercise of the employment relationship.[41] But the scope (and reach) of employer authority comes under discussion and, within the assumption, the right to privacy also covers professional life and work relationships (*see* below).

The privacy concept can feed into the meta-juridical labour law debate. Nevertheless, positive law reflects the tension between privacy on the one hand and authority and subordination on the other hand. This is (at least partly) based on mechanisms underlying fundamental rights protection. It may be interesting to advance the labour law discussion on 'subordination' in relation to the framework of Article 8 ECHR, in which limitations to the right to privacy should be legitimized, while justifications may result from the specific context(s) of an employment relationship. There exist different opposing rights and interests, including those of the employer, of colleagues, of clients or of the wider public. Justifications in reference to 'the protection of the rights and freedoms of others' may, in light of this, be seen as an open-ended ground for justifying interferences with the right to privacy in the interest of private parties in the employment relationship.[42] However, limitations cannot be *merely* justified on the basis of the *fact* that opposing legitimate rights and interests *exist*, it must take into account the principles of proportionality and legality.

Another justification, in *general terms*, of a legally subordinated relationship, could be the view that the employer's rights and interests follow from the worker's individual consent to the employment relationship, in which subordination is a contractually agreed term and condition. However, not only is free consent a problematic dimension in relation to privacy in the employment relationship, as 'GDPR' interpretations show but it should also be stressed that a full waiver of a fundamental right is problematic. The better discussion will focus on the limitations of privacy and the conditions under which this can be lawfully justified. A positive law discussion

4814449, at the time of writing forthcoming in *Comp. Lab. Law Pol'y J* Vol. 44(3), https://papers.ssrn.com/sol3/papers.cfm?abstract_id=4814449.

40. G. Davidov, 'Subordination Vs Domination: Exploring the Differences', *IJCLLIR* 2017, Vol. 33(3), 373 https://doi.org/10.54648/ijcl2017016.
41. Lord Wedderburn, 'Labour Law and the Individual in Post-industrial Societies', in Wedderburn et al., *Labour Law in the Post-industrial Era*, in *Studies in Modern Law and Policy*, Aldershot, Dartmouth, 1994, 39.
42. R.C.A. White and C. Overy, *The European Convention on Human Rights*, Oxford University Press, Oxford, 2010, 323.

may thus contribute to discussing the degree of, and the lawful exercise of, authority (directions, instructions, controls), in addition to a theoretical approach of subordination. The positive legal solution will also need to include an assessment of the role of the employer's fundamental freedom to conduct a business, as recognized in the European Union's Charter on Fundamental Rights of the EU.

Collins has addressed the tension between freedom and the institution of the employment contract in which the employer exercising authority creates a duty to obey and impacts the exercise by workers of civil liberties. He has also proposed that the tension should be well understood and that what is needed, in order to make it compatible with liberal values (including maybe freedom and autonomy), is a view of labour law that ensures 'that practical authority is always effectively constrained by strict and often mandatory boundaries on the content of the performance obligations, and on an employer's restrictions on workers' civil liberties, and on the use of disciplinary powers'.[43] It would seem that the integration of a privacy notion, and a fundamental right to privacy perspective, in light of this, contributes to a modernized view of employer authority with a view to reconcile it with concepts of freedom and autonomy.

§12.05 PRIVACY, IDENTITY AND PERSONAL DEVELOPMENT

The interdependency between privacy, freedom and autonomy is reflected in another legal dimension of the world of work. A broad understanding of privacy leads to the idea of self-development, personal integrity and self-respect. This should not only be seen from a purely individual perspective but it also includes a relational idea of privacy, encompassing human relationships as a condition to develop oneself as an individual and as a human. Fried has developed a privacy understanding that speaks to this dimension.[44] This understanding may also give a useful perspective to reflect on control and monitoring at work. This refers somewhat back to the feature of authority and subordination in the employment relationship, discussed above, but may be enriched with the view that self-development and freedom from judgment and control are aspects that belong to the guarantees offered by the right to privacy.

Hereafter, both the dimension of identity and self-development as well as the issue of monitoring and control will be elaborated in relation to the work context.

An understanding of privacy that aligns with a relational dimension of personal development can be found in the case law of the European Court on Human Rights. It shows that privacy and work are not contradictory notions, but are rather mutually reinforcing. This view reflects work as a way to develop one's identity, personal development and human relationships. This view means that work life *is* constitutive of the worker's private life, as it is protected under the right to privacy.

43. H. Collins, 'Is the Contract of Employment Illiberal?', in Hugh Collins et al. (eds), *Philosophical Foundations of Labour Law*, Oxford, OUP, 2018, 48-67.
44. Ch. Fried, 'Privacy', *Yale Law Journal* 1968, Vol. 77(3), 477 https://doi.org/10.2307/794941.

A milestone case where this view is supported is the case of *Niemietz v. Germany*, in which the European Human Rights Court held that 'there appears (...) to be no reason of principle why this understanding of the notion of "private life" should be taken to exclude activities of a professional or business nature since it is, after all, in the course of their working lives that the majority of people have a significant, if not the greatest, opportunity of developing relationships with the outside world'.[45] From this, it can be derived that a person's professional life, or work life, is part of this person's private life. An additional perspective was offered in *Antovic and Mirkov v. Montenegro*,[46] dealing with video surveillance in university lecture amphitheatres. The European Human Rights Court examined whether the applicant professors had a reasonable expectation that their privacy would be respected and protected. In its assessment, the Court provides an interestingly broad interpretation of the notion of private life. The Court noted that university amphitheatres are, of course, workplaces of teachers, but within that meaning it concerns a space where they not only teach students but also interact with them, and thus develop mutual relations and construe their 'social identity'. The idea of social identity refers to a relational self-concept, where work meanings include social meanings and the development of social life. Work, therefore, becomes an aspect of private social life.

It means that the privacy concept confirms work as holding a deeper meaning which goes beyond the mere commodified or market aspects of work. It also emphasizes that no clear separation between work and (private) life can be made. Work becomes private life, to the extent that it develops personal and social dimensions of life. Work is thus contributive, and perhaps essential, to self-determination. It might explain the importance of work in contemporary individual life as well as in our societies. Meaningful work, but also work as self-development and self-determination, dimensions of freedom and autonomy, are central to modern work understandings.[47]

The above does not mean that self-development cannot be reached without work. Work is not necessarily a purpose, it can also function as a means. The means-perspective on work is not problematic per se. A person engaged in work might also (and often will) do this for gaining an income, and to live a (good) life. The end of work may thus be found outside work itself. In modern labour law discourse, this is well captured through the notion of work-life balance. One of the possible views is that work and life should not necessarily be in conflict. It is, however, found that many people see 'work' as meaningful only in the function of life aside from work.[48]

Another dimension of the interdependency between privacy, freedom and autonomy, may be found in the issue of monitoring and control. With a world of work full

45. ECtHR, Judgment of 16 December 1992, No. 13710/88, *Niemietz v. Germany*, Series A, No. 251-B §29.
46. ECtHR, Judgment of 28 November 2017, No. 70838/13, *Antovic and Mirkov v. Montenegro*.
47. B.A. Allan, K.L. Autin & R.D. Duffy, 'Self-Determination and Meaningful Work: Exploring Socioeconomic Constraints', *Frontiers in Psychology* 2016, Vol. 7(71), 1-8 https://doi.org/10.3389/fpsyg.2016.00071, zie ook hoger aangehaald: C. Seemiller & M. Grace, *Generation Z: A Century in the Making*, New York, Routledge, 2019 (Figure 3.2.).
48. A. Onesto, 'What Makes a 21st Century Job?', in Anthony Onesto, *The New Employee Contract. How to Find, Keep and Elevate Gen Z Talent*, New York, Apress, 2022, p. 52 (110 p.).

of automation, computers, the internet, data processing, digital connection, wearables, data and location tracking, AI, and many other technologies, the workplace delivers a context in which employers can supervise workers intensively through technological means. Just as work has become more digital, the management and supervision of workers have become digital in many ways. Some have referred in this context to 'tele-subordination'.[49] The impact on privacy expectations is thus potentially enormous.

Technology in the work environment may improve freedom or autonomy. It can enable workers to work more autonomously. This is, for example, the case with remote work, working '*anytime anywhere*'. However, technology has also made it possible to supervise and monitor workers, including remote workers, in various ways, such as by using computer software or through specific mobile applications.[50] These surveillance technologies could track time, location and even (parts of) the workflow, by logging data, screen sharing, screenshots, keystroke measurement, mouse movements, visited websites, webcams, audio controls, or data entry.[51] Even in forms of so-called autonomous working, technology can be seen to increase levels of control, and thus reduce autonomy. The challenge may be seen as a 'technological paradox',[52] as workers may be working more independently from direct supervision, with the help of technology, but at the same time with an increased real risk of intensified control and monitoring due to this technological connection. The compatibility of intensive telework or remote work-monitoring mechanisms with the worker's right to privacy becomes, however, questionable.[53]

Monitoring and control issues link the concept of private life strongly to notions of identity and self-development. Under the influence of control, being free from external pressures or expectations becomes virtually impossible and this may exert significant influence on individual behaviour, one's freedom from judgment, and one's autonomy to define and shape one's own personal existence. The tensions between control, privacy, autonomy and freedom become even higher due to the blurring of boundaries, and the increasing overlap, between private life and work life. This impacts the scope and definition of what is the private sphere of individuals and impacts personal decisions regarding where and how to give meaning to one's personal life. The degree of control will influence personal vulnerability to work-related expectations, the employer's norms or social norms, and this can diminish or reinforce autonomy and (self-)control over one's private life. Respecting and protecting privacy

49. F. Morin, 'Nouvelles Technologies et la télésubordination du salarié', *Relations industrielles* 2000, Vol. 55(4), 725.
50. N. Fairweather, 'Surveillance in Employment: The Case of Teleworking', *Journal of Business Ethics* 1999, Vol. 22, 39.
51. J. Drolet & K. Lebnan, 'Les défis du télétravail à l'égard de la vie privée du télétravailleur', *Les Cahiers de droit* 2013, Vol. 54(2-3), 303-336; N. Fairweather, 'Surveillance in Employment: The Case of Teleworking', *Journal of Business Ethics* 1999, 41.
52. F. Hendrickx, 'From Digits to Robots: The Privacy-Autonomy Nexus in New Labour Law Machinery', *Comp. Lab. Law & Pol. Journal* 2019, Vol. 40, 365-388.
53. T. Katsabian, 'The Telework Virus: How the COVID-19 Pandemic Has Affected Telework and Exposed Its Implications for Privacy and Equality', *SSRN E-Journal* 2020, 19 https://doi.org/10.2139/ssrn.3684702.

could thus be seen to entail the acknowledgement of the diverse ways in which individuals seek to define and preserve their personal 'space', their identity and autonomy within a world of work which deploys external influences. The interplay between privacy, freedom, autonomy, and control thus confirms the fundamental value of a human need for space, where individuals can shape their identities free from undue external interference. In earlier scholarship, Westin defined, in this context, privacy as 'individuality', 'non-conformity', and 'independence' and brought this in relation to 'dignity' and 'free choice in life'.[54] Recognizing and respecting this is critical in fostering a work environment that gives meaning to both work and privacy.

With technologies including AI, algorithmic decision-making and robotics the debate brings the importance of freedom and autonomy to new horizons.[55] New 'intelligent' techniques not only accelerate the levels of personal data collecting and processing but can also be turned into workplace-relevant decision-making and monitoring tools. New forms of monitoring may require additional approaches, including references to new forms of vulnerability, the need to deal with information power and the agenda of humanization.[56] The concept of privacy is capable of capturing humanization as a foundation or purpose of labour law or as an explanatory component of the meaning of work.

§12.06 CONCLUSION

The evolving dynamics of work, shaped by global developments, including rapid technological advancements and the shift towards more flexible and digitalized working environments, bring the concepts of privacy, freedom, and autonomy into more central focus within labour law. As the lines between personal and professional life continue to blur, the understanding of privacy has expanded, transcending traditional notions of information privacy, whereas protection seeks to encompass deeper aspects of dignity, identity, and self-determination. Furthermore, meanings of privacy show that professional life is protected by the right to privacy and work life *is* constitutive of the worker's private life. This shift prompts a broader reflection on the meaning of work itself and its place in the human experience.

The explorations above show that the meaning of work itself is increasingly shaped by the degree to which privacy is recognized and develops. In many instances, autonomy and freedom are seen as major values in giving meaning to work, but also privacy can be seen as a prerequisite for meaningful work. Privacy is capable of underpinning the intrinsic values that workers may derive from their professional lives.

With the development of privacy as a vector of freedom and autonomy, labour law may have to go on new roads. Labour law, traditionally preoccupied with regulating subordination and the prerogatives of the employer, must now also concern

54. Westin, *supra* n. 33, 1967, 34.
55. Hendrickx, 'From Digits to Robots: The Privacy-Autonomy Nexus in New Labour Law Machinery', *supra* n. 52.
56. Cf. D.J. Solove, 'Privacy and Power: Computer Databases and Metaphors for Information Privacy', *Stanford Law Review* 2001, Vol. 53(6), 1393-1462.

itself with the protection and enhancement of the worker's freedom and autonomy. Work is thereby seen as more than an economic exchange, a source of income, or the mere creation of value. Work is personal, but not only. Work is fundamentally relational. It is a key arena in which individuals engage with others as well as with themselves. In this light, work becomes a medium through which personal and social identities are shaped, making the right to privacy not only an essential aspect of the employment relationship but also of a worker's personal self and of society. It allows privacy to take a strong place in giving meaning to work.

This also comes through in the monitoring and control dimension of privacy and labour law debate. The modern workplace, more and more becoming a virtual workplace, is increasingly dominated by data processing, AI, digital surveillance and connectivity. This challenges the conventional understanding of supervision and control. The employer's reach, now extending through various digital tools, has intensified monitoring practices. It raises profound questions about privacy, freedom and autonomy in work. The advent of technologies like AI and algorithmic decision-making complicates the interplay between privacy, autonomy, and control. While these technologies offer the promise of greater freedom and autonomy, they simultaneously introduce new forms of surveillance, creating a 'technological paradox.' This paradox highlights the need for labour law to evolve, ensuring that the dignity, individuality and self-control of workers are preserved.

Privacy, therefore, when viewed through the lens of freedom and autonomy, emerges as a cornerstone of what gives work its meaning. It provides the space for individuals to navigate through the complexities of modern work life, balancing the demands of professional responsibilities with the need for personal growth, identity and self-determination. As such, privacy should not be seen as a mere legal right but as an essential element of the human work experience, integral to a narrative of work – and of labour law – that recognizes freedom and autonomy, and the pursuit of a meaningful life. Labour law must, therefore, continue to evolve, fostering a work environment that respects and protects these fundamental values in an era of unprecedented technological change.

BCLR - BULLETIN OF COMPARATIVE LABOUR RELATIONS

Vol. Author/Title/Year/ISBN

1. Roger Blanpain, *Individual Employment Contracts: Collective Agreements*, 1970.
2. Roger Blanpain, *Social Planning*, 1971 (ISBN 90-312-0018-2).
3. Roger Blanpain, *Guaranteed Income Funds*, 1972 (ISBN 90-312-0019-0).
4. Roger Blanpain, *Employee Participation at the Level of the Enterprise*, 1973 (ISBN 90-312-0020-4).
5. Roger Blanpain, *Vastheid van Betrekking: Staking en Bezetting*, 1974.
6. Roger Blanpain, *Labour Law and Industrial Relations (International Bibliography)*, 1975 (ISBN 90-312-0023-9).
7. Roger Blanpain, *Multinational Enterprises*, 1976 (ISBN 90-312-0024-7).
8. Roger Blanpain, *Worker's Participation in the European Company*, 1977 (ISBN 90-312-0044-1).
9. Roger Blanpain, *Women and Labour*, 1978 (ISBN 90-312-0077-8).
10. Roger Blanpain, *European Conference on Labour Law and Industrial Relations: Multinational Enterprises*, 1979 (ISBN 90-312-0091-3).
11. Roger Blanpain, *Job Security and Industrial Relations*, 1980 (ISBN 90-312-0147-2).
12. Roger Blanpain, Greg Bamber & Russell Lansbury, *Technological Change and Industrial Relations: An International Symposium*, 1983 (ISBN 90-312-0205-3).
13. Roger Blanpain, James Janssen van Raay & A. Moulty, *Worker's Participation in the European Community: The Fifth Directive*, 1984 (ISBN 90-654-4187-5).
14. Roger Blanpain, *Equality and Prohibition of Discrimination in Employment*, 1985 (ISBN 90-654-4215-4).
15. Roger Blanpain, *Restructuring Labour in the Enterprise: Law and Practice in France, F.R. of Germany, Italy, Sweden and the United Kingdom*, 1986 (ISBN 90-654-4283-9).
16. Roger Blanpain & E. Kassalow, *Unions and Industrial Relations: Recent Trends and Prospect: A Comparative Treatment*, 1987 (ISBN 90-654-4294-4).
17. Roger Blanpain & Marco Biagi, *Trade Union Democracy and Industrial Relations*, 1988 (ISBN 90-654-4394-0).
18. Roger Blanpain & Jelle Visser, *In Search of Inclusive Unionism*, 1990 (ISBN 90-654-4439-4).
19. Roger Blanpain, *Flexibility and Wages: A Comparative Treatment*, 1990 (ISBN 90-654-4461-0).

20. Roger Blanpain, Stephen Frenkel & Oliver Clarke, *Economic Restructuring and Industrial Relations in Industrialised Countries,* 1990 (ISBN 90-654-4488-2).
21. Roger Blanpain & Friedrich Fürstenberg, *Structure and Strategy in Industrial Relations,* 1991 (ISBN 90-654-4559-5).
22. Roger Blanpain, Amira Galin & Ozer Carmi, *Flexible Work Patterns and Their Impact on Industrial Relations,* 1991 (ISBN 90-654-4572-2).
23. Roger Blanpain, *Workers' Participation: Influence on Management Decision-Making by Labour in the Private Sector,* 1992 (ISBN 90-654-4600-1).
24. Roger Blanpain, Brian Brooks & Chris Engels, *Employed or Self-Employed,* 1992 (ISBN 90-654-4613-3).
25. Roger Blanpain & Tiziano Treu, *Industrial Relations Developments in the Telecommunications Industry,* 1993 (ISBN 90-654-4642-7).
26. Roger Blanpain & Marco Biagi, *Industrial Relations in Small and Medium Sized Enterprises,* 1993 (ISBN 90-654-4696-6).
27. Roger Blanpain & Marco Biagi, *Participative Management and Industrial Relations in a Worldwide Perspective,* 1993 (ISBN 90-654-4769-5).
28. Roger Blanpain, Jacques Rojot & Hoyt N. Wheeler, *Employee Rights and Industrial Justice,* 1994 (ISBN 90-654-4804-7).
29. Roger Blanpain & Ruth Ben-Israel, *Strikes and Lock-Outs in Industrialized Market Economies,* 1994 (ISBN 90-654-4841-1).
30. Roger Blanpain, Kazuo Sugeno & Yasuo Suwa, *The Harmonization of Working Life and Family Life,* 1995 (ISBN 90-411-0064-4).
31. Roger Blanpain & Laszio Nagy, *Labour Law and Industrial Relations in Central and Eastern Europe,* 1996 (ISBN 90-411-0298-1).
32. Roger Blanpain, *Labour Law and Industrial Relations in the European Union,* 1997 (ISBN 90-411-0527-1).
33. Taco Van Peijpe, *Employment Protection under Strain,* 1998 (ISBN 90-411-0528-8).
34. Roger Blanpain, Takashi Araki & Ryuichi Yamakawa, *The Process of Industrialization and the Role of Labour Law in Asia,* 1999 (ISBN 9-041-1104-7-X).
35. Roger Blanpain & Marco Biagi, *Non-standard Work and Industrial Relations,* 1999 (ISBN 90-411-1117-4).
36. Roger Blanpain, *Private Employment Agencies: The Impact of ILO Convention 181 (1997) and the Judgment of the European Court of Justice of 11 December 1997,* 1999 (ISBN 90-411-1118-2).
37. Roger Blanpain, *Multinational Enterprises and the Social Challenges of the XXIst Century: The ILO Declaration on Fundamental* Principles *at Work, Public and Private Corporate Codes of Conduct,* 2000 (ISBN 90-411-1280-4).
38. Roger Blanpain, Ryuichi Yamakawa & Takashi Araki, *Deregulation and Labour Law: In Search of a Labour Concept for the 21st Century,* 2000 (ISBN 90-411-1370-3).
39. Roger Blanpain, *The Council of Europe and the Social Challenges of the XXIst Century,* 2001 (ISBN 90-411-1543-9).

40. Roger Blanpain, *On-Line Rights for Employees in the Information Society, Use & Monitoring of E-Mail & Internet at Work*, 2002 (ISBN 90-411-1626-5).
41. Roger Blanpain, *The Evolving Employment Relationship and the New Economy: The Role of Labour Law & Industrial Relations*, 2001 (ISBN 90-411-1691-5).
42. Roger Blanpain, *Involvement of Employees in the European Union, Works Councils, Company Statute, Information and Consultation Rights*, 2002 (ISBN 90-411-1760-1).
43. Michele Colucci, *The Impact of the Internet and New Technologies on the Workplace: A Legal Analysis from a Comparative Point of View*, 2002 (ISBN 90-411-1824-1).
44. Roger Blanpain, *White Paper on the Labour Market in Italy: The Quality of European Industrial Relations and Changing Industrial Relations*, 2002 (ISBN 90-411-1841-1).
45. Roger Blanpain, Russell D. Lansbury & Young-Bum Park, *Impact of Globalisation on Employment Relations: A Comparison of the Automobile and Banking Industries in Australia and Korea*, 2002 (ISBN 90-411-1850-0).
46. Roger Blanpain & Antoine Jacobs, *Employee Rights in Bankruptcy: A Comparative-Law Assessment*, 2002 (ISBN 90-411-1942-6).
47. Roger Blanpain, Takashi Araki & Shinya Ouchi, *Corporate Restructuring and the Role of Labour Law*, 2003 (ISBN 90-411-1949-3).
48. Roger Blanpain, *Collective Bargaining, Discrimination, Social Security and European Integration*, 2003 (ISBN 90-411-2010-6).
49. Roger Blanpain & Luis Aparicio-Valdez, *Labour Relations in the Asia- Pacific Countries*, 2004 (ISBN 90-411-2239-7).
50. Roger Blanpain & Ronnie Graham, *Temporary Agency Work and the Information Society*, 2004 (ISBN 90-411-2252-4).
51. Roger Blanpain, *The Actors of Collective Bargaining: A World Report*, 2004 (ISBN 90-411-2253-2).
52. Roger Blanpain & Michele Colucci, *The Globalisation of Labour Standards: The Soft Law Track*, 2004 (ISBN 90-411-2303-2).
53. Roger Blanpain, Takashi Araki & Shinya Ouchi, *Labour Law in Motion: Diversification of the Labour Force & Terms and Conditions of Employment*, 2005 (ISBN 90-411-2315-6).
54. Roger Blanpain, *Smoking and the Workplace*, 2005 (ISBN 90-411-2325-3).
55. Roger Blanpain, *Confronting Globalization: The Quest for a Social Agenda*, 2005 (ISBN 90-411-2381-4).
56. Roger Blanpain, Thomas Blanke & Edgar Rose, *Collective Bargaining Wages in Comparative Perspective: Germany, France, the Netherlands, Sweden and the United Kingdom*, 2005 (ISBN 90-411-2388-1).
57. Roger Blanpain & Anne Numhauser-Henning, *Women in Academia & Equality Law: Aiming High - Falling Short?*, 2006 (ISBN 978-90-411-2427-6).
58. Roger Blanpain, *Freedom of Services in the European Union: Labour and Social Security Law: The Bolkestein Initiative*, 2006 (ISBN 978-90-411-2453-5).
59. Roger Blanpain, Frans Pennings & Nurhan Sural, *Flexibilisation and Modernisation of the Turkish Labour Market*, 2006 (ISBN 978-90-411-2490-X).

60. Roger Blanpain & Boel Flodgren, *Corporate and Employment Perspectives in a Global Business Environment*, 2006 (ISBN 978-90-411-2537-X).
61. Roger Blanpain, Shinya Ouchi & Takashi Araki, *Decentralizing Industrial Relations and The Role of Labor Unions and Employee Representatives*, 2007 (ISBN 978-90-411-2583-3).
62. Roger Blanpain, *European Framework Agreements and Telework: Law and Practice: A European and Comparative Study*, 2007 (ISBN 978-90-411-2560-4).
63. Roger Blanpain, Jim Kitay, Leanne Cutcher & Nick Wailes, *Globalization and Employment Relations in Retail Banking*, 2007 (ISBN 978-90-411-2620-1).
64. Roger Blanpain, Russell Lansbury, Jim Kitay, Nick Wailes & Anja Kirsch, *Globalization and Employment Relations in the Auto Assembly Industry:* A *Study of Seven Countries*, 2008 (ISBN 978-90-411-2698-6).
65. Roger Blanpain & Michele Tiraboschi, *The Global Labour Market: From Globalization to Flexicurity*, 2008 (ISBN 978-90-411-2722-8).
66. Roger Blanpain, Michele Colucci & Frank Hendrickx, *The Future of Sport in the European Union: Beyond the EU Reform Treaty and the White Paper*, 2008 (ISBN 978-90-411-2761-7).
67. Roger Blanpain, Linda Dickens, *Challenges in European Employment Relations: Employment Regulation, Trade Union Organization, Equality, Flexicurity, Training and New Approaches to Pay*, 2008 (ISBN 978-90-411-2771-6).
68. Roger Blanpain, Hiroya Nakakubo & Takashi Araki, *New Developments in Employment Discrimination Law, 2008* (ISBN 978-90-411-2782-2).
69. Roger Blanpain, Andrzej Marian wiątkowski, *The Laval and Viking Cases: Freedom of Services and Establishment v. Industrial Conflict in the European Economic Area and Russia*, 2009 (ISBN 978-90-411-2850-8).
70. Roger Blanpain, William Bromwich, Olga Rymkevich, Silvia Spattini, *The Modernization of Labour Law and Industrial Relations in a Comparative Perspective*, 2009 (ISBN 978-90-411-2865-2).
71. Roger Blanpain, Juan Pablo Landa & Brian Langille, *Employment Policies and Multilevel Governance*, 2009 (ISBN 978-90-411-2866-9).
72. Roger Blanpain, European Works Councils; *The European Directive 2009/ 38/EC of 6 May 2009, 2009* (ISBN 978-90-411-3208-6).
73. Roger Blanpain, William Bromwich, Olga Rymkevich & Silvia Spattini, *Labour Productivity, Investment in Human Capital and Youth Employment: Comparative Developments and Global Responses*, 2010 (ISBN 978-90-411-3249-9).
74. Greg J. Bamber & Philippe Pochet, *Regulating Employment Relations, Work and Labour Laws: International Comparisons between Key Countries*, 2010 (ISBN 978-90-411-3199-7). General Editor: Roger Blanpain.
75. Roger Blanpain, Desislava Nikolaeva Dimitrova, *Seafarers' Rights in the Globalized Maritime Industry*, 2010 (ISBN 978-90-411-3349-6).
76. Roger Blanpain, Hiroya Nakakubo & Takashi Araki, *Regulation of Fixed- Term Employment Contracts*, 2010 (ISBN 978-90-411-3356-4).

77. Roger Blanpain, William Bromwich, Olga Rymkevich & Iacopo Senatori, *Rethinking Corporate Governance*, 2011 (ISBN 978-90-411-3450-9).
78. Roger Blanpain & Frank Hendrickx, *Labour Law between Change and Tradition: Liber Amicorum Antoine Jacobs*, 2011 (ISBN 978-90-411-3424-0).
79. Roger Blanpain, Thomas Klebe, Marlene Schmidt & Bernd Waas, *Trade Union Rights at the Workplace*, 2012 (ISBN 978-90-411-3460-8).
80. Roger Blanpain, William Bromwich, Olga Rymkevich & Iacopo Senatori, *Labour Markets, Industrial Relations and Human Resources Management: From Recession to Recovery*, 2012 (ISBN 978-90-411-4004-3).
81. Roger Blanpain, Hiroya Nakakubo & Takashi Araki, *Systems of Employee Representation at the Enterprise: A Comparative Study*, 2012 (ISBN 978-90-411-4080-7).
82. Roger Blanpain & Frank Hendrickx, *Temporary Agency Work in the European Union and the United States*, 2013 (ISBN 978-90-411-4769-1).
83. Roger Blanpain, Toker Dereli, Y. Pınar Soykut-Sarıca & Aslı en-Tabaı, *Emerging Patterns of Work and Turkish Labour Market Challenges under Globalization: Readings on Labour and Employment Relations*, 2014 (ISBN 978-90-411-4983-1).
84. Roger Blanpain, Pablo Arellano Ortiz, Marius Olivier & Gijsbert Vonk, *Social Security and Migrant Workers: Selected Studies of Cross-border Social Security Mechanisms*, 2014 (ISBN 978-90-411-4770-7).
85. Roger Blanpain & Nikita Lyutov, *Workers' Representation in Central and Eastern Europe: Challenges and Opportunities for the Works Councils' System*, 2014 (ISBN 978-90-411-4746-2).
86. Roger Blanpain, Ulla Liukkunen & Chen Yifeng, *China and ILO Fundamental Principles and Rights at Works*, 2014 (ISBN 978-90-411-4984-8).
87. Roger Blanpain, *The Use of Languages and Employment Relations*, 2014 (ISBN 978-90-411-5606-8).
88. Roger Blanpain, Hiroya Nakakubo & Takashi Araki, *Protection of Employees' Personal Information and Privacy*, 2014 (ISBN 978-90-411-5608-2).
89. Roger Blanpain, Jan Wouters, Glenn Rayp, Laura Beke & Axel Marx, *Protecting Labour Rights in a Multi-polar Supply Chain and Mobile Global Economy*, 2015 (ISBN 978-90-411-5662-4).
90. Roger Blanpain & Stefania Marassi, *Globalization and Transnational Collective Labour Relations: International and European Framework Agreements at Company Level*, 2015 (ISBN 978-90-411-4748-6).
91. Roger Blanpain, Frank Hendrickx & Petra Herzfeld Olsson, *National Effects of the Implementation of EU Directives on Labour Migration from Third Countries*, 2016 (ISBN 978-90-411-6257-1).
92. Roger Blanpain, Frank Hendrickx & D'Arcy du Toit, *Labour Law and Social Progress: Holding the Line or Shifting the Boundaries?* 2016 (ISBN 978-90-411-6747-7).

93. Roger Blanpain & Frank Hendrickx, *Reasonable Accommodation in the Modern Workplace: Potential and Limits of the Integrative Logics of Labour Law*, 2016 (ISBN 978-90-411-6258-8).
94. Roger Blanpain, Frank Hendrickx & Bernd Waas, *New Forms of Employment in Europe*, 2016 (ISBN 978-90-411-6239-7).
95. Roger Blanpain, Frank Hendrickx, Hiroya Nakakubo & Takashi Araki, *The Notion of Employer in the Era of the Fissured Workplace: Should Labour Law Responsibilities Exceed the Boundary of the Legal Entity?*, 2017 (ISBN 978-90-411-8470-2).
96. Elena Sychenko, *Individual Labour Rights as Human Rights: The Contributions of the European Court of Human Rights to Worker's Rights Protection*, 2017 (ISBN 978-90-411-8629-4).
97. William Bromwich & Olga Rymkevich, *Improving Workplace Quality: New Perspectives and Challenges for Worker Well-Being*, 2017 (ISBN 978-90-411-8628-7).
98. Sarah De Groof, *Work-Life Balance in the Modern Workplace: Interdisciplinary Perspectives from Work-Family Research, Law and Policy*, 2017 (ISBN 978-90-411-8630-0).
99. Sylvaine Laulom, *Collective Bargaining Developments in Times of Crisis, Second Edition*, 2025 (ISBN 978-94-035-0628-9).
100. Frank Hendrickx & Valerio De Stefano, *Game Changers in Labour Law: Shaping the Future of Work*, 2018 (ISBN 978-90-411-9953-9).
101. Ivana Palinkaš, *The Legal and Institutional Framing of Collective Bargaining in CEE Countries: Between Europeanisation and Decentralisation*, 2018 (ISBN 978-90-411-9199-1).
102. Jeremy Waddington, *European Board-Level Employee Representation: National Variations in Influence and Power*, 2018 (ISBN 978-90-411-9202-8).
103. Jan Pichrt & Kristina Koldinská, *Labour Law and Social Protection in a Globalized World: Changing Realities in Selected Areas of Law and Policy*, 2018 (ISBN 978-94-035-0093-5).
104. Matthew W. Finkin, *American Labor and the Law: Dormant, Resurgent, and Emergent Problems*, 2019 (ISBN 978-94-035-0654-8).
105. Giuseppe Casale & Tiziano Treu, *Transformations of Work: Challenges for the Institutions and Social Actors*, 2019 (ISBN 978-94-035-0891-7).
106. Miguel De la Corte-Rodríguez, *EU Law on Maternity and Other Child-Related Leaves: Impact on Gender Equality*, 2019 (ISBN 978-94-035-1452-9).
107. Valeria Pulignano & Frank Hendrickx, *Employment Relations in the 21st Century: Challenges for Theory and Research in a Changing World of Work*, 2020 (ISBN 978-94-035-1764-3).
108. Matteo Bottero, *Posting of Workers in EU Law: Challenges of Equality, Solidarity and Fair Competition*, 2021 (ISBN 978-94-035-2860-1).
109. Bernd Waas & Christina Hießl, *Collective Bargaining for Self-Employed Workers in Europe: Approaches to Reconcile Competition Law and Labour Rights*, 2021 (ISBN 978-94-035-2373-6).

110. Mathias Wouters, *International Labour Standards and Platform Work: An Analysis of Digital Labour Platforms Based on the Instruments on Private Employment Agencies, Home Work and Domestic Work*, 2022 (ISBN 978-94-035-4024-5).
111. Luca Ratti, *In-Work Poverty in Europe: Vulnerable and Under-Represented Persons in a Comparative Perspective*, 2022 (ISBN 978-94-035-4996-5).
112. Silvia Rainone, *The Role of the Court of Justice in EU Labour Law: A Case Study on the Transfer of Undertakings Directive*, 2023 (ISBN 978-94-035-2896-0).
113. Frank Hendrickx, Elena Gramano & David Mangan, *Privacy@work: A European and Comparative Perspective*, 2023 (ISBN 978-94-035-3106-9).
114. Elena Sychenko & Adalberto Perulli, *Employment Law and the European Convention on Human Rights: The Research of the Recent Jurisprudence of the ECtHR Related to Employment Law (2017-2021)*, 2023 (ISBN 978-94-035-3556-2).
115. Ilda Durri, *Casual Work Arrangements and Platform-Based Work: The Casual Work Agenda as a Way to Enhance the Labour Protection of Platform Workers*, 2023 (ISBN 978-94-035-3107-6).
116. Charalampos Stylogiannis, *Collective Labour Rights for Self-Employed Workers: A Human Rights-Based Approach of Platform Work*, 2023 (ISBN 978-94-035-0667-8).
117. Heather Kurzbauer, *Employment Vulnerabilities in the World of Orchestral Musicians: Symphonic Metamorphoses*, 2023 (ISBN 978-94-035-2737-6).
118. Natalie Videbæk Munkholm, Vincenzo Pietrogiovanni & Karsten Engsig Sørensen, *Managers in European Law: Rights and Duties of Executive and Non-executive Managers in a European Perspective*, 2024 (ISBN 978-94-035-3286-8).
119. Frank Hendrickx & Christina Hiessl, *The Meaning of Work: A Labour Law Perspective*, 2025 (ISBN 978-94-035-0579-4).

www.ingramcontent.com/pod-product-compliance
Lightning Source LLC
Chambersburg PA
CBHW071434230926
51846CB00001B/231
* 9 7 8 9 4 0 3 5 0 5 7 9 4 *